HEART OF OAK

G. J. MARCUS

HEART OF OAK

A survey of
British sea power in the
Georgian era

LONDON
OXFORD UNIVERSITY PRESS
NEW YORK   TORONTO
1975

Oxford University Press, Ely House, London W.1

GLASGOW NEW YORK TORONTO MELBOURNE WELLINGTON
CAPE TOWN IBADAN NAIROBI DAR ES SALAAM LUSAKA ADDIS ABABA
DELHI BOMBAY CALCUTTA MADRAS KARACHI LAHORE DACCA
KUALA LUMPUR SINGAPORE HONG KONG TOKYO

ISBN 0 19 215812 0

Printed in Great Britain by
The Camelot Press Ltd, Southampton

CONTENTS

ILLUSTRATIONS

MAPS

PREFACE

THIS book might, perhaps, be properly described as the anatomy of the sea power of Great Britain in the Georgian era. Its aim is to bring out the full significance of certain important factors which, in the usual narrative treatment of naval history, are likely to be overlooked altogether, or, at best, somewhat inadequately covered. With this object in view the various elements and aspects of our sea power in the period under review are set out in as lucid and as logical sequence as possible.

Beginning with the raw materials of naval strength—the oak and other timbers for shipbuilding, masts, cordage, naval stores, etc.—the survey goes on to treat of the major problems of strategy and tactics; then matters of seamanship and navigation, and the very important issue of maritime rights. There follow several chapters dealing with the personnel of the Service, the administration of the Navy, and the intimate connection between seaborne trade and sea power; then a series of chapters on the social and geographical background of officers and men; and lastly, a chapter on the aftermath of the great war of 1793–1815.

In the formulation and execution of naval strategy a decisive factor as a rule was accurate and timely intelligence. This was closely associated with two other crucial factors in naval warfare—namely, speed and surprise. On the collection, collation, interpretation, and distribution of intelligence great issues frequently hinged. In two of the most momentous campaigns in our annals—those of Quiberon Bay and Trafalgar—intelligence was a supremely important factor.

A commonly neglected branch of naval history is seamanship. This may be largely attributed to the pronounced academic aversion to the subject, which has manifested itself in a number of ways. It is hardly surprising, indeed, that the practice of excluding seamanship from their calculations has occasionally landed the learned in an untenable position. The following is a fair example. The late Mr. A. B. Rodger, then Senior Fellow of Balliol, once showed the present writer a list of questions which he had just prepared for the Special Subject section of the Final Examination in the Honours School of Modern History at Oxford; and the present writer noted with interest that one of these questions, *if properly answered*, would involve a knowledge of seamanship which not a member of the Board possessed. The same situation may well have arisen in other public examinations. The general neglect of this highly important subject is all the more to be regretted in that the loss to naval history is probably irreparable. The age of sail is now far behind us. Already much of what Mahan and his professional brethren took for granted is today virtually incomprehensible to the majority of scholars, knowing as they do little or nothing of the 'sea affair'. It can be confidently predicted that the next generation of historians will labour under the heavy handicap of being unable to check their conclusions with the assistance of professional seamen: for by then there will be no experienced sailors left.

The interrelation of various factors in naval history is of high significance and should be carefully studied. Thus, the effectual exercise of our maritime rights was closely linked with seamanship and also with prize money. Again, the manning of the Fleet in war-time necessitated an immense intake of seamen—partly as volunteers, but more generally as pressed men—from the mercantile marine and fisheries: the demands of the Navy, the need for commerce protection, the circumstances of particular trades, the situation in individual rivers and sea-ports, and the activities of the press-gang were all, therefore, closely related.

Generally speaking, the war on trade has scarcely received the attention it deserves. It was a major factor in a number of conflicts; and in the Napoleonic War a decisive one. Admittedly, it is by no means so dramatic a subject as the great battle scenes of the Revolutionary and Napoleonic eras; nevertheless, on the one side the *guerre-de-course* was in certain years a severe threat to British seaborne trade, and on the other the stranglehold which the Navy maintained on the enemy's commerce was ultimately the *causa causans* of Napoleon's overthrow.

This leads on to the problem of trade defence. As a result of their long experience of operations at sea the Admiralty had evolved tolerably effective methods of trade defence; the principal element of which was the convoy system. In spite of oft-recurring criticism of its disadvantages, convoy remained in fact the general rule throughout a long series of maritime wars. However, in the century of peace which ensued after Napoleon's downfall, and the severance of the living tradition of naval warfare, these lessons of experience were forgotten; and it was supposed at the Admiralty that the convoy system had become obsolete. (It is an amazing but undeniable fact that the Admiralty not only forgot the lessons of 1793–1815 in the course of the long Victorian peace, but also, in certain respects, even those of 1914–18 in the much shorter interval which elapsed between the First and Second World Wars.)

The social background of the personnel is for various reasons a matter of considerable interest and significance. Certain of the problems involved are never likely to be resolved, owing to the lack of evidence. A great deal is known about the background of many of the officers; comparatively little about that of the seamen. The subject teems with difficulties. For instance, as regards the matter of promotion from the lower deck, there is always a tendency nowadays for a writer to deviate from the strictly factual and objective viewpoint of naval history to a sociological approach and the current popular obsession with 'social justice' (whatever that may mean). Then there is the influence of Service politics; 'keeping one's nose clean', as it is commonly called. M. A. Lewis in his most interesting and illuminative work, *The Social History of the Royal Navy, 1793–1815*, discourses frankly and freely about politics, 'Interest', and social class: but he is significantly silent about the rigid exclusion of Catholics from the commissioned ranks of the Navy. Now the writer in question was much too careful and painstaking a historian to have completely overlooked this aspect of the operation of the Test Act. The presumption can only be that the good Professor, who had been in Admiralty service all his working life, chose rather to shun the delicate subject of religious discrimination altogether. After all, the spirit of the Test Act was still alive in the Navy. (There was a notable manifestation thereof in *Vernon*, in the middle of the last war, which had to be hurriedly hushed up by higher authority.) On a far greater scale there has from time to time been gross distortion of the facts of history through this intrusion of Service politics.

As a fitting conclusion to any study of the classic age of British sea warfare, it would be only right to emphasize the incalculable debt owed by Victorian England, at the very apogee of her influence, power, prosperity, and prestige, to that absolute and unquestioned maritime supremacy, upon which our position as a World Power in the main depended, achieved for this country by the Royal Navy and mercantile marine in the Revolutionary and Napoleonic Wars.

Hartland
N. Devon
1975

ACKNOWLEDGEMENTS

I AM greatly indebted to the following for advice and assistance on particular points: the late Captain John Creswell, R.N., the late Mr. Geoffrey Hunt, Captain H. A. Jewell, the late Professor Richard Pares, Captain Bertram Pengelly, R.N., Captain W. J. Slade, and Lieut.-Commander D. W. Waters, R.N.

My grateful thanks are due to the Staffs of the Public Record Office, the Reading Room of the British Museum, the National Maritime Museum, the University of London Library, and the Oxford University Press.

I have to thank the Navy Records Society for permitting me to reproduce excerpts from a number of their publications, and also the Bodley Head Ltd. for granting me a like permission with regard to J. H. and H. C. Hubback's *Jane Austen's Sailor Brothers* (1906).

One of my other books, *The Formative Centuries* (1961), has been laid under contribution in the present work, which originated in a suggestion made to me by the late Dr. J. A. Williamson.

━━━━━━━━━━━━━━━━━━━━━━━━━━━━━━━━━━━━━━━

CHAPTER 1

THE WOODEN WALLS

O N a gently rising slope above the banks of the Beaulieu River, in Hampshire, about seven miles inland from the Solent, there stand two rows of ancient Georgian houses divided by a remarkably wide street, which is no more than a hundred yards long. This is the village, or rather hamlet, of Buckler's Hard, set in the midst of meadows and woods. Down by the water's edge are sundry green mounds and hummocks, the rotting remnants of once stout timbers and decaying slipways—all that remains of what was formerly an important private shipyard. Beyond the shining reaches of the Beaulieu River, ridge after ridge of tree-tops extend to the distant horizon.

Buckler's Hard presented certain natural advantages to the shipbuilder. To this point the river was navigable at all tides; the spot was well sheltered from the prevailing south-westerly winds; there were places on the bank where the gravel bed would support a slipway, and the depth of water in the river was sufficient for launching. Last but not least, there was easy access to ample supplies of great and compass timbers.

The oak woods along the Beaulieu River formed part of the great oak belt which stretched across the south of England from the Severn to the Thames estuary. The four royal forests intimately associated with naval shipbuilding were, in order of importance, first, the Forest of Dean, next the New Forest, then Alice Holt, and finally the Forest of Bere. However, through neglect and other causes the crown lands had long since ceased to be the main source of supply to the royal dockyards. The extensive private woodlands belonging to the Dukes of Norfolk and Richmond, Lord Egremont, and others would supply more timber than was usually received from the Forest of Dean or the New Forest. Ashdown Forest, likewise privately owned,

Oak tree showing the curved or compass timbers which were indispensable to the construction of wooden ships.

furnished a considerable volume of oak for the Navy. From the county of Hampshire, formerly one of the most densely wooded regions in the kingdom, came the timber for the construction of a considerable number of the 'wooden walls'. The oak is at its best on the deep, sandy loam of the region. Further, the groves lay near to water transport. The great woods of oaks and beeches covered many thousands of acres; and in the parks and fields and along the lanes around flourished the rugged hedgerow oaks from which were obtained the best knees and other curved pieces. It was on the edge of this thickly wooded region, in the vicinity of Portsmouth and other

The building of H.M.S. Agamemnon *at Buckler's Hard shipyard in 1780; drawing by Harold Wyllie.*

lesser shipyards, that, early in the eighteenth century, the new yard was established under the patronage of the Marquis of Beaulieu.

From 1744 onwards Buckler's Hard was a busy centre of naval and mercantile shipbuilding. On the banks of the Beaulieu there stood a quay, a dock, a storehouse, and a counting-house. There were residences for the master shipwright and his work-people. (The former lived in the house, still standing, which is nearest the river.) Henry Adams came from the King's Yard at Deptford to act as overseer at the new yard. He later left the King's service, took over the lease of Buckler's Hard, and secured contracts on his own account. His first contract was for a sloop, the *Mermaid*, 24 guns. Adams, a skilled craftsman and an able business man, is said to have built more men-of-war for the Admiralty than any other private shipbuilder in the country. In all, he was responsible for the construction of no less than forty-three warships, large and small. Adams was by all accounts an exacting employer. In his later years he was accustomed to keep a close watch over his work force by means of a large telescope mounted at the top of his house; and he devised an elaborate system of signals to summon, for instruction or admonition, any particular man to attend him there. Adams died at the great age of ninety-one, just before the news of Trafalgar was received in England, and was succeeded by two of his sons. To the end of the Napoleonic War the Adamses were the shipbuilders of Buckler's Hard.

Adams launched three frigates in 1773, and in the following year his first ship of the line, the *Vigilant*, 64. In the next decade the yard produced one of the most famous ships in our naval annals. 'Was launched', recorded the *Salisbury and Winchester Journal* on 10 April 1781, 'at Buckler's Hard the *Agamemnon*, a fine 64-gun ship, built by Mr. Adams of that place.' This was the ship Nelson was to describe as 'the finest 64 in the service'. It was in the *Agamemnon*, in the celebrated action with the *Ça Ira*, that he first made his name. From Buckler's Hard, too, came the *Euryalus*. She was built in 1803 and, like the *Agamemnon*, took part in the battle of Trafalgar. The active life of this shipyard spans nearly the whole of the greatest age of our naval history.[1]

Some twenty miles to the eastward the *Victory* lies in her last resting-place, on the site of the oldest graving dock in the world. For more than a century she lay at anchor in Portsmouth harbour; then in 1922 she was placed in No. 2 Dock, and restored to the appearance she bore at Trafalgar. Every year thousands come to visit her there. With all the proud memories and associations that surround her, she may well stand for a monument to the world-wide maritime ascendancy exercised for centuries by Great Britain.

In 1758 the Cabinet had decided on an extensive shipbuilding programme, headed by a first-rate which was to surpass even the *Royal George*, the most famous ship of her day. She was designed by Thomas Slade, the Senior Surveyor of the Navy, and she was built at Chatham under the supervision of the Master Shipwright. Her keel was laid on 23 July 1759—'the Great Fifty-Nine', the Year of Victories. The *Victory* was launched on 7 May 1765. She succeeded the fourth ship of that name, launched in 1737, which was lost with all hands in 1744. In January 1771 the *Victory* was lying in the Medway where she must have been seen by the twelve-year-old Horatio Nelson when he came to join his first ship, the *Raisonnable*, commanded by his maternal uncle, Captain Maurice Suckling. The *Victory* at that time was not as we know her today. At the outset of her career, like many of her kind, she was fitted with open stern galleries. Her original and highly ornate figurehead was a group comprising the bust of King George III, with Britannia on his right, and the British lion *couchant* behind her, and, on the opposite side of the King, Victory holding out a crown of laurels, followed by Fame with her trumpet.

Wearing the flag of Admiral Augustus Keppel, the *Victory*, 100, took part in the indecisive action off Ushant on 27 July 1778. Subsequently she wore the flags of Admirals Hardy, Geary, Hyde Parker, Kempenfelt, Howe, and Jervis. As Lord Howe's flagship she had assisted in the relief of Gibraltar in 1782; wearing the flag of Admiral Sir John Jervis, she had taken part in the action off St. Vincent in 1797.

In 1801 she went into dock for an extensive refit. The open galleries were removed and the stern made 'flat'; she was also fitted with the figurehead that we see today. On the renewal of the war with France in the spring of 1803 she was Nelson's flagship during the long vigil off Toulon. Two years later she sailed for the West Indies in pursuit of the Combined Fleet and returned in August 1805 with the Admiral to England. When shortly after Nelson was re-appointed to the Mediterranean command it was in the *Victory* that he sailed from Portsmouth and rejoined the fleet off Cadiz, where on 21 October he achieved his last and greatest triumph.

After the battering she had endured at Trafalgar it was years before the *Victory* was again fit for service. In 1809 she assisted in the operations on the north coast of Spain which culminated in the evacuation of the British Army from Corunna. During the ensuing years she was the flagship of the strong squadron under the command of Saumarez in the Baltic. In 1812 her active career ended.

Throughout the greater part of the eighteenth century British naval construction was usually inferior to that of France and Spain. Compared with ours, the enemy's ships were large in tonnage, and correspondingly large in scantling, with massive frame-timbers and stout oaken sides not easily pierced by shot. Outside the Service, however, this was not properly understood. 'The thinking populace are too free to censure without inquiry into the reasons of things', Admiral Knowles remarked during the war of 1739–48, 'and imagine it strange that an English ship of war of 70 guns cannot take a French ship of the same force, whereas it is pretty apparent that our 70-gun ships are little superior to their ships of 52 guns.' Shortly before the first action off Finisterre, in the spring of 1747, Admiral Warren observed in similar terms to Anson: 'I am greatly pleased to hear it has been proposed, with a prospect of success, to augment the number of ships and weight of metal in all the different classes of our ships, to put them on a par with those of the French.' 'The Spanish men-of-war we have taken', Rodney informed his wife after the Moonlight victory in 1780, 'are much superior to ours.' The French vessels in particular were faster, better-proportioned, and, class for class, larger and more powerful than their British opponents. The French frigate *Aurore*, captured in 1758, was considered markedly superior to the best of our British frigates. The *Tonnant, Malta*, and *Canopus*, all 80-gun ships, taken at the battle of the Nile, were declared to be the 'finest on two decks ever seen in the British navy; their ports were generally seven feet a-midships, and their qualities in sailing and carrying sail have rarely, if ever, been surpassed'; and the *Egyptienne*,

Lord Anson in full dress uniform;
oil painting by the studio of Reynolds, c. 1764.

taken at Alexandria in 1800, 'the finest ship on one deck we ever had'. The excellence of French shipbuilding was, however, in general much more than counter-balanced by the superior strategy, seamanship, and discipline of the British Navy.

The truth was that the art of naval construction was studied far more carefully across the Channel than over here, where the rule-of-thumb methods of shipwrights, rather than scientific principles, usually prevailed. 'It is a bare act of justice to the fame of the French shipbuilders', Charnock declared, 'that to their studious exertions and experiments is primarily owing the energetical improvement made in modern times on the form, dimensions, and general contour of vessels, be the purpose to which it was intended they should be applied whatsoever it might.'[2]

According to Charnock, the several deficiencies of British shipbuilding 'which had long been discovered' were, at last, generally admitted as facts at the beginning of 1746. 'The first attempt towards emancipation from the former servitude', he went on, 'was the construction of the *Royal George*. . . . The services rendered by this ship to the public were of the most important kind. Her force nominally exceeded that of any vessel then possessed either by France, Spain, or any other country in the universe.'[3] The *Royal George* was laid down in Woolwich in 1749 and launched in 1756. Altogether forty ships of the line were added to the Navy during the Seven Years War, representing a substantial improvement on previous construction.

Under Anson's administration a new class of 74-gun ships was introduced in place of the old 70s, and of 64-gun ships in place of the old 60s: these were of 1,500 and 1,200 tons respectively. Later, in 1758, two 74s of still larger design were laid down on the lines of the French prizes captured by Anson and Hawke in the two victories off Finisterre in 1747. 'The advancement of more than three hundred tons at one stroke', says Charnock, 'in vessels of the same rate, was undoubtedly a grand stroke of mechanics.'[4]

Arising out of the experience of the Austrian Succession and the Seven Years War, important innovations were made in the organization of the Fleet. Hitherto no clear line of demarcation had existed between the line-of-battle ships and cruisers, and there had been a considerable proportion of hybrid types which were not strong enough to lie in the line of battle or sufficiently fast to serve as cruisers, but now the tendency was towards a classification of ships according to function, and, generally speaking, a simplification and specialization of the three main types of fighting ships. The fire power of the battleships was increased; the cruisers became faster and more seaworthy; and, for inshore work and subsidiary services, large numbers of flotilla craft were constructed.

The first- and second-rates were three-deckers of 90 guns and upwards. The third- and fourth-rates, comprising the bulk of the Fleet, were two-deckers, usually of 74 and 64 guns. Altogether ten 74s were constructed during the Seven Years War; and, towards the close of the century, this was to become the standard line-of-battle ship. Anson's term of office also saw the development of the fast-sailing, single-decker frigate, which amply proved its value in the actions of the Seven Years War. Twenty-two new 28-gun frigates were laid down; and there was a numerous class of 32-gun frigates. In 1757, under the superintendence of Sir Thomas Slade, a new class of 36-gun frigates was begun. According to Charnock:

A new class of vessels was introduced into the British navy. They carried 36 guns, and were of about 730 tons burden. They were constructed with every possible attention to their being swift sailers. The endeavours of the builders proving by no means unsuccessful, the few that were built by way of experiment, became regarded with an admiration bordering almost on enthusiasm, so that the command of them was coveted as highly as that of the most powerful and complete ships in the British service.

Between the frigates, and the sloops and lesser flotilla craft, a wide gap was forming, as between the line-of-battle ships and the frigates. At the same time Anson set to work to eliminate a number of intermediate classes, such as the small battleships and slow cruisers. Again to quote Charnock:

> The superior class of ships in the fifth rate mounted 44 guns, on two decks, and certainly were the worst vessels which, at that time, composed any part of the British navy. Long use had caused the continuance of their construction, and experience of their manifold defects proved scarcely sufficient to abolish the ridiculous and absurd custom.[5]

It is worth noting that no less than twelve 60s, eight 50s, and ten 40s were broken up during the Seven Years War.

The practice of sheathing a ship's bottom with copper to obviate the need of frequent cleaning was first tried, on Anson's orders, with the *Alarm* frigate in 1761. The experiment proved so successful that, during the next twenty-five years or so, almost every ship in the Navy was 'coppered'. There had been fears at first that copper would have a corrosive effect upon the iron bolts by which the frames were secured. 'But the industry and superior knowledge of the present Comptroller of the Navy [Sir Charles Middleton] adopted and recommended a preservative,' declared Lord Sandwich, the First Lord, 'well proved and attested to have answered every purpose expected for the space of nine years, which effectually preserves the fastenings of the ships from the corrosion of copper sheathing; and upon that foundation the whole Fleet of England, from a first rate to the smallest cutter, has now a copper bottom, except the very few ships that are not yet returned from foreign stations, and as a conclusive proof of our conviction on this subject we are returned to iron bolts and have in great measure laid aside the copper ones.'[6] 'For God's sake, and our country's,' observed Captain Young to Sir Charles Middleton in 1779, 'send out copper-bottomed ships to relieve the foul and crippled ones.'[7] Rodney's Moonlight victory of 16–17 January 1780 against a Spanish squadron off Cape St. Vincent was the reward of consummate seamanship, superior gunnery, and—last but not least—the speed of his coppered ships.

'I perceive you cry out loudly for coppered ships', Sandwich wrote to Rodney after the action; 'and I am therefore determined to stop your mouth. You shall have copper enough.'[8] It was found by experience that copper-sheathing not only preserved the bottom planking of a vessel, but also materially improved her sailing qualities, especially in light airs. Despite its high cost, the practice before long spread to all large merchantmen sailing to the tropics.

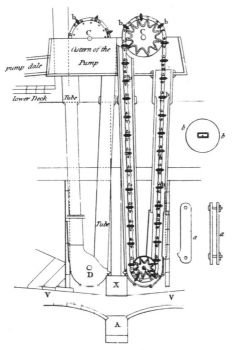

William Cole's chain pump of 1764, shown fitted in a British frigate; diagram from E. Chambers's Cyclopaedia, *1786.*

Among the various inventions and improvements which increased the material efficiency of the Georgian Navy must be mentioned the chain pump introduced by William Cole in 1764. It was discovered by experiment that whereas the old pump required seven men to pump out a ton of water in 76 seconds, the new pump would pump out the same quantity of water with but four men in not much more than half this time. Cole's pump was soon in common use throughout the Service. For steering large vessels the tiller was now generally replaced by the wheel. Lightning conductors were fitted to warships, at Anson's instance, in the early 1760s. Stills for producing fresh water from salt were introduced, on a small scale, in the last half of the century. During the same period an increasing number of our ships were equipped with ventilating apparatus. The method invented by Samuel

Sutton of extracting the foul air out of ships by means of pipes and a furnace was the one in general use; though a rival method of ventilation, through a system of fans operated by windmills, which was developed by the Rev. Stephen Hales, also had its advocates, among whom was Admiral Boscawen.

Internally the sides of British men-of-war were painted scarlet. A uniform scheme of external painting was long in arriving. On the eve of Trafalgar, the 'Nelson chequer' of black and yellow bands, with black port-lids, became common, though by no means universal. The familiar black and white chequer was introduced during the final phase of the Napoleonic War.

During the period under survey there were also very important developments in rigging and sail-plan. Early in the eighteenth century the bowsprit was lengthened by the addition of a jib-boom to carry the new triangular jib, which, with the foretopmast staysail, gradually superseded the old spritsail-topsail. To hold the bowsprit down to the stem a bobstay was fitted. The introduction of jibs into the three-masted ship constituted an innovation of the highest importance. Such a feat as Anson's beat down Channel in the face of a strong head-wind in the autumn of 1740, and, still more, his westward beat round the Horn several months later, would have been quite impossible with the old spritsails and spritsail-topsails. Staysails between the masts were fully developed by the middle of the eighteenth century. The ensuing decades witnessed the evolution of the spanker, or driver, from the old lateen mizen. Towards the close of the century the mizen-mast was prolonged by a topgallant-mast in order to carry a topgallant-sail; royals were introduced on all three masts, and studding-sails were set on the foremost and mainmast. 'An ocean-going ship', G. S. Laird Clowes has observed, 'with her masts and sails was incomparably the most elaborate mechanism which the mind of man had yet evolved.'

During the latter half of the eighteenth century the rigs in common use in the British merchant service were those of the ship, barque, brig, snow, brigantine, pink, schooner, ketch, lugger, and dogger. The larger East Indiaman, which had increased from about 400 tons burden in 1708 to 1,200 at the end of the century, was of course ship-rigged and resembled externally a 64. It carried royals and staysails and was pierced for fifty-six 18-pounders. The West Indiaman, which was also ship-rigged, was a good deal smaller than the East Indiaman (even at the end of the century it did not exceed 500 tons); it was built for maximum carrying capacity, and was a slow sailer. Generally speaking, ship-rigged merchantmen of under 300 tons had by now been replaced by two-masters such as brigs, snows, pinks, schooners, and ketches. The majority of our colliers and Baltic traders were either brigs or snows. There were also a large number of single-masted vessels with gaff-sails like the sloop and the hoy. The lug-sail was *par excellence* the fisherman's rig—the great advantage of this being the facility with which sail could be shortened. The three-masted Yarmouth luggers were reputed the fastest of all our east coast fishing craft. But the cutter rig was also fairly common among the fishing fleets. The Barking, Brixham, and other trawlers were cutter-rigged, as were also most of the Isle of Man herring fleet.

As the eighteenth century advanced the timber problem came increasingly to the fore. It was an article of faith among British shipwrights that oak was immeasurably superior to all other timbers for shipbuilding. Its rugged, massive trunk was endowed with a rock-like strength. It was 'tough, bending well, strong and not too heavy, nor easily admitting water', as John Evelyn had rightly claimed; his concern was lest the Navy should be diminished in strength for want of sufficient stout oaks in our forests; and for that reason he put the Oak in the forefront of his *Sylva*. Our shipwrights firmly believed that the best oak was English oak, and, moreover, that the best of this timber came from Sussex. It was thought so highly of that it was quite usual for naval contracts to specify 'good, sound Sussex oak'. Earlier in the century Daniel Defoe had discoursed confidently of the oak-groves of south-eastern England as 'an inexhaustible Store-house of Timber'; and he went on rather rashly to assert, 'nor can all the Ship-building the whole Kingdom are able to build, ever exhaust those Counties'. However, it had become apparent that the new growth of oak by no means kept pace with the ever-increasing demand. An oak-tree took about one hundred years to attain maturity. The great-grandson of the man who planted was usually the one who reaped the benefit. It is to the credit of our landed gentry that the majority had sufficient family feeling and self-restraint to permit their oaks to attain full development.

The consumption of suitable timber was enormous. Some 2,000 loads of timber were used in building a 64 like the *Agamemnon*. The construction of a 74 required about 3,000 loads. The produce of the royal forests being altogether inadequate to meet the requirements of the Fleet, the mainstay of the supply was the timber raised on private estates.

At the same time the increasing use of oak timber and plank from the American colonies helped to some extent to relieve the demand on English oak. American oak, it is true, never found favour with the Navy Board; but it was imported in considerable quantities for mercantile shipbuilding and was also used on a large scale in domestic architecture. Soft woods, such as white pine and spruce from the forests of New Hampshire and Maine, also provided timber admirably suited to shipbuilding. Early in the eighteenth century the New Englanders had built up an extensive shipbuilding industry of their own and exported large numbers of vessels annually to England. Close to the water's edge were most of the raw materials for shipbuilding. 'Masts of white pine or fir, logs of oak fifty feet long, clear of knots, and straight-grained for ship timbers and planks, pitch pine for tar and turpentine, and hemp for cordage furnished almost all the materials needed in the construction of a wooden sailing vessel.'[9] Towards the end of the colonial period American-built ships comprised no less than one-third of the total British registry.

By the end of the Austrian Succession and Seven Years War the oak plantations of the southern counties had been stripped nearly bare of timber suited for shipbuilding. 'It is most certain', wrote a contemporary authority, Roger Fisher, 'that there is a very great decrease in the quantity of large timber in all the neighbouring counties; in particular those of Surry, Kent, and Sussex. In the Wield of each, within the compass of forty years, almost all the principal timber is taken down, and in general only small remains; and but little regard is paid to the improvement of the growth of timber. . . . The counties I mention are so adapted by nature for the growth of timber, that I have often seen a field that had been ploughed and laid up for the summer fallow, if no cattle has been in it to browse off the heads, there has been young oaks enough appeared to have made it a wood, if suffered to grow.'

Fisher quotes various timber dealers and shipwrights in support of his conclusions. 'Indeed, so great has the consumption been that one of the most eminent timber dealers of the county of Sussex now living, has declared to me, that there is not now, as he verily believes, more than one tenth part of the full grown timber, standing or growing, as there was when he entered into business, forty-five years ago.' In the neighbouring county of Hampshire a timber dealer declared, 'That there is a great decrease in large oak timber is visible to everybody; and I am inclined to think that there is not in Hampshire one-fourth of the quantity standing, fitting for the navy, that there was forty years ago'. A leading timber dealer in Surrey delivered a similar opinion. 'I have been a dealer in the timber way for twenty years; and since my time I do think, that three-fourths of that size are cut down.' Fisher also quotes the letter of a master-shipwright of Hull ('by whose river most of the sea-ports on the eastern and northern side of the kingdom are supplied') in answer to 'a brother chip'—'As to the large timber. from thirty to forty years ago it has decreased much, by the navy being so much augmented. It may be now about a fifth part, or thereabouts, upon an average.'[10]

In the summer of 1768 the Navy Board addressed a letter to the Admiralty to the effect that it was now extremely difficult to procure supplies of English oak, not only on account of the enormous quantity felled during the late war for the Navy, but also owing to ever-growing demands of the East India Company. The problem was greatly intensified, towards the turn of the century, by the increase in the size of line-of-battle ships and East Indiamen. The main difficulty was the demand for 'great' and 'compass timbers' for stern-posts, wing transoms, common knees, and wing-transom knees. Owing to the increasing size of the vessels on charter to the Honourable Company, these 'great' and 'compass timbers' were needed for the East Indiamen as well as for the ships of the line. Because of the large-scale grubbing of coppices and hedgerows the growth of the vital crooked timber was seriously curtailed.

The unprecedented demands made on the forests of England during recent years had in fact almost denuded the land of seasoned timber for the construction of ships, with the result that there was not enough sound oak available either for shipbuilding or for repairs. The timber problem, together with the whole matter of naval stores, was destined to become one of the crucial factors in the War of American Independence. On the outbreak of hostilities in 1775 it was out of the question for Great Britain to restore her lost 'two-power' standard. It was the timber shortage which was primarily responsible for the long delay in fitting out squadrons against the Brest and Toulon fleets when France entered the war in 1778. Throughout the war the Admiralty experienced the greatest difficulty in preparing and maintaining as many as 100 sail of the line. The Bourbon States had at least half as many again in commission.

The majority of our line-of-battle ships had been rotting in reserve during the past fifteen years and were unable to go to sea. A good many of the battleships laid up in 'Rotten Row' were mere stacks of decayed timber, consumed with dry rot and covered with toadstools. This was largely the result of building vessels with unseasoned timber during the Seven Years War and afterwards.[11] There were numerous cases of vessels foundering in the course of the American War. The most spectacular of these disasters was the loss of the *Royal George*, on 29 August 1782, at Spithead. As she lay at anchor, 'slightly careened', undergoing some repairs, the ship's frames being completely decayed, the bottom suddenly dropped out of her . . . and 'Down went the *Royal George*, With all her crew complete'. Not surprisingly the Admiralty suppressed the findings of the ensuing court-martial.[12]

A view of the Royal dockyard at Deptford showing a frigate in the act of taking in her masts alongside a sheer hulk; engraving by R. Dodd, 1789.

The timber crisis was not only in respect of oak supplies. For the keel and keelson large numbers of elms were needed. Several elms were required for each keel (seven elms were needed for building the *Victory*'s keel, each section being about 28 feet long). Elms suitable for keels had become scarce towards the close of the eighteenth century; and for elm there was no substitute.[13]

Another serious handicap was in the matter of masts. For well over a century past, practically all the great masts needed for ships of the line had come from the virgin pine forests of New England. The Navy had in fact become largely dependent upon these American sticks. But the supply of masts was cut off after 1775 and no adequate substitutes were to be found on the shores of the Baltic. The Navy Board was lethargic in taking action. The piecing together of composite masts had become a lost art and was not effectively revived until 1780. There was the usual three years' supply on hand, comprising some 400 'great sticks' in the British dockyards in 1775; but as Middleton observed, 'Although His Majesty's magazines are at present well supplied with masts, there are but few large masts due upon contract, and the present contractor apprehended difficulty in procuring further supplies'. As the war went on the mast-ponds of Portsmouth and Plymouth were gradually depleted of the 'great sticks' so urgently required for the Fleet. These spars were normally due for replacement every ten years. Through the exhaustion of the mast-ponds, however, ships had to be fitted out with old sticks whose natural strength and resilience had long since departed. For want of the tall New England masts and bowsprits many a vessel was to be crippled during the most critical phase of the struggle.[14]

On the French intervention in 1778 a squadron comprising thirteen of the line under the command of Rear-Admiral Byron, 'Foul-Weather Jack', sent out to reinforce Howe at New York, ran into a gale in mid-Atlantic and suffered severe damage. The old masts with which many of these ships appear to have been fitted were cracked or sprung. Byron's squadron was completely dispersed, and most of his vessels were dismasted.

The shortage of masts continued to exercise the Admiralty throughout the war. After the terrific hurricane of 13 October 1780 in the West Indies, when a 74 disappeared without trace, several other warships were lost, and dozens of ships dismasted, the Commissioner in Antigua wrote to Sir Charles Middleton at the Navy Board: 'What we shall do for masts, sails, and stores to repair all these damages we know of, and those we have yet to learn, I know not.' Two years later, on his arrival at Port Royal in Jamaica after the victory of The Saints, Rodney was obliged through lack of masts to send away nine of the damaged battleships (among them several of his prizes), with a convoy of close on a hundred merchantmen. Off the Grand Banks of Newfoundland they were presently caught in a heavy gale, and five of the battleships, including the captured French flagship, the *Ville de Paris*, were lost.

In the matter of masts, nevertheless, with the exception of the five years or so of scarcity referred to above, the British enjoyed a substantial advantage over the French. The great sticks which they regularly imported, first, from the virgin pine forests of New England and, latterly, after the revolt of the American colonies, from Canada, were superior in practically all respects to the 'made masts' on which the French relied.[15] In the Revolutionary War the convoying of the mast ships was one of the most important tasks to be laid upon the Halifax squadron.

Because of the continued dependence of Great Britain on the Baltic for timber and naval stores, it was an object of cardinal importance to the Admiralty to keep open the Sound to British shipping, and to prevent the Baltic from falling under the domination of any one Power. The supply of Swedish iron was another major consideration. The importance of the Baltic to Great Britain was greatly increased by the loss of American supplies. An interesting report was made to the Earl of Shelburne by Lieutenant John Blankett, who visited Russia between the wars, on the outbreak of the American revolt.

I must premise that almost all these stores we were used in better times to take from America, we must now take from Russia, such as Pitch, Tar, Rosin, Turpentine, Tallow, Masts, Yards, Spars, Compass Timber & a variety of other articles used in Ship building. When it is said that Denmark & Sweden can supply those articles, it is true only in part. Sweden can export a great quantity of Pitch & Tar, but the connections of Sweden are too well known to place much dependence on a supply of Naval Stores from thence. We can only depend on Denmark for the Norway timber, some turpentine, & Rosin. But we must owe our Naval existence to Russia for a supply of Hemp, Sail Cloth, Masts, & some other articles which no other Country can furnish us.

By the turn of the century there was not enough English oak to meet more than a fraction of the Navy's demands. The long-pending and long-expected exhaustion of the oak groves was at this stage far more complete than ever before. Collingwood predicted that if country gentlemen did not make it a point to plant oaks wherever they would grow, the time would not be very distant when, to keep our Navy, 'we must depend entirely on captures from the enemy'. As before, the most pressing scarcity was that of curved or compass timbers. The cost of stern-posts, rudder pieces, wing transoms, common knees, and wing transom knees rose to unprecedented heights during the timber crisis of 1804. Even so, some of the most valuable pieces were actually being wasted. At a Commission of Inquiry, according to one report, 'In the yards we see the noblest oak of the forest, worthy to have formed the ribs of the proudest three-decker of Great Britain, sawed and hacked and chipped to make the floor of a sloop'; and it was stated that 'the shipwrights would deliberately build and repair small vessels with timber of the highest classes'.[16]

St. Vincent's over-drastic measures to reform the dockyards only made matters worse; for the all-powerful timber contractors, who virtually monopolized the supply of home-grown oak, were thereby antagonized and retaliated by withholding all available oak supplies from the dockyards. 'The rigid measures that were passed at this time', Barham was later to observe, 'would have produced much good to the service if they had been delayed till the peace was established; and I am persuaded that Lord St. Vincent must have thought it secure when he attempted this measure of reformation. On any other ground it was madness and imbecility in the extreme.'[17]

When Pitt returned to office in May 1804 he chose Melville as his First Lord, who at once reversed St. Vincent's policy and placated the contractors. By these measures he succeeded in securing sufficient oak to patch up 39 of the line, or about one-third of the total battle fleet. 'We must be limited by the deficiency which may exist in the amount of our naval stores', Melville observed. '. . . With a view both to our present exigencies, and to be able to meet future contingencies, we must, for some years, live on expedients. We must take first in hand those ships that can be repaired in the shortest time after they are taken in hand. We must have recourse to every substitute in order to spare our best timber, and we must be contented with less permanent repairs than would satisfy us in less pressing moments.' When Melville was replaced in 1805 by Barham, the latter immediately applied himself to the task of getting as many of the ships laid up in the dockyards to sea as possible; and in the nick of time the Fleet was reinforced. Three battleships were fitted out and sent to Nelson within a month of Trafalgar.[18]

In the later years of the Napoleonic War the Admiralty drew much of its timber from overseas. Some idea of the immensity of the problem may be gauged from the fact that close on a thousand ships of all classes were maintained in commission during the decade succeeding Trafalgar. Much of our oak timber was procured from Canada and the Maritime Provinces. Lesser sources of supply which were developed were India, West Africa, and New Zealand. Before the end of the war less than one-quarter of the timber used for naval shipbuilding was drawn from our own forests. First-rate masts were readily forthcoming from British North America. From about 1795 onward nearly all the masts used by the Navy came from New Brunswick, until, in 1804, the centre of the industry shifted to the St. Lawrence valley. About the same time masts of New Zealand kauri pine were fetched home in transports which would otherwise have made the return passage in empty ballast.

CHAPTER 2

STRATEGY AND TACTICS

THE main lines of our naval strategy, determined by centuries of experience of naval warfare, were already in being by the early part of the eighteenth century. During the ensuing decades, notwithstanding occasional failures and reverses, the hold of the Admiralty and of our leading commanders on certain strategical maxims and principles became increasingly assured. By the middle of the century the interrelation of the major factors in our naval strategy—British dispositions in the Channel and Mediterranean *vis-à-vis* those in the East and West Indies, North America, and other overseas stations, as well as the protection of convoys and conjunct expeditions—were fully apparent.

The pivotal factor of British naval dispositions in home waters was the Western Squadron, whose main and ultimate function was to hold the approaches to the Channel and to counter any hostile attempt from Brest. It was the Western Squadron which effectively secured the British Isles against invasion. In this era navigational conditions in the Channel were decidedly unfavourable to France. East of Brest there was no port for heavy ships—only tidal harbours which could take no more than a limited number of small craft. It was consequently impossible for their transports to get across until their battle fleet came up into those waters and cleared the way for the passage of their army. But the battle fleet was held firmly in check by the Western Squadron.

It was in large measure owing to the skilful dispositions pressed by Vernon on a sluggish and reluctant Admiralty that the rising of the 'Forty-five ended as it did. It was Vernon's policy to maintain a strong squadron of heavy ships in the western entrance of the Channel and a smaller force in the Downs. 'It was always my opinion', as he later declared, 'that a strong

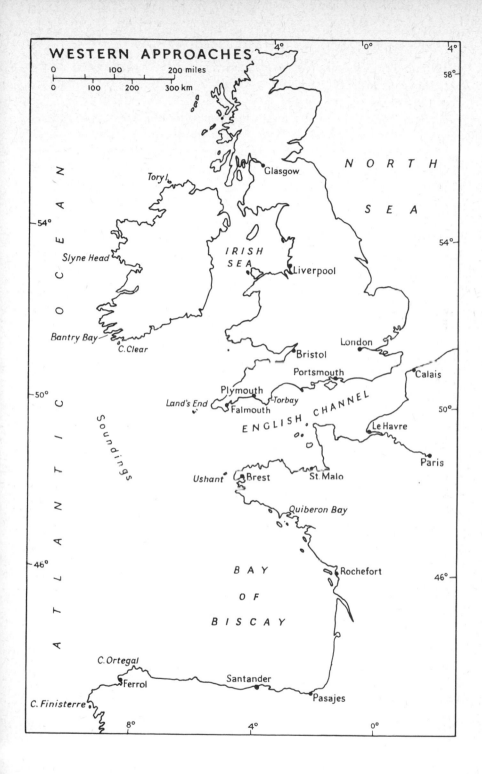

WESTERN APPROACHES

0   100   200 miles
0   100   200   300 km

N O R T H

S E A

Glasgow

Tory I.

58°

54°

54°

I R I S H

S E A

Liverpool

Slyne Head

London

Bantry Bay

C. Clear

Bristol

Portsmouth

Calais

50°

Plymouth

Land's End

Torbay

Falmouth

E N G L I S H   C H A N N E L

50°

Le Havre

Paris

Ushant

Brest

St. Malo

Quiberon Bay

46°

B A Y

O F

Rochefort

46°

B I S C A Y

C. Ortegal

Ferrol

Santander

C. Finisterre

Pasajes

8°

4°

0°

A T L A N T I C   *O C E A N*

Soundings

squadron kept at sea to the Westward, and a squadron of smaller ships in the North Seas, were the only secure Guardians to these His Majesty's kingdoms against Invasions.'[1]

From 1746 onwards the Western Squadron, which was at first concerned merely with the protection of British trade and the interception of hostile convoys, was progressively strengthened by Anson as the keystone of our naval strategy. The tactical and strategical weaknesses that had been revealed in the preceding years were now effectually remedied. The appointment of Anson to the command of the Western Squadron proved the turning-point of the War of the Austrian Succession. Severely critical of the defective strategical dispositions which had hitherto permitted the enemy to slip in and out of Brest, he had immeasurably improved the efficiency of the squadron and reorganized it for victory. The decisive actions fought by Anson and Hawke off Finisterre, in the spring and autumn of 1747 respectively, followed as the result of the new strategy.

In the Seven Years War, Anson continued to put his trust in a strong Western Squadron. 'The best defence for our colonies,' he declared in 1758, 'as well as our coasts, is to have a squadron always to the westward as may in all probability either keep the French in port, or give them battle with advantage if they come out.'

In the crucial year of the war, 1759, there emerged a development of the first importance. Throughout the first three years of the war—1756, 1757, and 1758—the Admiralty had relied on the time-honoured system of watching Brest from one of our western ports. But in the spring of 1759 Sir Edward Hawke, then in command of the Western Squadron, initiated a revolution in naval strategy. The situation confronting him at Brest was, in his judgement, too critical for him to retire with the squadron from the vital post off Ushant; and in the campaign of 1759 he abandoned the old policy altogether in favour of the new strategy of the close blockade. All our defensive and offensive operations throughout that year turned, in the last resort, on Anson's dispositions. The blockading squadrons off the hostile arsenals and the fleet which carried Wolfe and his army to their final triumph on the Plains of Abraham all made part of the same strategic plan.

'The first great and acknowledged object of naval defence in the country,' observed the Earl of Chatham during the Falkland Islands crisis of 1770, 'is to maintain such a superior naval force at home, that even the united fleets of France and Spain may never be masters of the Channel. . . . The second naval object with an English minister should be to maintain at all times a powerful western squadron. In the profoundest peace it should be respectable; in war it should be formidable.'

Lord Spencer; mezzotint after Copley, 1801.

In the War of American Independence, however, the policy of close blockade was not continued by Hawke's successors, who believed in keeping the Channel fleet in harbour during the winter months, leaving the enemy (as Kempenfelt observed) 'to the mercy of long nights and hard gales'. The Admiralty made no attempt either to blockade or mask the enemy's fleets in Brest and Toulon, with the result that the British control of sea communications on the North American and West India stations was continually being threatened by the arrival of reinforcements from Europe. In the Revolutionary War, Lord Howe was similarly opposed to the policy of keeping ships at sea in all weathers, blockading a port from which, he observed, 'the enemy can always be in readiness to escape after a gale of wind, by which the blockading squadron has been driven off and dispersed, the ships must be damaged in their masts, sails, and rigging, and their crews disheartened and disgusted'. The First Lord, Earl Spencer, was also loth to expose the fleet to winter gales.

In practice, the policy favoured both by Howe and his successor, Lord Bridport was open to grave objections. The advantages to be gained by keeping their ships in port during 'the bad weather months' by no means justified the choice of so unfavourable a strategic position. The policy of open blockade not infrequently played into the hands of the enemy. As a result of these dispositions Howe and Bridport ran the risk of allowing the French to get away to sea without their knowledge, until it was too late to intercept.

*Earl of St. Vincent; oil painting from the studio of
L. Abbott.*

On his appointment, in the spring of 1800, to the command of the Channel fleet, St. Vincent revived the policy of close blockade. The rendezvous of the main body of the squadron was henceforth changed from eight leagues west of Ushant to 'well in with Ushant in an easterly wind'. The strength of the force on the blockading station was increased to between 24 and 30 of the line. As in earlier wars, a strong and active Western Squadron was the pivot of our naval strategy. When in February 1801 St. Vincent became First Lord in Addington's ministry, he was succeeded by Admiral William Cornwallis, under whom the same rigorous investment of Brest continued.

During the early years of the Napoleonic War it was the close and unremitting grip of the blockade that effectually prevented a great combination such as Napoleon continually, but ever in vain, strove to achieve. In the event of any of the enemy's detachments slipping past the blockading forces, orders were given for the outlying British squadrons to fall back on their strategic centre off Brest, so as to follow the French either to Ireland or up the Channel. However they might for a time evade the vigilance of the blockading squadrons, a strong British force would be ready to bring them to action as they approached the vital point. For months Napoleon contrived ingenious but impracticable plans to disperse the British concentration; but without getting any nearer to his goal. To the last the problem of invasion over an uncommanded sea defied every attempt at solution.

Thus, in the very crisis of the campaign of 1805, the Navy still retained its advantage of interior lines, and our admirals were still guided by the historic tradition of British strategy: to fall back, in the hour of danger, on the vital position at the mouth of the Channel. While Villeneuve was still in mid-ocean. Barham so disposed our forces that Napoleon's intended concentration was rendered impossible. So confident in fact were the Board of Admiralty in the soundness of their dispositions that they were a good deal more concerned for the safety of our convoys than for any threat of invasion.

After Trafalgar, the overwhelming superiority of the British Navy effectively confined the French hegemony to Continental Europe. Despot of the Continent as he was, Napoleon's power stopped short at the water's edge. Our Mediterranean fleet continued to cover Sicily and Malta and to prevent the French from advancing eastward against the Ottoman Empire and India. In the North, Saumarez's powerful squadron protected British interests in the Baltic. Strategically, the continual blockade of the enemy's ports and coasts secured the small detachments and single ships guarding our innumerable convoys, as well as our overseas bases and depots, conjunct expeditions, great and small, and all the far-flung territories of the British Empire. One after the other Napoleon's grandiose designs were baulked by British sea power. In the entire train of significant developments between Nelson's last and greatest victory and the crucial Russian campaign of 1812 the abiding and decisive factor in the contest was the maritime supremacy of Great Britain and the unremitting blockade of the enemy's ports.

At the eastern entrance of the Channel the proximity of the Rhine delta to our shores presented a perennial strategical problem. This was the quarter from which England was most vulnerable. The situation in the Netherlands was the abiding preoccupation of the rulers of this country. Of necessity the domination of the ports of the Scheldt and the Rhine by a great military Power must entail a standing threat to our island security. In Antwerp, above all, such a Power would have an incomparable base for an invasionary army. From the days of Elizabeth to our own a cardinal principle of British policy was therefore involved.

When Louis XIV strove to extend the frontiers of modern France to the furthest limits of ancient Gaul, and to gain possession of the left bank of the Rhine, he inevitably excited the strong hostility of England. One of the principal causes of the War of the Spanish Succession was his seizure of the barrier fortresses in Flanders. At the Peace of Utrecht the southern Netherlands were annexed to Austria, which was not a maritime Power. One of the prime British objectives in the War of the Austrian Succession was the restitution of the Austrian Netherlands, which had been overrun by the French.

The recurrent menace of the Rhine delta was revived in 1792 when the Republican army occupied the Austrian Netherlands and took possession of the ports of the Scheldt and the Rhine. The retention by France of this vital region was a major contributory cause of the breakdown of the short-lived Peace of Amiens. It is worth noting that, towards the end of the Napoleonic War, Castlereagh and Aberdeen secured their object in advance of the general settlement. Ministers were determined that Antwerp must not be left in the hands of France. Of all the ports of the Netherlands, it presented the most likely possibilities for a swift and deadly attack. 'I must particularly entreat you', Castlereagh urged Aberdeen in the autumn of 1813, 'to keep your attention upon Antwerp. The destruction of that arsenal is essential to our safety. To leave it in the hands of France is little short of imposing upon Great Britain the charge of a perpetual war establishment.'

The Baltic always played a significant part in British naval strategy throughout the age of sail, since the destruction of the balance of power around its shores would endanger not only our important commercial interests there, but also the supply of Baltic spars, oak, and other timber for shipbuilding, and, above all, the naval stores without which the Navy could not move. Consequently, when in 1716 Sweden was menaced by a hostile coalition, Great Britain acted promptly and decisively to assist her against the Danish fleet; and after the restoration of peace in the region it was the settled policy of the British government to maintain the balance of power among the Baltic States. To achieve this end, throughout the eighteenth and early nineteenth centuries British squadrons were again and again sent out to the Baltic to keep open the Sound.

The Duke of Marlborough may be accounted the first Englishman to grasp the true potentialities of fleet action in the Mediterranean. In the War of the Spanish Succession a strong Anglo-Dutch squadron effectively supported the allied forces on land and wrested the control of the great inland sea from the French.

A highly important element in naval strategy was the location of bases in relation to those of the enemy and to the theatre of operations. It was the possession of well-defended and adequately equipped bases which enabled a squadron to operate in distant waters, where it could lie in sheltered anchorages to revictual and refit, and obtain fresh water, provisions, and naval stores. Naval operations in the Mediterranean depended in large measure upon the possession of such bases.

The idea of taking and holding Gibraltar, 'the key to the Levant', had long been entertained in England. The old stronghold had fallen into decay and was weakly garrisoned. It was attacked and taken by a powerful allied squadron on 23 July 1704. It is to be remembered that at the time Gibraltar was no more than an open roadstead: but it was potentially one of the key fortresses of Europe.

For want of a port within the Straits on which the allied fleet might be based the whole year round our winter squadron had been obliged to withdraw every year to Lisbon to refit. It was for this reason that in 1708 the conquest of Minorca, with its deep, land-locked harbour of Port Mahon was decided upon. By the early autumn of that year Port Mahon was in allied hands. 'I heard from General Stanhope on the 30th of last month to the effect that the fortress of Mahon surrendered to him the day before', Marlborough wrote at the end of October. '. . . There is no doubt that we shall now be able to keep a good squadron in the Mediterranean throughout the winter.' The naval stores and dockyard gear were speedily transferred from Lisbon to Port Mahon, which henceforward took the place of Lisbon as a base where our squadrons could winter and refit. Great Britain had now a first-class naval base within the Straits. Strategically, Port Mahon was ideally situated for masking Toulon and controlling trade within the western Mediterranean and, in conjunction with Gibraltar, made Great Britain the undisputed mistress of the inland sea.

The importance of Gibraltar from the strategic angle is convincingly revealed during the Seven Years War. In 1758 a squadron under Sir Henry Osborne, based on Gibraltar, held the Straits and prevented the Toulon fleet from getting across the ocean to the help of Louisbourg. In 1759 Boscawen, warned of the passage of Clue's fleet through the Straits, got away from

Gibraltar in the nick of time to destroy the enemy in Lagos Bay. This was a striking example of the immense strategic importance of the Rock. As Lord Shelburne later declared, 'Gibraltar has been described as that happy spot, which in the possession of Great Britain, divides France from France, and Spain from Spain, and consequently as a place which ought not on any account to be relinquished'. The strength of Gibraltar was conclusively established in the historic siege of 1779–83. 'The failure of the great siege of 1779–83', a modern American historian observes, 'established more firmly than ever the tradition of Gibraltar's invulnerability. Gibraltar, in short, became a symbol of British power and invincibility.'[2] Under the aegis of St. Vincent, Gibraltar developed into a major naval base. Shortly afterwards, Saumarez's brilliant victory over a Franco-Spanish squadron off Algeciras again underlined the strategic importance of the Rock and confirmed the truth of Shelburne's observation quoted above that Gibraltar, in the hands of Great Britain, 'divides France from France, and Spain from Spain'.

In the eastern Mediterranean, Malta passed into British hands as one of the prizes of the Nile. The wise governorship of Captain Ball (one of the famous 'band of brothers') firmly cemented the British hold on the island; which, despite the provisions of the Treaty of Amiens, was retained after the restoration of peace. 'There is no quarter', observed Lord Mulgrave, 'in which the naval power of Great Britain is more necessary to check the further progress of French ambition on the Continent during the war, or counter-act the sudden revival of its activity during peace, than the Mediterranean. The particular possession in these seas by which the means of naval exertion in the Common Cause can be most securely provided is Malta.' The prediction was fulfilled in full measure during the Napoleonic War when Malta played a leading part in British naval dispositions to bar the eastward expansion of Napoleon's empire. The island was also retained at the general peace settlement of 1814–15. Henceforth Malta in the strong possession of the Mediterranean fleet stood out in the eyes of Europe 'as the visible embodiment of the mastery of the Mediterranean by England'.

On the other side of the Atlantic, Halifax served as a base for the North American station and the port of assembly for the convoys to and from Europe. Upon the escort vessels provided by the small North American squadron depended the safety of the vital mast ships *en route* for England.

In the West Indian theatre, naval strategy was in large measure determined by the constant factor of the easterly trade winds, which gave fleets or squadrons based on the Windward Islands a substantial advantage over those based on the islands to the leeward. In Fort Royal (Martinique) the French had a first-class windward base and in Cap François (Haïti) a base which lay to windward of the principal British base, Kingston (Jamaica), while the Spaniards had a fine natural harbour at Havana with shipbuilding facilities. In this respect, therefore, the British, having no suitable station to the eastward, were at a serious disadvantage. Another crucial factor in naval operations in the West Indies was the incidence of the hurricane season in June, when the main fleets of the belligerents were accustomed to sail northward up the east coast of North America. In October, when winter conditions set in in North American waters, they would return to the West Indies. The North American and West Indian theatres of the war were therefore intimately connected.

It is significant of the high commercial importance of the West Indian islands in the eighteenth century that both Great Britain and France allotted for these operations in the Caribbean naval forces roughly three times as great as those employed in the Indian Ocean. For the same reason it not infrequently happened that purely military objectives had to give place to the defence and prevention of trade.

The possession of the Cape (captured from the Dutch in 1795; restored at the Peace of Amiens; retaken in 1806) was invaluable to Great Britain for securing the sea-route to India. It was additionally useful as a place of refreshment and convalescence for the sick. As the anchorage in Table Bay was a bad one, the naval base was situated in the neighbouring Simon's Bay. Henceforward the Cape would not only cease to supply Mauritius and Bourbon Island, but would also serve as a base for the British blockading squadrons there.

As in North America and the West Indies, the strategic factor that was ultimately decisive in the East Indian theatre was sea power. In the Seven Years War, Dupleix's designs for establishing a great French principality in southern India were defeated by the presence of a superior British squadron. Similarly it was the tenacious and on the whole effective campaign which Hughes waged against the brilliant and resourceful Suffren that, coupled with the efforts of Hastings and Coote, successfully preserved the British possessions in India in the hour of peril.

Trincomalee, with the finest natural harbour in the Indian Ocean, was, as the experience of the American War had shown, a serious embarrassment to our East India squadron. On the Coromandel coast there was no harbour at all, the other anchorages being merely open roadsteads. On the approach of the north-east monsoon, or trade-wind, there was therefore no safe refuge on the eastern coast for the British squadron. Early in the Revolutionary

War, in 1795, it was taken from the Dutch by Rainier, and retained at the peace.

The possession by the French of Mauritius, with its secure and spacious harbour of Port Louis, was a constant threat to the British territories and commerce in the East. Throughout the Revolutionary and Napoleonic Wars the problem of trade protection was the main preoccupation of the Commander-in-Chief on the East India station. Based on Mauritius and the Dutch ports in the East Indies, the enemy privateers exacted a heavy and continuous toll from the rich traffic of the Bay of Bengal, the Straits of Malacca, and other focal areas. Mauritius was taken from the French in 1810, and retained at the peace settlement of 1814–15 (as Castlereagh explained), 'because in time of war it was a great maritime nuisance, highly detrimental to our commerce'.

The importance of intelligence as a factor in naval warfare can scarcely be rated too highly. The formulation of a sound strategy depends to a great extent on exact knowledge of the enemy's situation—his plans, his *matériel*, his morale, and his movements, present and pending. In the period under survey such information was eagerly sought and carefully scrutinized by commander-in-chief and Admiralty alike. Such is its crucial importance that in modern times a special organization, the Naval Intelligence Department, was created at the Admiralty to deal with it.

With timely and accurate information a commander-in-chief may be able so to dispose his forces as to achieve a superior concentration at the decisive time and place. With inadequate or conflicting reports he may not know when, where, or how to move. This factor stands out very clearly in such episodes as Nelson's pursuit of the French fleet in the campaign of the Nile and Collingwood's failure to track down the enemy following Ganteaume's incursion into the Mediterranean in 1808.

The right interpretation of intelligence was therefore one of the most necessary and important responsibilities laid upon a commander. In strategy and tactics so much depended on it. In the later stages of this era, through the accumulated experience derived from the almost continuous warfare of the past century, the faculty of interpretation had attained to its most complete powers. The channels by which intelligence was obtained were many and various. One of the most important duties of our frigates and smaller cruisers was to gather this intelligence. Scouting frigates were often sent out in pairs—one to dog the enemy, the other to carry the report to the commander-in-chief. Reports on fleet bases were usually obtained by regular reconnaissances by cruisers and, occasionally, by ships of force. Merchantmen—British, allied, or neutral—frequently supplied useful information. The reports regularly forwarded by the Committee of Lloyd's were always a valuable source of intelligence. From time to time most important information would be communicated by British consuls and secret agents in neutral and enemy countries.

Intelligence and orders for the commander-in-chief were conveyed by the Admiralty messenger to the port on which his squadron was based and, if he were at sea, put on board a cruiser, which was usually a fast and handy cutter. This procedure was supplemented, during the war of 1793–1815, by the manual telegraph, which was used for transmitting brief messages to and from the Admiralty and the principal naval ports. In the later years of the war a chain of signal stations was set up around the shores of Great Britain and Ireland to strengthen the existing system of trade protection.

The campaign in home waters in 1759 provides a good illustration of the use and distribution of intelligence at the crucial stage of the Seven Years War.

During the blockade of the principal French arsenal, first Captain Robert Duff and later Captain the Hon. Augustus Hervey were ordered to look into Brest to procure for the Commander-in-Chief, Sir Edward Hawke, intelligence of the enemy's strength, and the condition of his spars and sails (which would reveal to a seaman, with reasonable accuracy, his readiness for sea). On 1 July, Duff duly reported that he had counted there 'Twenty ships of two decks, one snow, one schooner, & one cutter, with French colours hoisted. . . . The ships with their yards and topmasts struck, and topgallant yards down; one of the ships without topgallant masts. About fifteen of the ships had their topsails bent, but no courses.' When Duff was succeeded on the inshore station by Hervey he was ordered to cruise close in with Brest and look in on the enemy fleet as often as he could, and to send the Admiral frequent reports of their situation. Meanwhile intelligence continued to reach the Admiralty from our agents across the Channel of the straitening effect of Hawke's blockade on the enemy's principal base; and towards the end of July the master of a Dutch dogger which had just come out of Brest reported that ' 'Twas surprizing the price of everything, and no white bread scarce to be had'. From time to time Hervey was able to view the enemy at close quarters, and it is clear that he did not rate their seamanship highly. About the middle of July he stood off the entrance to the Goulet and watched the French 'exercising their people at loosing & working their sails—which they do surprisingly badly indeed'. Hervey's ships were in fact the eyes and ears of the fleet, enabling Hawke to cruise far out to the westward in the full knowledge and confidence that he would receive timely warning of any impending move on the part of the enemy.[3]

*Battle of the Nile at about 6.30 p.m. showing
the* Goliath *and the* Zealous *attacking the French ship*
Guerrier; *oil painting by Nicholas Pocock
who was present at the action, 1798.*

At the crisis of the campaign an intercepted letter from Choiseul, the French minister, reached the British government, containing the vital information that d'Aiguillon and his troops were to sail immediately to invade this island and that the Brest fleet under Conflans had been ordered to cover the passage 'au risque d'un combat'. From a supply-ship, the *Love and Unity*, Hawke learned on 16 November that on the previous day Conflans's fleet had been sighted about seventy miles west of Belleisle. Both from the intelligence lately communicated to him from Whitehall and from the report of Duff's squadron stationed in Quiberon Bay it was certain that Conflans's destination must be the Morbihan, where d'Aiguillon's troops and transports were assembled in readiness for the invasion project. 'I have carried a press of sail all night,' Hawke observed in his dispatch, 'with a hard gale at south-south-west, in pursuit of the enemy, and make no doubt of coming up with them at sea or in Quiberon Bay.'[4]

Timely and accurate intelligence gave the Admiral the incalculable advantage of speed and surprise. Four days later, as we know, Conflans was brought to action in the narrow waters of Quiberon Bay and Hawke gained one of the greatest victories in the annals of the sea.

The campaign of the Nile exemplifies the almost insuperable difficulties

with which a commander-in-chief was confronted in the absence of certain news and in face of conflicting reports. Nelson's three frigates had parted company in a gale; about the same time as this, Bonaparte's army, escorted by de Brueys's squadron, had sailed from Toulon. Naples and Sicily had been mentioned in Nelson's orders as the enemy's most probable objectives; but on receiving news of the French fleet passing Sicily and arriving off Malta, Nelson rightly deduced that they were bound for Egypt. Crowding all sail, his squadron reached Alexandria within six days. But for lack of the missing frigates, 'the eyes of the Fleet', he twice failed to intercept the enemy: first, during the hazy night of 25 June, when his squadron was so close to their quarry that the enemy heard the boom of the British signal guns in the mist and altered course to the northward; second, on the 29th on the arrival of the French at Alexandria, which occurred in a matter of hours after his own departure from that port. For the squadron had overrun its prey; and, finding no sign or news of the French in Egypt, Nelson at once stretched over to Asia Minor. Three weeks later, inquiring fruitlessly in Sicily for news of the French, he wrote to Sir William Hamilton: 'It is an old saying, "The Devil's children have the Devil's luck": I cannot find, or to this moment learn, beyond vague conjecture, where the French Fleet are gone to.' Still it was evident that they were, after all, somewhere to the east of him. Not until more than a week later did he learn from some Greek fishermen that the enemy had been seen off Crete about a month earlier, standing to the south-east. It was clear that the French had gone to Egypt, and it was equally clear how he had missed them there. Once again his squadron sailed for Alexandria.

In short, for lack of intelligence it had taken Nelson nearly two and a half months from the time of de Brueys's departure from Toulon to track down and destroy the enemy in Aboukir Bay.

The campaign of Trafalgar similarly illustrates the portentous issues which often hinged upon the intelligence factor.

On the renewal of hostilities in the spring of 1803, Napoleon embarked upon preparations for an invasion of the British Isles on a scale more formidable than that of anything hitherto attempted. Meanwhile Pitt was patiently pursuing the negotiations which finally brought into being the Third Coalition: the crux of the bargain his government struck with the Tsar being the dispatch of an expeditionary force to the Mediterranean to co-operate with the Russians in Italy.

Early in 1805 Napoleon, after considering and abandoning in turn his former plans for getting his army across the Channel, evolved his third and final design for the invasion of England. The root idea was still to disperse the British squadrons; but this time he envisaged a concentration on the further side of the Atlantic. Ganteaume was to put to sea with the Brest squadron, raise the blockade of Ferrol, and then sail in company with the Spanish squadron to the West Indies, there to join forces with Missiessy. At the same time Villeneuve with the Toulon squadron was to slip past Nelson, release the Spanish squadron blockaded in Cadiz, and shape a course for the same destination. The entire armada, under the command of Ganteaume, would then return to Europe and appear in overwhelming force at the entrance of the Channel, to cover the passage of the Grand Army.

When Villeneuve's fleet broke out of Toulon on 30 March, Nelson's overriding anxiety centred on his ignorance of the enemy's intended objective. Once again, as in the summer of 1798, he strove desperately to obtain news of the enemy fleet. Shaking off the pursuing British frigates during the night of the 31st, Villeneuve stood out of the Gut with a favouring wind. Two hours later the *Fisgard* frigate, then at Gibraltar, sailed for Ushant to warn the Channel fleet. In the Bay of Biscay dispatches were put on board a Guernsey lugger, which was forthwith ordered into Plymouth. On 25 April it was known at Admiralty that the Toulon fleet had passed the Straits. Barham at once took steps to secure the safety of the expeditionary force which had been dispatched to the Mediterranean. A week later he rightly concluded that Villeneuve's destination was the West Indies, and ordered a small squadron to follow him there.

Meanwhile Nelson took his station midway between Sardinia and the African coast, covering the vital positions to the eastward, and there remained until he had certain news that the enemy had gone to the westward. Owing to a series of westerly gales it took him a whole month to reach the Straits; and not until 9 May did he learn of Villeneuve's departure for the West Indies. His squadron arrived off Barbados in little more than three weeks. Misled, however, by a message from Brigadier-General Brereton in St. Lucia that the enemy had lately been sighted steering southward for Trinidad, Nelson followed in pursuit; and thereby missed coming up with them off Martinique. On 13 June, after sending a sloop to England with dispatches and another vessel to warn Calder off Ferrol of the enemy's return, Nelson sailed for Gibraltar, arriving off the Spanish coast several days ahead of Villeneuve. Early on 9 July, Barham received certain intelligence that Villeneuve was making for the Bay of Biscay, which enabled him to make the dispositions that effectively undermined Napoleon's elaborate paper strategy. Barham moved so swiftly that Napoleon was completely baffled. It was apparent that the latter's whole plan of campaign for the invasion of England had collapsed.

Though the Admiralty had never shared the apprehension entertained by the general public at the presence of the Grand Army encamped within forty miles of our shores, it was seriously concerned about the threat to our convoys. The intelligence system covering our defences against a hostile descent had shown itself remarkably efficient: but as regards trade-protection there was much room for improvement. In the latter half of August 1805 Barham and Nelson together took steps to secure measures for more effective communications and protection of commerce. A line of frigates was ordered to cruise between Finisterre and St. Vincent, for the dual purpose of intelligence and trade protection.

To forestall the allied offensive in Italy, Napoleon ordered the Combined Fleet into the Mediterranean to co-operate with St-Cyr's army in southern Italy. That was the immediate cause of the Combined Fleet's departure from Cadiz which resulted in the battle of Trafalgar. But Napoleon's grand strategy for the overthrow of Great Britain had been defeated, in fact, many weeks before when Villeneuve in despair abandoned his attempt to join hands with the Brest fleet and took refuge in Cadiz.

In able hands intelligence, as we have seen, was often a factor of decisive importance. However, it was quite a different matter when the commander was a Byng, a Man, a Bridport, or a Colpoys. To what purpose would intelligence concerning the vulnerability of the enemy's transports and supply-ships in Minorca, and their communications with France, have availed Byng when his one idea, as is apparent from the proceedings at the council of war following the indecisive action with Galissonière, was to retire immediately to Gibraltar? In the same way it may be suspected that no intelligence in the world would have nerved Man to face a difficult and dangerous situation off the Spanish coast in 1795. 'Poor Admiral Man has been afflicted with such a distempered mind during the last nine months that imaginary ills and difficulties are continually brooding in it. . . . When the Blue Devils prevail,' Jervis declared, 'there is an end of resource and energy.' The most urgent intelligence would scarcely have caused Bridport to act with energy and promptitude, as is seen by the almost incredible series of blunders on his part during the French expedition to Bantry Bay in 1796 and Bruix's incursion into the Mediterranean in 1799. Colpoys's negligent attitude to intelligence may be gauged from the fact that in the invasion crisis of 1796, despite all the reports that reached him to the effect that the French were on the point of sailing, he had actually quitted his rendezvous when Pellew's cruisers arrived with the expected and urgent intelligence that the enemy were at sea.[5]

Throughout the first half of the eighteenth century the Fighting Instructions issued by Russell in 1691 and Rooke in 1703 were supplemented by a series of Additional Fighting Instructions. Vernon seems to have been the first commander to perceive the inadequacy of the old system of Fighting Instructions and to supplement it by the Additional Fighting Instructions. The evidence for this is contained in a pamphlet written about 1744, in which the following passage appears:

> Mr. V[ernon], that provident, great admiral, who never suffered any useful precaution to escape him, concerted some signals for so good a purpose, widely foreseeing their use and necessity, giving them to the captains of the squadron under his command. And lest his vigilance should be some time or other surprised by an enemy, or the exigencies of his master's service, should require him to attack or repulse by night, he appointed signals for the line of battle, engaging, chasing, leaving off chase, with many others altogether new, excellent, and serviceable.[6]

The work of Vernon was afterwards carried on by Anson, who, as First Lord, issued the best of Vernon's additions, throughout the Fleet, and added a few of his own. Although this admiral was never to fulfil the hopes that his disciples had entertained of his achieving a general improvement in tactics, the effect of Anson's additions—and of the later Additional Fighting Instructions evolved successively by Hawke, Boscawen, Rodney, and Hood—was to make tactics a great deal more flexible and elastic.

In the scientific study of naval tactics our writers, indeed, lagged far behind the French. The marked improvement of battle tactics was not the least important aspect of the French naval renaissance which took place between the American and French Revolutionary Wars. Nothing like Morogues's *Tactique Navale* (1763) or de Villehuet's *Le Manœuvrier* (1765) was published on this side of the Channel until a generation later.

The first important original work on tactics to appear in English was Clerk of Eldin's *An Essay on Naval Tactics* (1797). This made no major contribution to the subject, but did much to propagate the hard-bought lessons of experience among naval officers. Nelson is said frequently to have 'expressed his approbation' of Clerk's work.

Our commanders throughout this period were faced with a twofold problem. In the first place, the proficiency of British and French alike in forming and maintaining the close-hauled line of battle ahead almost invariably led to stalemate. Secondly, the unwillingness of the French commanders to accept decisive action presented our own with the tactical problem of fixing the enemy. The problem seemed to Captain John Jervis in 1778 virtually insoluble. 'I have', he informed the Secretary of the Admiralty, 'often told you that two fleets of equal force can never produce decisive events unless they are equally determined to fight it out, or the commander-in-chief of one of them so bitches it as to misconduct his line.'

In the War of American Independence, it was mainly owing to their want of tactical skill and the inadequacy of their signalling system that the British as a rule failed to force the French to close action and so produce a mêlée, with the result that many an engagement degenerated into a mere artillery duel. In these encounters the French were accustomed to take the lee-gauge and, aiming at their opponents' masts and rigging, retire before the British could come near enough to resort to the rapid fire at point-blank range in which they excelled. 'They have formed a system of tactics', observed Kempenfelt to Middleton, 'which are studied in their academies and practised in their squadrons.'

The method by which the British eventually forced the French to continue an action once begun was by breaking the enemy's line. In the action off The Saints in 1782, Rodney, as a result of a sudden shift of the wind, succeeded in doing this from the leeward position—and though the main body of the enemy's fleet got away, individual groups of French vessels were effectually fixed. In 1783 the manœuvre of breaking the enemy's line, now fully understood, was given a corresponding signal by Hood.[7] The usual procedure, however, was for a British fleet to attack from to windward. In spite of the grave risks of this mode of attack against an opposing fleet of approximately equal strength and efficiency and willing to fight it out, the tactic of breaking the enemy's line became a virtual necessity if British commanders were to obtain a decision in face of the elusive tactics developed by the French. It was this procedure—a completely new manœuvre—which Howe adopted on the Glorious First of June.

Howe's plan was to 'divide the enemy, at all points, from to windward'. Each of his vessels was to cut through under the stern of her opposite number in the enemy's line and engage her from to leeward. The advantages of this method of attack, if successful, would be twofold: first, his ships would be able while passing through the enemy's line to pour a heavy raking fire into the hulls of their opponents, and, secondly, the retreat of disabled Frenchmen would thereby be cut off, since a crippled ship could only retire to leeward. In the event the seamanship of most of the British fleet was not equal to this manœuvre, and the intervals between certain of the enemy's ships were in any case too narrow: only seven of Howe's ships out of twenty-six, in fact, succeeded in piercing the enemy's line. Even so, this sufficed to bring on a desperate mêlée and prevented the French from disengaging.

British tactics in the age of sail may be said to have reached their highest development in the three great victories achieved by Nelson. All three were preceded by the most careful planning and preparation. Thus, during the long pursuit of the French fleet which ended in the battle of the Nile, provision had been made for every conceivable combination of circumstances in which they might encounter the enemy. 'There was no possible position', Nelson's flag-captain declared, 'in which they could be found that he did not take into his calculation, and for the most advantageous attack of which he had not digested and arranged the best possible disposition of the force which he commanded.' Speed and surprise played an essential part in this brilliant victory. The enemy's van was attacked by an overpowering force and obliged to strike. His centre was then engaged by a superior concentration and overwhelmed in like manner. Victory was not a name strong enough for such a scene, Nelson himself observed; he called it a conquest.

At Copenhagen, there was the same skilful adaptation of tactics to the circumstances. The enemy line was to be attacked at its weakest point. The southernmost Danish ships were to be engaged by a superior force and overwhelmed; after which an overpowering concentration was to be

The Victory *breaking the line at Trafalgar, 21 October 1805;*
aquatint by W. J. Huggins, 1837.

brought to bear on the next part of the enemy line. In effect the Danish fleet
was to be attacked and destroyed in detail. In the event, however, both the
navigational difficulties of the channel where the enemy were moored and
the Danish resistance had proved greater than was anticipated. The action of
Copenhagen was in fact a close-run thing and had come near to being lost.

In Nelson's last and greatest action his intention was to bring such an
overwhelming force against a part of the enemy line (*the rear and centre*) as to
destroy it in time to deal with the remainder (*the van*) before nightfall. This
was to be done by dividing the fleet into two squadrons, one of which was to
surround and destroy the enemy's rear, while the other first contained the
van and then overwhelmed the centre. The overriding importance of the
time factor is seen in the emphasis laid on 'bringing the Enemy to Battle in
such a manner as to make the business decisive', to which end it was laid
down that 'the Order of Sailing is to be the Order of Battle'. 'Something
must be left to chance,' continued Nelson in the famous Memorandum;
'nothing is sure in a Sea Fight beyond all others . . . but I look with
confidence to a Victory before the Van of the Enemy could succour their
friends [in the Rear].'[8] Such in essence was the 'Nelson touch', embodying as
it did a daring and revolutionary method of attack based on a right

assessment of the fighting value of the British ships compared with that of their opponents.

The development of tactics was closely bound up with the system of signals. The restrictions imposed by the inadequacy of the old signal book had for long been a drag upon tactical progress. Our signal code, in fact, formed part of the Fighting Instructions issued by Russell and Rooke, which, even with the Additional Instructions already mentioned, seriously circumscribed a commander's tactical control in action. The signal book allowed of only a strictly limited number of signals, and was, moreover, easily put out of commission by damage to masts and rigging.

From the Master's Journal, Euryalus; *this page records Nelson's historic message before Trafalgar.*

The French were actually first in the field with the highly efficient method of signalling invented by Mahé de la Bourdonnais. It was not, however, the French but their British adversaries who profited chiefly by these new developments. To Howe in collaboration with Kempenfelt belongs most of the credit for the revolutionary improvement in our system of signalling towards the close of the eighteenth century. In 1781 there appeared *General Instructions for the conduct of the ships of war, explanatory of, and relative to the signals contained in the signal-book herewith delivered by Rear-Admiral Richard Kempenfelt.* It was not enough to devise an efficient method of signalling; it was also necessary to get it generally adopted. 'I therefore followed in great measure Lord Howe's mode,' observed Kempenfelt, 'he being a popular character.' In 1782 Howe brought out his early Signal Book, somewhat on the lines of the numerary system already devised by the French, entitled *Primer of Speech for Fighting Ships*; in 1790, when he resumed command of the Channel fleet, there appeared his *Signal Book for Ships of War*, embodying various improvements, which was generally adopted throughout the Service.[9] Howe's first and second Signal Books superseded the old rigid system of Fighting Instructions, thereby giving the admiral, for the first time, full tactical control of his fleet. The new system of signals went far towards solving the main tactical problem of the eighteenth century—namely, that of 'fixing' the enemy and forcing him to close action. The year 1799 saw the official Signal Book on the new system printed and issued by the Admiralty. By this means elasticity in naval tactics was at last achieved. A year later Sir Home Popham's *Telegraphic Signals or Marine Vocabulary* marked a further step forward. For the first time the Commander-in-Chief was able to say exactly what he pleased by signal. The new code came rapidly into general use. Nelson's immortal signal at Trafalgar, *England expects that every man will do his duty*, was made with Popham's code.

The striking progress in gunnery made by the British Navy in the last two decades of the eighteenth century was due in the main to important improvements introduced by Sir Charles Douglas, Rodney's Captain of the Fleet. Douglas substituted flannel for silk as a cartridge-casing and utilized steel springs to control the recoil of the guns. He was similarly responsible for the invention of the gun-lock. As a result of these and other improvements in serving the guns the gunners were able to fire as many as two rounds in three minutes; and, by means of a system of blocks and tackles, it became possible for the first time to employ oblique fire. The improvements were officially approved by the Admiralty early in 1781 and introduced in the West Indies squadron at Rodney's special request. The efficacy of these new methods was apparent at the action of The Saints, in 1782, when more men were killed in the French flagship, the *Ville de Paris*, than in the entire British fleet. 'I can aver from my own observation that the French fire slackens as we approach,' wrote Dr. Gilbert Blane, who was present at this action, 'and is totally silent when we are close alongside.' The carronade,[10] which was a short piece with a large bore, light and easy to handle in close-range fighting, was first introduced into the Navy in 1779. It played a leading part at The Saints (the first great carronade action), the Glorious First, Camperdown, St. Vincent, Nile, Copenhagen, and Trafalgar; all of which actions were fought at close range. Throughout this period the carronade substantially increased the fire-power of the battle fleet under such conditions and contributed to an important degree to the great roll of British victories in the Revolutionary and Napoleonic Wars. In the last two decades of the century the majority of the British frigates were fitted with carronades. The carronade gradually became larger in calibre and, in the smaller British cruisers, often comprised the entire armament of the vessel with the exception of a pair of bow-chasers.

CHAPTER 3

SEAMANSHIP
AND NAVIGATION

IN the age of sail, the importance of seamanship as a factor in naval warfare can scarcely be set too high. It was intimately linked with survival in face of 'the dangers of the sea'; with the protection and destruction of trade; with the collection and diffusion of intelligence; with the blockade of the enemy's ports; with the conduct of conjunct expeditions, and with the enforcement of our maritime rights. Since the defeat of the Armada the superiority of British seamanship had played a crucial part in a great many of our actions. How supremely important seamanship was reckoned among the qualities of an officer, may be gauged from the testimony of James Anthony Gardner and others. A revealing anecdote is told of one of Nelson's captains in his later years, then an Admiral, and Commander-in-Chief at Plymouth. A certain lieutenant, in command of a small brig, had been ordered to proceed to the Sound. Because the wind was rather scant, he had rashly requested the Admiral to allow his brig to be towed out of Hamoaze by a steamship. The Admiral (Sir William Hargood) thereupon informed the lieutenant that when in command of the *Belleisle*, 'had he not worked out of Hamoaze with the wind two points more against him, he should not have been at Trafalgar; and concluded by recommending the lieutenant to find his way to the Sound without delay'.

Though the French on numerous occasions displayed fine seamanship—notably in the war of 1778–83 and in the *guerre de course* of 1793–1815—they scarcely attained the same high level of excellence as the British. Still less did the Spaniards, whose efforts our own officers were accustomed to regard with tolerant contempt. In the summer of 1793 Nelson noted how our Spanish allies were unable, after several hours of manoeuvring, 'to form anything which could be called a Line of Battle ahead'. In the same year Gardner observed how, when he was in the *Berwick*, they fell in with a dismasted Spanish frigate, to whose crew they were able to render some much-needed assistance; 'as they appeared to be deficient in nautical knowledge', was the British officer's acid comment, 'or, in other words, the vilest set of lubbers that ever were seen. They positively did not know how to get a jury mast up.' But Gardner was no less severe on his own countrymen when, owing to the negligence of the pilots, the *Blonde* frigate narrowly escaped disaster on the Shipwash Sand in the winter of 1799, arriving (as he observed) at Sheerness the following evening:

> Ragged, and shabby, and all forlorn,
> By wind and weather tattered and torn,
> Occasioned by pilots who treated with scorn
> The good advice that was given that morn;
> For which a rope their necks should adorn,
> The damnedest lubbers that ever were born.[1]

The British superiority in seamanship revealed itself over and over again in the long struggle with France. The *Mermaid*, 40, manœuvring in pursuit of the *Vigilant*, 64, off Louisbourg in 1745; the high standard of disciplined skill necessitated by Anson's evolutions, two years later, in the first action off Finisterre; the passage of the Traverse by Saunders's fleet and the landing of Wolfe's troops in the ships' boats under the Heights of Abraham; Boscawen's squadron clearing from Gibraltar only four hours after the signal 'Enemy in sight' had been received; the *Royal George* and the *Magnanime* sweeping into Quiberon Bay in a rising gale under topgallant-sails, in headlong pursuit of Conflans (Hawke's victory was a victory of seamanship, if ever there was one); the outmanœuvring of a superior French squadron by Howe, in the summer of 1778, off the North American coast; Rodney's fleet running before a fresh westerly gale between the Spaniards and a dead lee shore, and then, during the day and night following the Moonlight action, clawing off the shoals of San Lucar; Hood steering under the enemy's guns into the anchorage off St. Kitts vacated by de Grasse; Kempenfelt cutting in between de Guichen and his convoy; the rounding of Ushant by the *Formidable* and eleven more of Rodney's squadron in a January gale in 1782; Howe working between his convoy and a superior French squadron lying in Algeciras Bay at the third relief of Gibraltar; Fremantle in the *Inconstant* frigate manœuvring in pursuit of the huge *Ça Ira*; St. Vincent's infinite capacity for improvisation while on the Mediterranean station, and the matchless sail-drill of the squadron under his command; the *Alexander* towing the dismasted *Vanguard* into St-Pierre's anchorage, off Sardinia, and the refitting of the latter vessel within four days; Blackwood in the *Penelope* frigate pursuing the *Guillaume Tell*, 80, and severely damaging her in the long night action of 30 March 1800; the passage of the Hollænder Deep by Nelson's division before the battle of Copenhagen; Sir Charles Pole, in the following spring, bringing a British squadron for the first time through the winding channels of the Great Belt and against contrary winds; the landing of Abercromby's troops in Aboukir Bay in the face of strong enemy resistance; Nelson's fleet beating through the Straits of Messina in chase of Villeneuve; the rapid pursuit of the Combined Fleet from Lagos Bay to the West Indies, and back again to Gibraltar; the conduct throughout the war of 1793–1815 of innumerable convoys, landing-parties, and cutting-out expeditions—are all instances of that fine seamanship which so often had a decisive influence upon the course of operations.

Above all, the masterly handling of British ships and squadrons was made manifest in the investment of the enemy's coasts and ports—in the close blockade of Brest by Hawke in 1759; revived, at the turn of the century, by St. Vincent and later continued by Cornwallis: in the investment of the Texel by Duncan; of Cadiz by St. Vincent, Keith, and Collingwood; of Ferrol, by Pellew, Cochrane, and Calder; of Toulon, by Nelson, Collingwood, Cotton, and Pellew, in the Revolutionary and Napoleonic Wars.

On the advanced station, close in with the perilous, iron-bound Brittany coast, the arduous, grim blockading duty was a searching test of seamanship. Well might Cornwallis declare that 'the officer in charge of those ships [the inshore squadron] should have a particular turn for that kind of service'. It took a cool and resourceful seaman to discover the passage off Béniguete, whereby the batteries near Conquet were avoided. It took a bold seaman to run for Douarnenez Bay in a rising gale, with mortar batteries crossing each other from the Bec du Chevre and the Bec du Raz, and with a shoal in the middle of the entrance. The day-to-day routine of the inshore squadron—perpetually on the alert for the vagaries of the weather, currents, and tidal streams; their watchful care of their anchors and cables; the countless risks they ran to watch the motions of the enemy in Brest, to cut out gun-boats and *chasse-marées*, and to prevent timber and other supply ships from getting into Brest—bred up an incomparable race of seamen. How often, on the other hand, in the course of these wars, was a French squadron, on leaving port, incapacitated or even obliged to return to harbour again, through stress of weather.

In the later years of the Napoleonic War the seamanship of the Navy does not appear to have suffered any such general deterioration as its gunnery had. The dangers of the sea were in truth sufficiently formidable to keep the crews ever on the alert. In the continual cruising and blockading, ships were often obliged to work to sea to avoid being driven on shore—it is significant that references to 'club-hauling' begin to appear in nautical manuals about this time. John Boteler in his *Recollections* relates how, when he was a midshipman in the *Dictator*, 74, in February 1811 Captain Williams successfully club-hauled his ship off the Scottish coast.

> In beating into Inchkeith we got close in on a lee shore, Kirkaldy; and I saw an evolution performed, that may be the luck of one sailor's lifetime to witness, i.e. to 'club-haul' the ship. We were so close in, that the chance was, the ship might not go about, with the little sail she could shew, and there was decidedly no room to wear. So that when all was ready and good way put on the ship, 'down with the helm', when head to wind 'let go the anchor' and so check her on the other tack, then cut the cable and the ship was safe round—we made two or three tacks after, then safely anchored in Leith Roads. . . .[2]

The following year was distinguished by one of the finest feats of seamanship in naval history. This was another case of club-hauling, and in exceptionally hazardous circumstances. The *Magnificent*, 74, Captain John Hayes, lay, on the evening of 16 December, in the entrance to Basque Roads. The wind was westerly, and freshening, and the topgallant yards and masts were got down. With the wind still freshening, the lower yards and topmasts were struck; the ship lay in ten fathoms, with the sea breaking heavily on a neighbouring reef, about a quarter of a mile astern. At any moment the cables were liable to be cut on the surrounding rocks. With the wind at W.S.W. it blew a gale, with a lee tide and a heavy sea setting right on the reef. In these desperate straits the captain presently resolved to club-haul the ship, which was successfully done. 'And now', related one of the officers on board, 'for the first time, I believe, was seen a ship at sea under reefed courses, and close-reefed top-sails, with yards and topmasts struck. The sails all stood remarkably well; and, by this novel method, was saved a beautiful ship of the line, and five hundred and fifty souls.'[3] For the rest of his life Captain Hayes was renowned throughout the Service as the 'Magnificent Hayes'.

In North America as in Europe the exigencies of the blockading service were a searching test of seamanship. On certain parts of the coast of New England the navigational conditions presented well-nigh insuperable difficulties to an effective blockade. The fact was that during the winter months neither Boston nor Narragansett Bay could be closely and continually blockaded; and on 'dark blowing nights' and again in a blizzard there was always the chance of a frigate or a sloop slipping out to sea. The *Shannon* and *Tenedos*, according to Captain Capel, in the spring of 1813, were 'invariably as close off the Port of Boston as the circumstance of the weather would permit, but the long continued fogs that prevail on this part of the coast at this season of the year give the enemy great advantage'.[4] Though for many months Captain Charles Stewart was locked up in Boston, a northerly wind at last gave him the opportunity for which he had been waiting; and he got away to sea.

Decatur in the United States had similarly hoped to slip out from New York, in the stormy spring weather, by way of Sandy Hook, but was never given the chance; for a strong British force remained continually off the bar. In the final phase of the war the 'Magnificent Hayes', commanding the division blockading New York to prevent the escape of Decatur and his squadron, gave yet another example of consummate seamanship. Though repeatedly blown off the coast by winter gales he was careful to take up his post on that point of bearing from the Hook that he judged likely, under the prevailing weather conditions, would be the enemy's track. So it came about that when late on 13 January 1813 Hayes's ships were blown out to sea in a blizzard, and unable, with the wind blowing fresh from the W.N.W. next day, to get in with the Hook again, he successfully intercepted the enemy on the track he expected them to take, with the result that the *President* was severely damaged and forced to strike.[5]

The handling of British frigates was responsible for some remarkable feats of seamanship. Sir Edward Pellew, of whom Mahan justly writes, 'a seaman inbred, if ever there ws one', was, perhaps, the frigate captain *par excellence*.[6] A midshipman who had served under his command on the Newfoundland station between the American and the French Revolutionary Wars records the following anecdote:

> Wherever there was exertion required aloft, to preserve a sail or a mast, the captain was foremost in the work, apparently as a mere matter of amusement, and there was not a man in the ship that could equal him in personal activity. He appeared to play among the elements in the hardest storms. I remember once, in close-reefing the main topsail, the captain had given his orders from the quarter-deck and ordered us aloft. On gaining the topsail yard, the most active and daring of our party hesitated to go upon it, as the sail was flapping violently, making it a service of great danger; but a voice was heard from the extreme end of the yard, calling upon us to exert ourselves to save the sail,

which would otherwise beat to pieces. A man said, 'Why, that's the captain: How the —— did he get there?' He had followed us up, and, clambering over the backs of the sailors, had reached the topmast head, above the yard, and thence descended by the lift,—a feat unfortunately not easy to be explained to landsmen, but which will be allowed by seamen to demand great hardihood and address.[7]

Another celebrated frigate captain, who greatly distinguished himself in the Mediterranean during the Napoleonic War, was Patrick Campbell of the *Unité*. Under his command, it was claimed, the *Unité* became 'the smartest ship in the sea'.

> In the *Unité*, so ready was every individual to his station, and so confident was the First Lieutenant of everyone's abilities and exertion, that, instead of saying, hoist away this, that, and the other, sail, he had only to say two words—'Make sail'—and in a few moments the ship from appearance as a naked tree would be as a cloud, in so short a time that a landsman would hardly credit his own sight, was he to be a spectator.[8]

Similar examples of fine seamanship are to be seen in the handling of the *Amazon* frigate by Captain Riou in the Baltic campaign of 1801, the admirable scouting work of Captain Blackwood and the other frigate captains on the eve of Trafalgar, the brilliant achievement of the *Impérieuse* under Captain Cochrane in 1808, the Channel cruise of the *Pique* against French privateers in 1811–12, and the operations of Popham's frigates off the north coast of Spain in the later stages of the Peninsular War.

Finally, attention must be drawn to the world-wide experience gained by the captains and officers of so many frigates, sloops, and smaller cruisers. A vessel might be ordered from the Channel to the Caribbean, from the Caribbean to the Bay of Fundy, from the Bay of Fundy to the North Cape. Large numbers of our officers accordingly came to be familiar with navigational conditions and local weather, not only in the North Sea, Channel, and Mediterranean theatres in which the great majority of them served, but also in many different and distant parts of the globe: with the signs of a pampero off La Plata; with the 'table cloth' that presaged a south-easter in Table Bay, with its dreaded shift to the N.W.; with the hurricane season in the West Indies; with the monsoons of the Bay of Bengal and the innumerable hazards of the China Sea and its approaches; with the fogs and gales off Newfoundland; with the lowering Arctic skies and the strong indraught which invariably set on the Murman coast; with the intricate navigation of the Belts and of the Malmö passage. The testimony of one mariner, of whom mention has already been made, gives some idea of the immense range of experience that was possessed by many in the Service during the era in question. 'My life', declared John Nicol, 'for a period of twenty-five years, was a continued succession of change. Twice I circumnavigated the globe; three times I was in China; twice in Egypt; and more than once sailed along the whole landboard of America from Nootka Sound to Cape Horn; twice I doubled it.'[9]

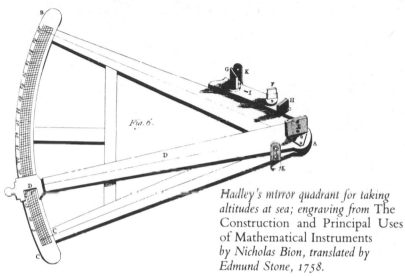

Fig. 6.

Hadley's mirror quadrant for taking altitudes at sea; engraving from The Construction and Principal Uses of Mathematical Instruments *by Nicholas Bion, translated by Edmund Stone, 1758.*

The eighteenth century witnessed various developments of outstanding importance which ushered in a new era in navigation. To this fact, indeed, was largely due the remarkable accuracy of Captain Cook's observations during his voyages of exploration in the South Pacific.

There had been little change in the structure of the quadrant since the late Tudor age. It had remained subject to a considerable degree of error resulting from the motion of the sea. The difficulty was finally overcome by John Hadley, in 1731, with his reflecting quadrant. This was a great improvement on the crude instrument used by Elizabethan mariners.

With this Instrument, though the Ship rolls ever so much, provided the Instrument be kept in or near an upright Posture, though it be leaned forward or backward therein, yet the Image of any Object, when once brought by sliding the Index [alidade] to appear on the edge of the Sea, will there remain absolutely immoveable as long as the Index continues in the same Place, without being stirred, and the Observer has the same Advantage of making the Observation as if he took it in smooth Water, and the Instrument was held still without motion.[10]

John Harrison's chronometer; this one made c. 1765.

It was from Hadley's reflecting quadrant that the modern sextant was evolved by John Campbell in 1757. Hadley's instrument was in point of fact a measure of ninety degrees: the principle of construction remained the same in Campbell's instrument, but the latter extended the circular arc so as to be able to measure up to one hundred and twenty degrees.

With the swift expansion of British merchant shipping in the opening years of the eighteenth century, the need to discover a solution to the problem of longitude determination became so urgent that, in 1714, an Act of Parliament was passed setting up the Board of Longitude and providing for a reward of £20,000 to be paid to any person or persons who should devise a sufficiently accurate method of calculating a ship's longitude. Various attempts to use the variation of the compass as a basis for ascertaining longitude at sea had indeed been made for centuries; but this procedure had been proved unreliable. The ingenious method evolved by the Astronomer-Royal, Dr. Nevil Maskelyne, of determining the longitude by lunar observations, involving as it did certain complicated mathematical calculations, was scarcely practicable in the ordinary way. Still it was a distinct improvement on dead reckoning and was used by a number of enterprising masters. James Cook on his first voyage to the South Pacific (1768–71) employed the lunar method with remarkably accurate results. No really practical method existed of determining longitude at sea until well on in the eighteenth century:[11] the vast majority of mariners continued to trust to their dead reckoning, or calculation of course and distance run; and, since

John Harrison; oil painting by T. King.

this at best was extremely uncertain, recourse was had to latitude sailing. At last came the solution of the problem. For centuries it had been known that if a clock could be constructed which would accurately keep the time of the port of departure throughout a long voyage, it would become possible to ascertain the longitude: but this knowledge was in fact of no more than academic interest, seeing that not until the fourth decade of the century did any such time-piece exist. The first chronometer was invented and constructed, in 1735, by a village carpenter, John Harrison—'Longitude Harrison', as he was called. Harrison constructed a second in 1739 and a third ten years later. Duplicates of this third chronometer were carried by Captain Cook on his second and third voyages. The marvellous accuracy of Harrison's instruments marked a revolutionary advance upon anything that had hitherto been achieved. By the close of the eighteenth century his time-keeper had virtually superseded all other methods of getting Greenwich time. In the last two decades of the century chronometers were being produced commercially. Their cost, however, was high; and it was not until many years later that they came into general use.

As the result of an inquiry following the disaster to Clowdisley Shovell's squadron in 1707, the Admiralty decided that brass instead of wooden compass bowls should be used in future. In the latter half of the eighteenth century the compasses manufactured by Dr. Gowin Knight, which were fitted with very strongly magnetized needles and proved considerably more accurate than the others then available, were adopted by the Navy and a number of merchantmen. Knight's method of manufacturing artificial magnets was so successful that they speedily replaced the lodestones formerly used for re-magnetizing compass needles. Towards the close of the century his compasses, however, were being superseded by those made by Ralph Walker, which marked a further advance.

Among the more important navigational works of the period were Joshua Kelly's *The Modern Navigator's Compleat Tutor* (1724), Captain Daniel Newhouse's *The Whole Art of Navigation* (1727), N. Colson's *The Mariner's New Kalendar* (1746), John Robertson's *Elements of Navigation* (1754), Dr. Nevil Maskelyne's *The British Mariner's Guide* (1763), and J. H. Moore's *New Practical Navigator* (1793)—this last ran through nearly twenty editions before the end of the great war of 1793–1815. An outstanding contribution to the advance of modern scientific navigation was the publication, in 1767, of the first number of Maskelyne's *Nautical Almanac*—a work of amazing and unprecedented accuracy. Maskelyne continued to compile the *Nautical Almanac* during the rest of the century.

It would be difficult to exaggerate the dangers of the unlighted, unbuoyed coasts of these islands in early times. In the hazardous approaches to not a few of our ports ships might well be lost within sight of their destination. The most important landfall on our coasts—the Lizard—was for many years unlighted. In the western approaches the Bishop, Seven Stones, and the Wolf were all unlighted; as were also, in the Channel, the Runnelstone, Manacles, and the Needles. The Goodwin Sands[12] and the banks and shoals off the east coast were very inadequately lighted. What a toll of wrecks and strandings must these unseen rocks and banks have claimed!

On the Isle of May, in the entrance to the Firth of Forth, a coal fire was exhibited for 181 years. It was privately owned, like so many of the lighthouses throughout the seventeenth and eighteenth centuries. Several of the earliest lighthouses came into being through the needs of the busy collier traffic passing up and down the coast. Two lighthouses were erected in 1607 at Caister, near Yarmouth, which not only indicated the position of shoals, but also assisted shipping to keep in the right channels. At about the same date there were lighthouses on the North and South Foreland, and for a few

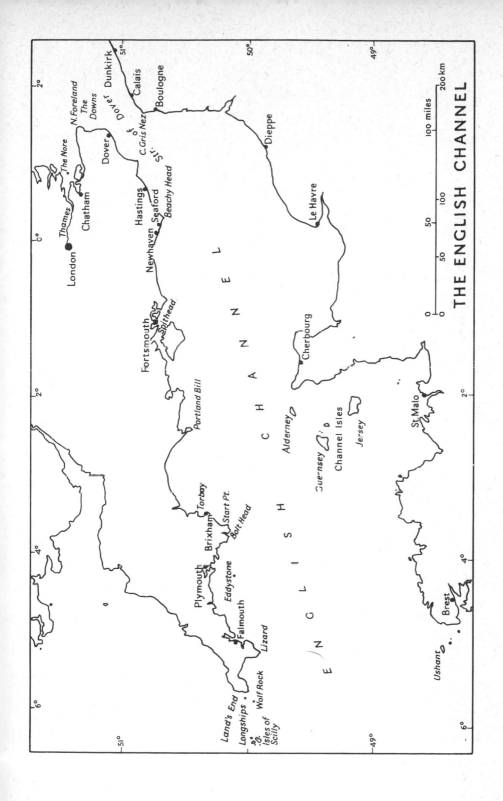

THE ENGLISH CHANNEL

Bell Rock lighthouse;
nineteenth-century engraving.

years a light was shown on the Lizard. Lighthouses did not in fact exist in significant numbers until after 1700. The Skerries (on the direct route of ships making the Mersey) were lighted in 1715; a lighthouse was erected at Portland Point in 1716, another at Foulness in 1720, and another on the Casquets in 1723.

Nowhere in British waters was there a greater danger to shipping than the Eddystone reef, which lay about 16 miles S.S.W. of Plymouth. After the destruction by fire of Rudyard's wooden tower in 1753, the work of erecting a new lighthouse on the Eddystone was entrusted to the celebrated engineer, John Smeaton. The tower was begun in August 1756, and the last stone was laid three years later. It was constructed entirely of stone; the light being visible at a distance of 13 miles. Light was provided by 24 tallow candles until 1807, when the candles were replaced by oil lamps and reflectors. From 16 October 1759, when the new lighthouse first sent out its warning beams, Smeaton's tower continued in use down to within living memory.

In 1806 a lighthouse was constructed on Flamborough Head. This was an important point for a 'fix' on the east coast, with its outlying and extensive sands, which presented so many dangers to shipping. Light was provided by revolving oil lamps and reflectors giving alternate red and white flashes.

The year 1811 saw the completion of the lighthouse upon the Inchcape, or Bell Rock. This was a reef lying 11 miles off the Scottish coast. Captain Basil Hall, who was born nearby, related that wrecks on the Inchcape Rock were so numerous that 'ships bound for the Forth, in their constant terror of this dangerous reef, were not content with giving it ten or even twenty miles of elbow room, but must needs edge off a little more to the south so as to hug the shore in such a way that, when the wind chopped round to the northward, as it often did, these over-cautious navigators were apt to get embayed in a deep bight to the westward of Fast Castle'. He declared that sometimes as many as half a dozen ships would be wrecked every winter within a mile or so of his home.

In the early half of the Georgian era coal was the illuminant at most of the coastal lighthouses; but from 1788 on the Elder Brethren of the Trinity began to have argand lamps and parabolic reflectors fitted in their new lighthouses and to urge the managers of the older lighthouses to do likewise, so that by the close of the century the coasts of the British Isles could be accounted the best-lighted in the world.

Though far younger than the Corporation of Trinity House, the Commissioners for the Northern Lights, inaugurated by Act of Parliament in 1786, were fully as efficient, and accomplished a great deal in a relatively short period. They began by building a lighthouse on Kinnaird Head in 1787; they had constructed the lighthouse on the Inchcape Rock, which has already been mentioned, by 1811; they lighted Islay in 1825, Buchanness in 1827, Cape Wrath in 1828, and Tarbetness in 1829.

The administration of the Irish Lights was taken over by the Ballast Board in 1810. In 1819 the principal Irish lighthouses were those at Inishtrahull, Howth, Tuskar, Roches Point, Kinsale, Cape Clear, Loop Head, Aran, Clare Island, and Aranmore.

Other notable lighthouses erected or rebuilt during this era were the Farne (1776), Small Rock (1778), St. Catherine's (1780), Needles (1782), Portland (1788), Orfordness (1793), Longships (1795), and Scilly (1790).

The lightship at the Nore (1734) was the first to be moored off the English coast. It was followed, two years later, by another off the Dudgeon shoal, in Norfolk, and another off the Owers, in Sussex, in 1788. The earliest lightship at the Goodwin Sands dates from 1793: it was stationed at the north-east extremity of those sands on which so many British, and many more foreign vessels, had been cast away. The lightship moored in 1798 at the end of Sunk Sand, at the entrance of the North Channel into the Thames, was the means of preserving large numbers of ships entering or sailing out of the river which would otherwise have been lost. In 1803 a lightship was

View of Liverpool; aquatint by W. Daniell, 1815.

moored off the Galloper; in 1809, another, the Gull, marking the fairway behind the Goodwin sands; and in 1812, another off Bembridge Ledge at St Helens in the Isle of Wight.

In Queen Anne's reign the Gilkicker mark, near Gosport, was erected, and the Horse buoy laid at Spithead. The hazardous passage into the Hamoaze from Plymouth Sound was buoyed by about 1730. The buoyage of the Mersey and the Severn was also being taken in hand; but it was not until the final quarter of the century that the buoyage of the intricate outer passages of the Thames estuary was at last undertaken on a really large scale. By the same time the buoyage of the more important harbours of the British Isles was beginning to be fairly general.

The era under survey witnessed the construction and extension of various important port and harbour works. These developments as a rule were governed by the configuration of the coast.

The mouths of several of the principal rivers—notably the Thames, Tyne, Mersey, and Humber—formed good natural harbours, affording sheltered access to docks and quays. In many places, projecting headlands provided some measure of protection. This could sometimes be supplemented by a

Leith Pier and Harbour in 1798; engraving from a drawing by J. Waddell.

breakwater, facing the exposed direction, as at Plymouth. Harbours were also formed by two breakwaters projecting from the shore at some distance apart and converging at their extremities, so as to leave sufficient opening for the safe entrance of shipping. Of this type of harbour Tynemouth and Ramsgate are very good examples.

Before the close of the eighteenth century Liverpool, the second port in the kingdom, had been equipped with excellent docks and large warehouses; considerable progress had also been made in the buoying and lighting of the River Mersey. At Aberdeen, John Smeaton began to construct the north pier, which protected the harbour and increased the depth of water on the bar; another celebrated engineer, Thomas Telford, extended the same pier, and also the old south breakwater. At Dundee, the floating dock[13] was completed by Telford in 1825. Glasgow, which by the middle of the century was the centre of the British tobacco trade, had at last secured an outlet to the sea as a result of the systematic deepening of the Clyde through the scour of the current controlled by a series of jetties. The harbour at Leith was formed by two piers situated on each side of the river mouth, the 'Water of Leith'. In the late seventeenth and early eighteenth centuries these piers were reconstructed and extended. In 1800 work on Leith's first wet dock was begun, and completed in 1806, the second in 1817; and in 1828 the east pier was still further extended. The harbour at the mouth of the Tyne was formed by two piers projecting from the shore and converging at their extremities to induce scour across the entrance, also to afford shelter to vessels entering the river. At Whitehaven, quays and jetties were built under the shelter of the cliff close to the town. In 1768 Smeaton had made certain proposals for the enlargement of the harbour: but it was not until 1824 that the work was actually taken in hand. At Whitby, the west pier in 1734 was prolonged by 700 yards; and in 1814 it was extended still further. The year 1800 saw the construction, by Sir John Rennie, of the first dock at Grimsby, complete with entrance lock. It was presently provided with wharves and warehouses. For the excavation of the earliest docks at Hull, a few years afterwards, Rennie used a steam dredging machine. Selected as a port of refuge for the Downs in southerly gales, Ramsgate was protected by two piers converging by successive angles and enclosing a harbour of some 40 acres. The work was begun in 1748 and completed twenty years later; it owed much to the improvements suggested by John Smeaton. In 1791 the east pier was extended as a protection against easterly gales. At Plymouth, the construction of an immense breakwater across the middle of the Sound on the lines of Rennie's design, to supplement the natural protection of the headlands flanking the bay, was taken in hand in 1812 and completed in 1844.

In the last decade of the Georgian era a great many other port and harbour works on various parts of the coast were successfully undertaken, to the greater safety and convenience of our seaborne trade.

Starting with the publication of Captain Collins's charts of home waters towards the close of the seventeenth century, there was a striking and sustained advance in hydrography throughout the eighteenth century. With the aid of sextant, station pointer, and other instruments fitted for marine surveying, the position of reefs, banks, and shoals could be fixed with far greater precision; and in the latter half of the eighteenth century the Admiralty had a series of important surveys caried out in home waters, first by Murdoch Mackenzie (whose *Treatise on Marine Surveying*, published in 1774, laid the foundations of hydrographic surveying methods for a century to come), and subsequently by his nephew of the same name, assisted by Graeme Spence, and by Captain William Bligh, of *Bounty* fame.

On the outbreak of the Revolutionary War in 1793 the lack of an adequate supply of good printed charts was becoming a serious handicap to the Navy.

Steps were accordingly taken to remedy this deficiency. In 1795 the Hydrographic Office was inaugurated at the Admiralty by an Order in Council, in which reference was made to the great inconvenience to sea-officers arising 'from the want of sufficient information respecting the navigation of those parts of the world to which their services may be directed, and with which they are sometimes totally unacquainted'.

The first Hydrographer to be appointed was Alexander Dalrymple, formerly Hydrographer to the East India Company. The task which awaited him was formidable indeed. Masses of documents had been accumulating during the past century, including the important work done by the East India Company, the surveys carried out in home waters by the two Mackenzies, Spence, and Bligh, the various surveys of the North American coasts, the charts compiled by Cook and his disciples, and a great quantity of privately and commercially produced charts. There followed thirteen arduous years, not only of collecting, collating, and classifying existing material, but also of organizing a new department *ab initio*. Sea-officers with practical experience of navigation now worked in association with civilian cartographers. By the close of his term of office Dalrymple had assembled a nucleus of newly engraved copper plates from which copies 'could be expediently and economically provided by the Admiralty and printed instead of relying on purchases from various publishers'.[14]

Dalrymple was succeeded, in 1808, by Captain Thomas Hurd, who was the first of a continuous line of Hydrographers chosen from a number of senior officers with practical experience of surveying. As a young lieutenant he had found off Bermuda 'safe and secure anchorage among those islands for the whole Navy of England', and early in the Napoleonic War he had carried out a valuable survey of the approaches to Brest. He was to occupy the office of Hydrographer for fifteen years. To impress the Board of Admiralty with the magnitude of the task confronting his office, Hurd on 7 May 1814 declared, 'The return of Peace to this country makes me consider it as an official duty to represent to the Lords Commissioners of the Admiralty the great deficiency of our Nautical Knowledge in almost every part of the world, but more particularly on the coastline of our own Dominions'. He proceeded to list the areas which were still inadequately charted and urged the importance of 'acquiring a mass of valuable information that would not fail of being highly advantageous to us in any future War, and could otherways redound to the Credit and Glory of this great Maritime Empire, whose flag flies triumphant in every part of the World'.[15]

During these years the surveying service of the Navy became merged with the Hydrographic Office under the supervision of the Hydrographer, who was responsible to the Board of Admiralty. At the same time the surveying service was greatly increased. In 1814, two surveying ships appeared for the first time in the Navy List; when Hurd died, in 1823, there were twelve of them.

Hurd organized a regular system of surveys, selected and retained a band of officers specially qualified for the task, and throughout his term of office substantially increased the number of charts constructed and published. He later persuaded the Admiralty to make these charts available to the ships of the mercantile marine.

Major James Rennell, F.R.S., oceanographer; engraving by Ridley after Scott, 1802.

Late in the century the foundations of the science of oceanography were laid by Major James Rennell (1742–1830), an authority of European reputation on winds and currents, who was offered, but declined, the post of Hydrographer at the Admiralty. As an example of the kind of work he did, mention may be made of two papers read by Rennell before the Royal Society, in 1793 and 1815 respectively, on the subject of the variable northerly set off the entrance to the English Channel, subsequently known as Rennell's Current. Throughout his long life Rennell devoted much of his time to the systematic study of winds and currents; he brought together an enormous mass of materials, patiently assembled from the logs of his friends and correspondents; and the publication in 1832 of his posthumous *Investigation of the Currents of the Atlantic Ocean* was a landmark in the progress of modern scientific navigation.[16]

In the Georgian era exploration and discovery were recognized as an integral part of the functions of the Royal Navy. It is significant that, in their instructions to Captain John Byron, who was appointed to command a small expedition which they had dispatched on a voyage of discovery in 1764, the Lords of the Admiralty declared that 'nothing can redound more to the honour of this nation as a maritime power, to the dignity of the Crown of Great Britain, and to the advancement of the trade and navigation thereof, than to make discoveries of countries hitherto unknown'. Byron sailed across the Atlantic and, after taking formal possession of the Falkland Islands, rounded Cape Horn and crossed the Pacific. He returned home by the way of the Cape of Good Hope and anchored in the Downs in May 1766. The expedition of Wallis and Carteret in the *Dolphin* and *Swallow* (1766–8) resulted in the discovery of Pitcairn and various other islands. The latter half of the century also witnessed a great advance in the work of surveying and charting. In these activities Cook, Vancouver, Puget, Flinders, and Bass were prominent: but the greatest of all was Cook.

James Cook, a native of Cleveland, in Yorkshire, who had served his apprenticeship in the coasting trade, entered the Navy in 1755 and was shortly after rated master's mate. In the North American campaign which ended in the conquest of Canada, Cook made his name as a navigator and hydrographer. His work was so highly esteemed at the Admiralty that, in 1768, he received a lieutenant's commission and was sent out to Tahiti in the *Endeavour*, in command of a well-equipped expedition, ostensibly to observe the transit of Venus, actually to forestall the French in the search for *Terra Australis Incognita*, the great southern continent which was believed to lie somewhere to the south of the tracks of former explorers. Cook sailed from Tahiti to the Society Islands, and then stood southward in the direction of the alleged continent. He charted the coasts of New Zealand and the eastern seaboard of Australia, and established beyond doubt the fact that there could be no continental land north of latitude 40° S. between New Zealand and Cape Horn. Shortly after his return to England in 1771 Cook was promoted to the rank of commander and appointed to lead a second expedition of discovery in the Pacific. On his voyage of 1772–5 Cook completed the exploration of the southern hemisphere. He sailed further south than man had ever penetrated before, until, in latitude 71° 10′ S., his progress was stopped by ice. Sandwich Land was discovered in latitude 60° S.; but the theory of a vast southern continent was now finally disproved. Cook rapidly surveyed and charted the coasts of Tasmania, the Friendly Islands, and a number of other island groups, and also corrected his survey of New Zealand. The extraordinary accuracy of his charts, no less than his

meticulous attention to detail, entitles him to be regarded as the father of
modern hydrography. He explored many thousands of miles of hitherto
unknown coastline. He established a new standard in chart-making; some of
Cook's surveys were still in use at the end of the nineteenth century. On his
return he was promoted to post-rank, and elected a Fellow of the Royal
Society. The object of his third voyage to the Pacific (1776–9) was to settle
once and for all the question of a north-west passage from the Pacific to the
Atlantic Ocean. No such passage was in fact discovered; but he surveyed and
charted the Pacific coast of North America from latitude 44° N. to latitude
70° 44′ N., as well as both sides of the Behring Straits. As a result of Cook's
voyages Australia and New Zealand passed into British keeping.

Some time later George Vancouver, assisted by Peter Puget, made an
admirable survey of the intricate channels and inlets along the west coast of
North America, and he also charted the south-west coast of Australia.
Matthew Flinders, with the assistance of George Bass, surveyed the coast of
New South Wales and later charted the Gulf of Carpentaria.

CHAPTER 4

MARITIME RIGHTS

THE vital importance of maritime rights to a state like Great Britain was that by the exercise of these rights her superior sea power was enabled in war-time to throttle the enemy's commerce and thus progressively run down his economy. If the scope of these belligerent rights were for any reason materially weakened or restricted, the efficacy of her sea power would be much diminished.

In the early half of the eighteenth century maritime law was still confused and ill-defined. An authoritative and comprehensive code of international law did not exist. Attempts to regulate certain branches of commerce in war-time immediately engendered disputes about neutral and belligerent rights. Though some of these rights were virtually unchallenged, there was always a vast and tangled borderland in question. There were consequently wide divergencies in both precept and practice among the various maritime Powers. The Dutch were firm believers in the maxim of 'Business as usual' in time of war. Great Britain, possessing as she did the mastery of the seas, resolutely refused to admit the doctrine of the neutral flag covering the goods, or *Free ships, free goods*. Broadly speaking, the British position was that enemy goods in neutral ships might be condemned. As was to be expected, neutrals naturally favoured the Dutch position.

In the attack on enemy commerce during the War of 1739–48 the British developed the argument that a neutral must not in time of war engage in any traffic closed to him in peace (e.g. Spain's trade with her American colonies), while the Dutch found strong support for their claim of *Free ships, free goods* in the treaty which concluded the Third Dutch War. In 1746 the Admiralty had occasion to complain of the Dutch 'covering the seas with their ships carrying supplies of provisions with every destructive means of ruining our commerce, and even endangering our common safety'; and the next year the Earl of Chesterfield similarly complained of 'the great inconveniences which we have long so sensibly experienced from the latitude given to the Dutch by the 8th article of the Marine Treaty'.

'Might not those who fought the battles', observed the financier, Nicolas Magens, some years later, 'ask, what signifies our being masters at sea, if we shall not have liberty to stop ships from serving our enemies? And when we examine to the bottom of the thing, it appears very evident, that sea battles are fought not so much to kill people, as to be masters of trade, whereby people live; and by stopping their supplies, to compel our enemies in the end to live in friendship with us.'[1]

The vital issue of maritime rights reappeared during the Seven Years War. By 1757 the maritime neutrals were becoming increasingly restive at the restraints on their trade resulting from the belligerent rights claimed and enforced by this country. It was not that the rules laid down by Great Britain were so much harsher than those of other states that made the enforcement of her maritime rights so grievous to neutrals; it was because her naval power was incomparably greater. The geographical position of Great Britain was also a factor of prime importance. The trade of Holland, Denmark, Sweden, Russia, and northern Germany all passed through the Channel close to her ports: for in the days of sail the shipping usually hugged the English coast.

Throughout the war the carrying trade of neutrals was vitally important to France and Spain (it has been estimated that no less than two-thirds of the trade of France in the eighteenth century was carried in neutral bottoms); and neutral shipowners, particularly those of Holland, were not slow to exploit the situation. Thus in the latter stages of the war our cruisers based on the Downs found more employment from Dutch, than from French or Spanish shipping. 'The sea is full of ships,' wrote Boscawen in the spring of 1756, 'but all Dutch. These rogues carry on a swinging trade while the English and French languish in port, and laugh at us both.'

These differences were aggravated by the fact that France, to preserve her West India trade, had suspended her navigation laws and opened that formerly exclusive traffic to neutrals. Here, however, they encountered the strong and uncompromising resistance of British statesmen and judges, who now developed the Rule of the War of 1756, which had already been applied, in the War of 1739–48, in the case of Spain. The Rule of the War of 1756, which was strongly upheld by Pitt and Anson, was summarized as follows by Lord Mansfield, the Solicitor-General:

> All European nations exclude foreigners from their American colonies, and so things stood at the time of the treaty of 1674. It is the general rule still, and

cannot possibly be varied, except as a new invention fraudulently to screen French effects from capture, and the question is whether England shall suffer them to trade thither in time of war, without seizure, when the French themselves will not suffer them to trade thither, in time of peace, on that very account.[2]

With the Rule of the War of 1756 was linked the doctrine of Continuous Voyage. In the British view, whether a voyage had originated in a neutral or an enemy port, it made no difference if the neutral were engaged in a traffic closed to him in time of peace. What was in fact at issue were two conflicting interpretations of international law: for while the Dutch and certain others claimed that enemy goods in neutral ships were immune from capture, the British maintained that enemy goods were lawful prize everywhere at sea. The more pressing grievances of the neutrals centred on the increasingly lawless and violent activities of the British privateers: some of which, indeed, were little better than pirates. What Chaucer said of the *Shipman*, 'Of nyce conscience took he no kepe', would apply equally well to certain privateersmen. The Swedes had shown themselves hostile to Great Britain from the outbreak of the war. The Danes and Dutch were naturally unwilling to relinquish the lucrative West India traffic. Russia was already at war with our ally, Frederick II, and protested bitterly at the piracies committed by our privateersmen against her merchantmen. It was not only the Northern Powers that were growing restive. The Spanish protests at the depredations of our privateers became more insistent; while Choiseul was labouring to revive the Family Compact between the two Bourbon States.

In the years 1757–8 the blockade in the Channel became increasingly effective. Following upon the seizure of large numbers of Dutch and Danish merchantmen, intense indignation arose among those neutrals who had hoped to profit by the war: the traditional alliance with Holland became a dead letter and there was talk in Copenhagen of a maritime league of neutrals. Fortunately for Great Britain, these outbursts of neutral resentment were not simultaneous. First the Danes and the Swedes, then the Dutch, and lastly the Spaniards fulminated against our interference with their trade. The object of French diplomacy in the meantime was to bring about a maritime union against Great Britain; but the attempt failed. When the danger was at its height—between August 1758 and August 1759—Spain was paralysed by her internal politics; and the Dutch claim of *Free ships, free goods* was strongly and successfully resisted by Great Britain. Pitt's treatment of this most difficult question was a triumph of tactful but resolute statecraft. To the Russian Vice-Chancellor, Woronzow, our envoy expressed profound regret for the excesses of the privateers, but explained 'that they were the consequences of a maritime war, where the giving of commissions to privateers was necessary; and must unavoidably now and then fall into bad hands, as the persons who follow that trade are often not the people in the world of the best morals and strictest discipline; but that the Government were doing everything in their power to put a stop to these licentious proceedings'.[3]

Pitt stood firm on our traditional maritime rights, including the right of search; at the same time he brought pressure to bear upon the prize courts to release as many captured neutral ships as possible and did his utmost to restrain the worst excesses of the privateers by administrative and legislative action. 'England the Mistress of the Ocean should not act despotically there,' he told the House of Commons. '. . . The misfortunes accruing to this country from the robberies committed by privateers are such that, unless a step is timely made, the neutral nations would all be offended.' The Admiralty offered a reward of £500 for the discovery of the culprits, a number of whom were subsequently arrested, condemned, and executed for their crimes. The Bill which Pitt introduced in May 1759 to curb these abuses gave satisfaction to the maritime neutrals generally. The Danish government soon abandoned their claim to trade directly with the French West India islands. Sweden, though hostile, was not strong enough to act alone; and Great Britain carried on her Baltic trade unhindered. In the latter stages of the War of American Independence the exasperation of neutrals at British interference with their trade once again resulted in a crisis. To the Scandinavian peoples, in particular, the renewal of the struggle between Great Britain and France had brought a far larger share of the world's carrying trade and abounding prosperity. 'In the brilliant commercial period of 1775 to 1784.' says Mathenson, 'the country [Denmark] and its people gathered their activities to an admirable degree. The nation was thereby enabled to obtain for the future a not inconsiderable rank among the great seafaring Powers.'[4] For her part France was no less anxious to secure the services of neutral shipping since her own was in danger of being driven off the seas. Once again she strove to bring about the maritime league of neutrals which she had endeavoured in vain to raise up in the last war. This time she succeeded. At the outset of hostilities France had formally adhered to the principle that property belonging to the subjects of belligerents should be free on board neutral vessels, excepting merchandise of contraband. This had the designed effect on the northern neutrals. An unending series of protests poured in against the belligerent rights enforced by Great Britain. Finally, in 1780, Russia, Denmark, and Sweden joined together in the Armed

Neutrality to resist the British practice of seizing enemy goods carried in neutral bottoms. Our seizure of Baltic timber and naval stores destined for the enemy's navies was a determining factor in this decision. Within a few months the Baltic States had close on eighty of the line in commission; and the British government, following in the footsteps of Pitt in the previous war, was constrained to submit to the curtailment of our maritime rights. An important result of the Armed Neutrality was the partial replenishment of the French dockyards, which for long had been deprived of the vital Baltic stores.

The British recovery after the disastrous war of 1778–83 was rapid. During the next decade our imports and exports rose by more than 50 per cent. With the increasing use of the new machinery British industry was just then entering on a phase of progressive and unparalleled expansion. The swift recovery of our prosperity and prestige was largely due to the wise financial policy of the younger Pitt, who was also responsible for maintaining a strong Navy; so that on the eve of the next general war Great Britain had in home waters a substantial force in commission comprising twenty-five sail of the line and nearly fifty frigates. In these circumstances the crucial issue of maritime rights was certain to reappear.

At the outset of the Revolutionary War the British government proclaimed a blockade of the enemy's ports and added corn to the list of contraband. In 1793 orders were given for the seizure of 'all ships laden with goods the produce of any colony belonging to France, or carrying provisions or other supplies for the use of any such colony'. These orders were based on the Rule of the War of 1756. Several hundreds of American ships were then seized and taken into West Indian ports by British cruisers. To resolve the growing differences between Great Britain and the United States the President in 1794 appointed John Jay, Chief Justice of the Supreme Court, as his Envoy Extraordinary to London. In November of the same year there was signed the Treaty which is known by his name. Jay's Treaty was, in effect, a victory for British diplomacy; for though American shipping was henceforth permitted to engage in direct traffic between the United States and British possessions in the East and West Indies, they were still prohibited from carrying the produce of those colonies to foreign ports; and the Americans were obliged to acquiesce in the British doctrine of contraband.

To Sir William Scott (later Lord Stowell) belongs the credit of bringing unity and consistency to British prize law. Hitherto there had existed no corpus of jurisprudence by which judges or advocates could be guided. To

William Scott, Baron Stowell; drawing by G. Dance, 1803.

create such a body of prize law was Scott's lifework. In 1798 he was appointed Judge of the Prize Court, an office which he held for nearly thirty years. It was the long-drawn-out struggle at sea which gave him his opportunity. Year after year an apparently endless succession of cases in maritime law poured into the Prize Court for decision. They embraced such controversial questions as blockade, continuous voyage, contraband, and joint capture. Scott's judgements were so well reasoned, logical, and equitable that they commanded general approbation, not only in the legal profession, but also in the Service. These decisions made Scott a well-known figure during the Revolutionary and Napoleonic Wars. It was his achievement to establish within his lifetime a clear and authoritative body of British prize law.

One of the key decisions of the Prize Court, based on the Rule of 1756, was in respect to the doctrine of Continuous Voyage. Sir William Scott in 1800 observed:

Upon the breaking out of a war, it is the right of neutrals to carry on their accustomed trade, with an exception of the particular cases of a trade to blockaded places, or in contraband articles (in both which cases their property is liable to be condemned), and of their ships being liable to visitation and search; in which case, however, they are entitled to freight and expenses. I do not mean to say that in the accidents of a war the property of neutrals may not be variously entangled and endangered. . . . But without reference to accidents of one kind or another, the general rule is, that the neutral has a right to carry on, in time of war, his accustomed trade to the utmost extent of which that accustomed trade is capable. Very different is the case of a trade which the neutral has never possessed, which he holds by no title of use and habit in times of peace, and which, in fact, can obtain in war by no other title than by the successes of one belligerent against the other, and at the expense of that very belligerent under whose success he sets up his title; and such I take to be the colonial trade, generally speaking.[5]

Colonies, declared the judge, depended for their existence as colonies on foreign supplies. If they could not be supplied and defended they must fall to the belligerent of course; and if the belligerent chooses to apply his means to such an object, what right has a third party, perfectly neutral, to step in and prevent the execution?

Another of Scott's decisions disposed of the claim of a neutral to participate in the coastal trade of a belligerent. This became an important issue during the Revolutionary and Napoleonic Wars.

As to the coasting trade (supposing it to be a trade not usually opened to foreign vessels), can there be described a more effective accommodation than can be given to an enemy during a war than to undertake it for him during his own disability? Is it nothing that the commodities of an extensive empire are conveyed from the parts where they grow and are manufactured to other parts where they are wanted for use? It is said that this is not importing anything into the country, and it certainly is not; but has it not all the effects of such an importation? Supposing that the French navy had a decided ascendant, and had cut off all British communication between the northern and southern parts of this island, and that neutrals interposed to bring coals of the north for the supply of the manufactures and for the necessities of domestic life in this metropolis; is it possible to describe a more direct and a more effectual opposition to the success of French hostility short of an actual military assistance in the war?[6]

On the outbreak of the Revolutionary War the belligerent rights claimed by Great Britain had received general acceptance. Notwithstanding the concessions extorted from this country by the Armed Neutrality of 1780, the new doctrine of neutral rights which had then been enunciated was never established. But the war-time development of the carrying trade in the neutral Baltic States and the rapidly expanding commerce of northern Germany had brought those countries into frequent conflict with Great Britain. Enemy ships and cargoes had been protected in wholesale fashion by fictitious transfers to neutral subjects, who profited greatly in consequence. 'Merchants', wrote James Stephen in 1805, 'who, immediately prior to the last war, were scarcely known, even in the obscure sea-ports in which they resided, have suddenly started up as the sole owners of hundreds of ships, and sole proprietors of rich cargoes, which it would have alarmed the wealthiest merchants of Europe, to hazard at once on the chance of a market, even in peaceable times.'[7] The Danes had likewise profited from what Grenville, in 1794, described as 'the collusive and fraudulent commerce so openly carried on from the ports of the Baltic'. The Swedes had similarly benefited during this period remembered in the years to come as *den gode Tid*, 'the good time'.

As the years went by the clash of interests between Great Britain and the northern neutrals intensified. In 1798 a number of Swedish merchantmen, laden with contraband of war, were, though under convoy of a Swedish man-of-war, seized by our cruisers and condemned by our prize courts. The loss of these ships, valued at £600,000, inevitably gave rise to great indignation in Sweden. About two years afterwards a number of Danish merchant vessels, under convoy of the frigate *Freya*, encountered a British squadron cruising in the Channel. Having resisted the British proposal to visit the convoy, the Danes, after a fight, were obliged to yield to superior force and were escorted to the Downs. Later the *Freya* was released and a compromise agreement appeared to have been reached; but the question at issue was by no means resolved.

'All other questions of Maritime Law', Grenville commented to Whitworth in August 1800, 'will at once be superseded by this new principle, nor can any question of prize ever again be raised respecting merchant vessels, or a single capture be made by the British Navy, since all that will be required is that in the whole circle of the civilized world one Neutral State shall be found (however small) sufficiently well disposed to our enemies to lend its flag to cover their commerce, without risk to itself, and with the certainty of large pecuniary recompense.'

Towards the end of that year Bonaparte, playing upon the resentment of the Northern Powers at British interference with their trade, encouraged those States to revive the League of Armed Neutrality which, comprising Russia, Sweden, Denmark, and Prussia, was pledged to resist the belligerent rights at sea claimed and enforced by Great Britain. The customary rights of search and seizure were now boldly challenged.

The neutral rights thus proclaimed undermined the very foundations of British naval power and deprived us of the means of striking effectively at the continental enemy. 'Does he not know', Pitt declared, in reply to one of the Opposition leaders, 'that the naval preponderance, which we have by these means acquired, has given security to this country, and has more than once afforded chances for the salvation of Europe? In the wreck of the Continent and the disappointment of our hopes there, what has been the security of this country but its naval preponderance?'[8]

The leading principles affirmed by the League were, that neutral vessels were free to engage in the coasting and colonial trade of belligerents: that enemy property carried in neutral shipping was not subject to seizure, nor were vessels under convoy of a man-of-war liable to the belligerent right of search: and that naval stores were to be excluded from the category of contraband.

'Four nations', observed Pitt, early in 1801, 'have leaguered to produce a new code of maritime laws, and in defiance of the most solemn treaties and engagements, which they have endeavoured to force arbitrarily upon Europe. . . . The question is whether we are to suffer blockaded fleets to be furnished with warlike stores and provisions, whether we are to suffer neutral nations, by hoisting a flag upon a sloop or fishing-boat, to convey the treasures of South America to the harbours of Spain or the naval stores of the Baltic to Brest and Toulon.'[9]

Rejecting the League's demands point-blank, the British Cabinet dispatched a strong squadron to the Baltic under Admiral Sir Hyde Parker, with Nelson as his second-in-command, which destroyed the Danish fleet at Copenhagen and forced the Danes to come to terms. The victory of Copenhagen, followed as it was by the news of Tsar Paul's assassination, broke the back of the Armed Neutrality. A convention was signed on 17 June with Russia and some months later with Denmark and Sweden. The terms of the convention represented a compromise. Great Britain obtained an explicit acknowledgement of the Rule of 1756, prohibiting direct traffic between hostile Powers and their colonies by neutral intermediaries, and the renunciation, on Russia's part, of the doctrine that the neutral flag covered the enemy's goods; whilst renouncing, on our side, the claim to seize naval stores as contraband of war. In future the vital rights of search and seizure of enemy goods in neutral shipping were no longer contested by the Baltic Powers.

The issue of maritime rights was again to the fore during the long-drawn-out struggle centred around the Continental Blockade. By Napoleon's orders British goods were to be excluded from France and all her dependencies. Not only his subjects and allies, but neutrals as well, were to be forced to submit to these decrees. The British government thereupon proclaimed a counter-blockade of all ports which adhered to the Continental System, and, owing to the overwhelming preponderance of the Royal Navy, was able effectively to deny the carrying trade of Europe to neutrals.

Chief among the neutral carriers were the Americans, whose merchant marine, then and for long afterwards, was a formidable rival to our own. Since the turn of the century American re-exports had been steadily increasing in volume and value. The produce of the enemy's colonies was being carried in American bottoms to American ports and thence re-shipped to Europe in the guise of produce of the United States. The ports of the French West Indian islands were for years crowded with American shipping. The Rule of the War of 1756 had been virtually abrogated.

James Stephen's *War in Disguise, or The Frauds of the Neutral Flags*, which appeared in 1805, was full of characteristic and well-substantiated examples of wholesale evasion of the regulations by the guileful neutral. Stephen had seen much of these evasions while occupied with his legal practice at St. Christopher's, in the West Indies. In his pamphlet he developed the principle that a belligerent has the right to prevent neutrals from rendering assistance to his enemy. The assistance which the Americans were rendering the French was to carry their colonial trade for them, and also their coastal trade, thus affording to enemy property the protection of the neutral flag. Stephen's interpretation of the Rule of the War of 1756 was supported by certain significant judgements in the Prize Court.

'The fabrics and commodities of France, Spain, and Holland', Stephen declared, 'have been brought under American colours to ports in the United States; and from thence re-exported, under the same flag, for the supply of the hostile colonies. Again, the produce of these colonies has been brought, in a like manner, to the American ports, and from thence re-shipped to Europe.'[10]

During the whole of the Revolutionary and the opening years of the Napoleonic War, Great Britain had interfered very little with American commerce. The attitude of the British government now stiffened. In the spring of 1805 the *Essex* decision, reversing an earlier decision of the Prize Court, put a period to British toleration of the American re-export trade. Stephen's pamphlet, which was published under official auspices, had made out a very strong case for the more rigorous application of the Rule of the

War of 1756, which prohibited to neutrals all traffic closed to them in time of peace; and British attacks on the neutral carrying trade became alike more frequent and more aggressive. In 1807 the injury to American trade was extremely serious, and relations between the two countries deteriorated.

It was the high-handed British activities within sight of their own coast which particularly provoked the Americans. During 1807 our cruisers watched New York so closely that they stopped nearly every ship leaving the harbour. The British minister at Washington wrote:

I am persuaded that more Ill will has been excited . . . by a few trifling illegal Captures immediately off this Coast and some Instances of insulting Behaviour by some of His Majesty's Commanders in the very Harbours and Waters of the United States than by the most rigid Enforcement of the Maritime Rights of Great Britain against the Trade of the United States in other Parts of the World. It may easily be conceived to be highly grating to the Feelings of an Independent Nation to perceive that their coming in or going out of their Harbours examined rigorously in sight of the Shore by British Squadrons stationed within their Waters.[11]

American merchants maintained that the Rule of the War of 1756 had never formed part of international law; and they argued that—subject to the belligerent rights of blockade and contraband—neutrals were entitled in war-time to trade between any of the enemy's ports in all kinds of merchandise, whether or not that trade were open to them in time of peace. In reply to this interpretation of maritime law our Prize Court advanced the doctrine of Continuous Voyage, holding that a voyage from a foreign colony to its mother country was not made two voyages by putting in at an intermediate port in order to evade the law—but would, on the contrary, be regarded by the Prize Court as one continuous voyage. It was this doctrine which was propounded so strongly by James Stephen. The Anglo-American War of 1812 has sometimes been entitled 'Mr. Madison's War'. It might with equal justice have been called 'Mr. Stephen's War'; for *War in Disguise, or The Frauds of the Neutral Flags* was a significant contributory factor in the situation which led up to the outbreak of hostilities.

As has already been said, throughout the Napoleonic War the British government had tenaciously and effectively resisted the claims advanced by various neutrals which adversely affected our power to put economic pressure upon the enemy. The unfettered exercise of our maritime rights was a matter of life and death to Great Britain, since it was a vital and integral factor of our naval superiority, and as such played a decisive part in the long struggle against the Napoleonic empire. At the peace negotiations the government showed the same jealous insistence on our belligerent rights. Rather than relinquish any of those rights, it was announced that this country would withdraw from the Congress. 'Great Britain may be driven out of a Congress,' Castlereagh declared, 'but not out of her maritime rights; and if the Continental Powers know their business, they will not hazard this.' At a later stage Aberdeen assured the French plenipotentiary that 'no possible consideration could induce Great Britain to abandon a particle of what she felt to belong to the maritime Code, from which in no case would she ever recede'. In the end Castlereagh had this vital issue expressly excluded from the matters to be discussed at the Congress.

CHAPTER 5

THE OFFICERS OF
THE SERVICE

IT cannot be too strongly emphasized that the naval superiority of Great
Britain depended upon the excellence of the personnel, rather than that
of the *matériel*. Numerical superiority, in fact, did not always rest with the
British; and, as has already been said, not only the French, but also the
Spaniards, not infrequently built better ships than we did. Perhaps the
greatest and most decisive factor of all was the British superiority in the
quality of the officers. It would scarcely be too much to say that these officers
were the Navy—i.e. the regular, continuous-service Navy. The crews were
paid off after every commission—the officers remained. They formed the
permanent, effective cadre of the Service; they were imbued with the
strongest sense of professional pride and *esprit de corps*: even in time of peace
there were large numbers of them continuously at sea—far more than was
the case with the Bourbon navies.

The year 1748 saw the establishment of a regular uniform for certain
officers of the Royal Navy—namely, admiral, captain, commander,
lieutenant, and midshipman. Hitherto these officers had been accustomed to
dress more or less as they pleased. In his *Roderick Random* Smollett thus
described the appearance of Lieutenant Bowling:

> He was a strong built man, somewhat bandy-legged, with a neck like that of a
> bull, and a face which, you might easily perceive, had withstood the most
> obstinate assaults of the weather. His dress consisted of a soldier's coat, altered
> for him by the ship's tailor, a striped flannel jacket, a pair of red breeches,
> japanned with pitch, clean grey worsted stockings, large silver buckles, that
> covered three-fourths of his shoes, a silver-laced hat, a black bob wig in buckle,
> a check shirt, a silk handkerchief, a hanger with brass handle, girded to his
> thigh by a tarnished laced belt, and a good oak plant under his arm.

Divine Service on board a ship; oil painting by Augustus Earle, early nineteenth century.

According to tradition, the original uniform of the British naval officer was modelled on the riding habit worn by the Duchess of Bedford, which had happened to take the King's fancy. It would appear that uniform was but slowly and gradually adopted in the Service. The Lords Commissioners of the Admiralty were obliged to point out to the three commanders-in-chief at the home ports: 'As example is on these occasions extremely necessary, you are to cause every captain under your command to appear in the said dress, and we do expect that you yourselves shall constantly appear in the same.' It is said that when uniforms were first provided for lieutenants, there was but one uniform coat kept in the wardroom for the use of these officers, when sent on duty to other ships, or on shore. Epaulettes were brought in in 1795. As the century advanced, uniform was generally worn by all officers; though from time to time, as may be seen from the *Recollections of James Anthony Gardner*, considerable liberties might be taken by individuals.

> Our first lieutenant was a very droll and strange personage, in dress as well as in manners. When he commissioned the *Edgar* he had on a uniform coat made in days of yore, with sleeves that reached to his hips, a very low collar, huge

white lappels and cuffs, the buttons behind at a good fighting distance, and the skirts and pockets an enormous size. A red waistcoat, nankin breeches, and black worsted stockings, with great yellow buckles, on round-toed shoes, a hat that had been cocked, but cut round, with a very low crown, so that he was obliged to keep his hand to his head to prevent its blowing off in the lightest breeze.[1]

But these variations on the regulation theme were becoming rarer towards the end of the century. Gardner observed that about 1788 Captain Charles Thompson of the *Edgar*, whom he described as 'gruff as the devil' and 'very particular concerning dress', issued the following order: 'If any officer shall so far forget himself as to appear when on shore without his uniform, I shall regard it as a mark of his being ashamed of his profession and discharge him from the ship accordingly.' Gardner adds: 'He had very nearly caught some of us in Middle Street, Gosport, but fortunately an alley was at no great distance through which we made a hasty but safe retreat, and by that means prevented a few vacancies for midshipmen taking place in the *Edgar*.' In Gardner's next ship, the *Barfleur*, Captain Robert Calder was no less strict in the matter of dress. 'We dared not appear on deck without our full uniform,' said Gardner, 'and a round hat was never allowed; our side arms always on the quarter-deck ready for duty, and when exercising sails the midshipmen in the tops were to be in full dress.' Captain Thomas Hardy once cured his 'young gentlemen' of strolling round the deck with their hands in their pockets by having their pockets *sewn* up.

In 1805 surgeons attained to officer's status and were given a new uniform. Hitherto they had worn the uniform of a warrant officer. Two years later masters and pursers were also given an officer's uniform.

The century saw a gradual but sustained improvement in the manners and status of the British sea-officer. 'The last war', wrote Captain Edward Thompson in 1756, 'a chaw of tobacco, a rattan, and a rope of oaths were sufficient qualifications to constitute a lieutenant; but now, education and good manners are the study of all.' 'I will venture to say', the same writer went on to observe, 'that the gentlemen of the navy will bring more laurels to their country than were ever brought in any former time.'[2] In the latter half of the century this prediction was fulfilled in full measure.

The influence of Anson had much to do with this improvement. A significant proportion of the young officers under his command during the great voyage of 1740–4—notably Saunders, Saumarez, Denis, Brett, Keppel, Hyde Parker, and Howe—were afterwards to rise to the top of their profession. Between the Austrian Succession and the Seven Years War he had doggedly resisted the efforts of the Duke of Newcastle to draw the Navy within the orbit of his all-embracing system of patronage. 'He withstood recommendations of interest or favor more than any First Lord of the Admiralty was ever known to do,' the second Earl of Hardwicke wrote long afterwards. 'I must', observed Anson, on 15 June 1759, to the Duke, 'now beg your Grace will seriously consider what must be the condition of your Fleet if these borrough recommendations, which must be frequent are to be complied with. . . . My constant method, since I have had the honour of serving the King in the station I am in, has been to promote the lieutenants to command, whose ships have been successfully engaged upon equal terms with the enemy, without having any friend or recommendation: and in preference to all others, and this I would recommend to my successors if they would have a Fleet to depend on.'[3]

The quality of the post-captains varied greatly. There is ample evidence to show that the majority of them were good enough seamen; but in other respects they were often found wanting. 'We are likewise to recollect, that all commanders of men of war are not gentlemen or men of education,'[4] observed that keen observer, Captain Thompson: 'I know a great part are brave men, but a much greater seamen.'

'I expect a great deal from you,' wrote Captain Curtis Barnett, when Anson was appointed to the Admiralty in 1745. 'I am stupid enough to think that we are worse officers though better seamen than our neighbours; that our young men get wrong notions early, and are led to imagine that he is the greatest officer who has the least blocks in his rigging. I hope you will give a new turn to our affairs and form a society for the propagation of sea-military knowledge.' Much the same opinions are expressed in a paper, which has been attributed to Vernon, early in 1747.

> It is certainly necessary that a sea officer should have some natural courage; but it is equally just that he should have a good share of sense, be perfect master of his business, and have some taste for honour; which last is usually the result of *a happy education, moderate reading, and good company, rarely found in men raised on the mere credit of being seamen.* . . . The general notion about sea officers is that they should have the courage of brutes, without any regard to the fine qualities of men, which is an error themselves too often fall into. This levels the officer with the common seaman, gives us a stark wrong idea of the nature, design, and end of the employment, and makes no distinction between the judgment, skill, and address of a Blake, and a mere fighting blockhead without ten grains of common sense.[5]

Admiral Sir Edward Hawke; oil painting by
F. Cotes, 1768–70.

Hawke in his day did much to improve the manners and deportment of the British sea-officer. A protégé of his, the future Captain William Locker, declared many years later that he considered him 'as the founder of that more gentlemanly spirit, which has since been gradually gaining ground in the Navy. At the period when he first went to sea, a man of war was characterized by all the coarseness so graphically described in the novels of Smollett. Tobacco and a checked shirt were associated with lace and a cockade; and the manners of a British Admiral partook of the language and demeanour of a boatswain's mate. . . . His gentlemanly deportment and propriety of conversation effected a salutary improvement among his officers. He discountenanced the coarseness of language and demeanour which disfigured too many of the old school, and still clings to some of the present more enlightened age.'[6]

It was above all by personal influence and example that Hawke inspired his officers and raised professional standards to a pitch scarcely imaginable in former years. His influence extended far beyond the term of his life: between Hawke and Nelson the chain of tradition runs clear and unbroken. Pellew, also, was mindful of that great tradition when his frigate pursued the *Droits de l'Homme* close in with a dangerous lee shore and was all but embayed with her in Audierne Bay.[7]

There was a remarkably high proportion of first-rate commanders in the squadrons led by Hawke and Boscawen in 1759. Moreover, as the century advanced, it is evident from the observations of Gardner and others, that the proportion of commanders who were good captains as well as fine seamen steadily rose. The advantage that our officers enjoyed over their opponents in point of practical skill and experience was enhanced by the British policy that obtained in the latter half of the century of rigorously blockading the enemy's naval ports.

The appointment of Admiral Sir John Jervis to the command of the Mediterranean squadron marked an era in the history of the Navy. He established method and order, put down mutiny, and disciplined his whole squadron—officers and men alike—with a firm hand. He organized a sound commissariat. He restored the sickly crews to health. Slowly but steadily he raised the level of seamanship and gunnery throughout the whole fleet. It was, taken all in all, an astonishing achievement. 'Of all the fleets I ever saw', wrote Nelson in October 1796, 'I never saw one in point of officers and men equal to Sir John Jervis's.' It was with thirteen ships detached from this fleet that Nelson, his favourite pupil, achieved one of the most brilliant victories in naval history.

From the campaign of the Nile arose a new tradition of leadership. 'I had the happiness to command a band of brothers,' Nelson informed Howe after the victory. '. . . My friends readily conceived my plan.' 'Never could there have been selected a set of officers better calculated for such a service,' Ross observes; 'Nelson was fortunate in commanding them and they in being commanded by him.' As at the Nile, this leadership was destined to be a major and decisive element in the victories of Copenhagen and Trafalgar.

Socially the officers of the Royal Navy were a mixed lot. The middle class, especially the professional element, was strongly represented. The Anglican clergy, particularly the more affluent and influential among their number, provided a substantial quota. A very high proportion—as many as between 40 and 50 per cent—came apparently from seafaring stock: for the most part sea-officers. Service families tended to settle in and around Plymouth, Portsmouth, and Chatham. Devon supplied by far the largest quota of officers in the whole country; after Devon came Kent and Hampshire.

The aristocracy and landed gentry were also sending their sons into the Service. It is worth noticing that in the latter part of the period under review the increasing popularity of the Navy as a career for young men of family was regarded as a by no means unmixed blessing for other serving officers. In a letter of St. Vincent's, dated 9 July 1806, there is a significant allusion to the 'idle, licentious aristocrats who are taking away all the first-fruits of the Service, to the utter exclusion of friendless merit'. In Marryat's *Peter Simple* the hero overhears the First Lieutenant observe to the Captain:

> 'The Service is going to the devil. As long as it was not popular, if we had not much education, we at least had the chance that natural abilities gave us; but now that great people send their sons for a provision into the Navy, we have all the refuse of their families, as if anything was good enough to make a captain of a man-of-war, who has occasionally more responsibility on his shoulders, and is placed in situations requiring more judgment, than any other people in existence. Here's another of the fools of the family made a present to the country—another cub for me to lick into shape. Where's Mr. Simple? . . .'

Promotion from the lower deck to the quarter-deck (not always with the happiest results) was by no means unusual. The élite of the lower deck were often singled out for their officer-like qualities—the almost continuous warfare which went on throughout this period gave them their chance. There was a natural tendency for a captain who had himself come up from the lower deck to put on the quarter-deck others of like origin: just as a captain of good family would advance youngsters of his own class, and a Scottish or Irish Captain would promote Scots or Irishmen.

The life-story of Captain Robert Carkett, who, as first of the *Monmouth*, had so greatly distinguished himself in the 'Moonlight Action' of 28 February 1758 with the *Foudroyant*, illustrates both the pros and cons of promotion from the lower deck. There is no doubt that a certain prejudice in the Service against such promotion was in some cases fully justified. Of John Richards, one of the lieutenants of the *Barfleur*, Gardner observes: 'This man belonged to the *Boreas* at the time my father was on board; he was then before the mast. When Captain Thompson was appointed to the *Alcide*, 74, he took Richards with him in a low capacity, and afterwards put him on the quarter-deck; when his time was served he got made a lieutenant. He was a good sailor, but proud, insolent, and vulgar in his language; full of strange sayings and low wit, and overbearing to those of inferior rank.' The testimony of the future Admiral the Hon. Sir George Elliot is also worth noting. 'I suspect I was equal to at least two of the lieutenants,' Elliot declares, 'who had just been made from common seamen, and were neither used nor very fit to command. Four out of five of our lieutenants were made in that way, the distress for officers was so great; two were efficient, *one very good*, and the other two very much otherwise.' Elliot appears to have been reasonably objective in his judgement; he at least gives credit where credit is due.

One of the ablest of the commanders who served under Hawke during the campaign of 1759 had 'come up through the hawse-hole'. John Campbell, son of a Scottish minister, first went to sea in the coasting trade. While serving his apprenticeship, his coaster had been overtaken by the press-gang, and the whole crew, with the exception of the master and himself (who was exempt by his indentures), had been pressed into the Navy. The mate burst into tears at the prospect of being thus torn from his family, and young Campbell had asked if he might take his place. 'Ay, my lad,' was the gruff rejoinder; 'I would rather have a lad of spirit than a blubbering man.' Campbell had risen in the Service; on the return of Anson's *Centurion*, in which he had served as midshipman, master's mate, and master, he had passed the examination for lieutenant. During the long blockade of Brest in 1759 he commanded the *Essex*, and when in November Hawke shifted his flag to the *Royal George* Campbell was appointed his flag-captain.

Carkett and Campbell are well-known names; but there were very many other such cases of officers in the Georgian Navy who had successfully worked their way up in the Service. Of George Westcott, who fought and fell so gloriously as captain of the *Majestic* at the battle of the Nile, Byam Martin relates that he was born at Honiton in Devon of humble parentage: 'I could myself name many who, like Westcott, owed their advancement to their own personal merit'. The First and Signal Lieutenant of the *Victory* at Trafalgar—John Quillian and John Pascoe—had both come up from the lower deck. The former was a Manxman gathered in by the press; he was made lieutenant in 1798, and appointed first of the *Victory* by Nelson; after Trafalgar he was made a post-captain. The latter, acording to Byam Martin, had been their servant in the midshipmen's berth in which he messed on board the *Pegasus*. Both of them eventually reached flag-rank.

David Bartholomew, a Scot, had made several voyages before the mast in merchant vessels bound to the Baltic, West Indies, and also in the Greenland whale fisheries. Captured by the press in London in 1795, he attracted the notice of Sir Home Popham, who made him midshipman and master's mate. Before the Revolutionary War ended, Bartholomew had passed his lieutenant's examination. On the resumption of hostilities with France he applied to the First Lord for a commission, which was refused. He renewed his request—eight times in all. At last, in defiance of all custom and precedent, St. Vincent had him pressed in the entrance hall of the Admiralty. The scandal was considerable; and the case was referred to a Select Committee, which finally found in Bartholomew's favour. By this time, however, the latter was away at sea, employed as acting lieutenant. Then his old patron, Popham, applied for him and he obtained his commission. Bartholomew continued to distinguish himself in the Napoleonic War; in 1812 he was made commander and at the end of the war post-captain.

Many of the men who were thus promoted from the lower deck may be said to have been of middle-class origin. In his *Autobiography*, however, Cochrane singles out one of these 'upper topmen' who seem really to have risen from the ranks. On joining his first ship, the *Hind*, of which his uncle was captain, Cochrane relates how he was introduced to her first lieutenant.

> Jack Larmour—a specimen of the old British seaman little calculated to inspire exalted ideas of the gentility of the naval profession, though presenting at a glance the personification of its efficiency—Jack was in fact one of a not very numerous class whom, for their superior seamanship, the Admiralty was glad to promote from the forecastle to the quarter-deck, in order that they might mould into shipshape the questionable materials supplied by Parliamentary influence, even then paramount in the Navy to a degree which might otherwise have led to disaster. Lucky was the commander who could secure such an officer for his quarter-deck. On my introduction, Jack was dressed in the garb of a seaman, with marlin-spike slung round his neck and a lump of grease in his hand, and was busily engaged in setting up the rigging.[8]

One of the most striking examples of the remarkable catholicity of choice displayed by the Georgian Navy in its appointment of commanders is the case of the celebrated mulatto, John Perkins, of Jamaica. When in command of the *Punch* schooner during the War of American Independence, Lieutenant Perkins (as he then was) is said to have annoyed the enemy more than any other officer on the station by his repeated acts of daring and the immense number of prizes he took. His knowledge of the navigational conditions in the Caribbean was, perhaps, never equalled and certainly never excelled; and this he exerted to the great advantage of himself and his native island by the capture of the enemy's privateers and merchant shipping. 'Jack Punch' again distinguished himself during the French Revolutionary War. In 1800 he received his well-deserved promotion to post-rank; and three years afterwards he was appointed to the frigate *Tartar*, 32, on the Jamaica station.

In the *Recollections of James Anthony Gardner* the Old Navy lives for ever. 'His book', observes Dr. David Mathew, 'is in fact the classic account of the life of a sea-officer of the late eighteenth century.' Though it is clear from these memoirs that Gardner's messmates were all too frequently addicted to hard drinking, and occasionally to puerile and brutal horseplay, the general impression to be gained from the *Recollections* is one of good fellowship and abounding high spirits. Incidentally the work serves to reveal that Marryat's description of some of the amazing characters in his naval novels, such as 'Gentleman Chucks' the boatswain and Mr. Muddle the carpenter are in no way exaggerated. 'As I have said before,' remarked the author of the *Recollections*, 'every ship has its strange characters.'

When he was in the *Blonde* Gardner met Patrick Gibson, the purser of the *Pallas*, who had been a messmate of Gardner's father in the *Princess Royal*. The *Blonde* and the *Pallas* lying alongside the same hulk, the two saw a good deal of each other. From the account Gardner gives of his friend it would seem that the type of 'stage Irishman' who appears in *Peter Simple* was not entirely a figment of Marryat's imagination. Gibson was then (1799) eighty years of age and he lived for another thirty-one years. He had been at the taking of Quebec, and was one of those who helped to carry Wolfe off the field when mortally wounded. Gardner thus describes him: 'a tall raw-boned Irishman from the county Tipperary; very powerful, with an Herculean grasp, and woe betide those who got into his clutches if roused to anger. He was a very jovial companion, droll in his manner, full of anecdotes, and sung in the Irish language, of which he was a perfect master. He used to go on shore to bring off the drunken Irish who had stayed above their time, and I remember him saying to me, "Arrah, don't you think, my dear fellow, that it's a hard thing that nobody can manage those spalpeens but an ould man like me, now eighty years of age? Och, by the Holy Father, how I knocked their heads together, and left the mark of my fist upon their ugly podreen faces, bad luck to them."'[9]

In the unrivalled gallery of originals, cranks, and eccentrics portrayed by Gardner, particular mention must be made of the famous Billy Culmer, who prided himself on being the oldest midshipman in the Navy and looked upon young captains and lieutenants with contempt. 'Billy in person was about five feet eight or nine,' writes Gardner, 'and stooped; hard features marked with the small pox; blind in an eye, and a wen nearly the size of an egg under his cheek-bone. . . . He had a custom, when half seas over, of sounding a horn like a huntsman calling the hounds, and used to swear he would be in at the death.' 'When he went to pass for lieutenant,' Gardner recounts, 'one of the midshipmen and Marr the boatswain went up to London with him. They found it no easy matter to keep him in order, and he once swore to have them taken up as runaway soldiers. When he went to the navy board to undergo his examination he asked the commissioners the meaning of the word "azimuth" and told them he could never find any *wa wa* that knew a word about it. Some of the board had been shipmates with him and were well acquainted with his ways; and when putting him right when answering a question, he would say, "Go on, go on, my boy, that's the way; you are very right," as if he were passing them; and when they told him they had no more questions to ask, he said he was glad of it and would go back to his ship like a lark.'[10]

'Before leaving the *Berwick*', Gardner continues, 'I must mention a few droll hands that belonged to her; and first I shall bring forward old Bell, the mate of the hold. We pressed him and several mates of merchantmen out of a cartel from Marseilles to Gibraltar, and put them on the quarter deck. He was a hard-drinking man and also a hard-working man. We had a set on board full of fun; and when old Bell was half seas over, they used to paint his face with red ochre, his eyebrows blacked, large moustache, with a flaxen wig made from the fag ends of the tiller rope; a cocked hat over all, tied under the chin; his shirt off and his body painted like an ancient Briton. In this costume I have seen him chasing the midshipmen through the tier with a drawn sword, a fit subject for a pencil like Hogarth's.'[11]

Another of Gardner's messmates in the midshipmen's berth in the *Berwick* was 'old Collier, who drank like a fish, and when drunk used to sing the Thirty-fourth Psalm and prognosticate that the ship would founder with all hands'. Another of his shipmates was Johnny Bone, boatswain of the *Edgar*. 'This Johnny Bone was a devil of a fellow at Cap-a-bar,[12] and would stick at nothing. It is related that the late Lord Duncan, when he commanded the *Edgar*, once said to him, "Whatever you do, Mr. Bone, I hope and trust you will not take the anchors from the bows."' Of John Stiles, lieutenant of the *Salisbury*, Gardner wrote briefly, 'Fond of mastheading for little or nothing'; of John Roskruge, master of the *Edgar*, 'One that was better acquainted with rope-yarns and bilge-water than with Homer or Virgil. He said a man's ideas should go no further than the jibboom end'; of John Watson, mate of the same vessel, 'Sickly and crabbed as the devil. Cato the Censor never ended a speech without saying "Delenda est Carthago", and this man never ended a speech without saying "Damn your whistle"'; of Henry Foularton, midshipman, also of the *Edgar*, 'Drank very hard, and died regretting that a keg of gin (alongside of him) should see him out'; of Billy Chantrell, first lieutenant of the *Barfleur*, who in turning in at night used to say, 'Call me at six, and don't come bothering me about blowing and raining and all that damned nonsense'; of Jackson Dowson, lieutenant of the same ship, 'All jaw and singing from morn till night'; of Love Constable, first lieutenant of the *Queen*, 'The devil on board, but an angel on shore'; of Joseph Kemble, boatswain of the *Berwick*, 'A snappish cur'; of Alexander Mackenzie, midshipman of the same vessel, 'This man, when he was a midshipman, used to sneak after the lieutenants; when made a lieutenant, sneaking after the captains, and when made a captain, sneaking after the admirals. Had he lived to be made a flag officer, he would have sneaked after the devil.'

In the *Recollections* there is many a passage set out in vivid and revealing detail which brings the whole scene to life. For instance, there is the lively account of an alarming experience they had one night in the *Gorgon*, when they were overtaken by a gale off the entrance to the Channel, and the ship was taken aback 'in a thundering squall', with the wind shifting suddenly from S.W. to N.N.W. Gardner and the others were at supper afterwards when they heard a noise in the after-hold 'like the rush of many waters'. Everyone thought that a butt end had started and that they would founder in a few minutes.

> The alarm was given immediately. The sick and lame left their hammocks; the latter forgot his crutch, and leaped—not exulting—like the bounding roe. Down came the captain and a whole posse of officers and men. The gratings were instantly unshipped, and in rushed the carpenter and his crew, horror-struck, with hair standing on end, like quills on the fretful porcupine; when, behold, it was a large cask of peas as the ship rolled rushed alongside with a noise exactly like that of water.
>
> After looking at one another for some time the following ludicrous scene took place, which I was an eye-witness to:
> The captain shook his head, took snuff, and went upon deck.
> Old Edgar, first lieutenant, followed, and said, 'God bass 'e all.'
> Billy Chantrell gave a grin, and damn'd his eyes.
> The parson exclaimed, 'In the midst of life we are in death.'
> The carpenter said, 'Damn and b—— the peas.'[13]

In a good many families successive generations entered the Navy as a matter of course; a boy would follow in his father's footsteps, or, perhaps, in those of an uncle; in the Navy List the old familiar names constantly recur. A leading naval historian of the early nineteen-hundreds, discoursing of Rodney's action off The Saints, makes this point amply clear.

> It is an interesting instance of hereditary inclination—of how the naval spirit runs in families. Two-thirds of Rodney's captains, practically, are represented at the present hour in the Royal Navy by direct descendants. One had only to turn over the pages of the current Navy List to find Hoods and Inglefields and Parrys, and Graveses and Gardners, Fanshawes and Dumaresqs, a Buckner, a

Blair, a Burnett, a Balfour, a Savage, a Symons, a Charington, an Inglis, a Wallace, a Byron, a Cornish, a Truscott, a Saumarez, Knights and Wilsons, and Williamses and Wilkinsons and Thomsons, besides others, who either trace their descent directly from Rodney's captains or come of the same stock.[14]

Early inured to the hardships of their calling, many of these young officers attained to an astonishingly high level of professional skill and capability. Progressing for the most part by practical experience rather than by study, they acquired a thorough knowledge of the science of seamanship, rose promptly and coolly to an emergency, and learned to pit their strength and skill against every vagary of weather, wind, and sea. As will later appear, midshipmen would frequently pass for lieutenants while still in their teens. Frederick Marryat was not quite twenty when he led a party to cut away the main-yard of the *Aeolus*, when that ship had been laid on her beam ends in a heavy gale off the New England coast in September 1811.

Under the Anson regime, in the middle of the eighteenth century, Great Britain was entering upon a period of almost continuous warfare which was to raise the Royal Navy to its highest peak of power and glory. Rather less than half a century lies between Quiberon Bay and Trafalgar.

A factor of crucial significance in the development of British sea power in the latter part of this period was the living tradition of naval warfare inherited by so many officers of that generation, who had experience, not only of the War of American Independence, but also of the Seven Years War. On the outbreak of the last and greatest of our wars with France, covering the years 1793–1815, this country possessed a corps of sea officers that was unequalled in any other maritime Power in Europe, the veterans of Lagos and Quiberon Bay, of Finisterre and The Saints. 'There were giants in those days,' Captain Creswell rightly observes, 'not necessarily because they were more favoured at birth than the men of our generation, but because many of them had experience of two or even three wars and each man was carrying on a living tradition from the generation before him.'[15]

A striking example of the strength of this tradition may be seen in the letter written by Pellew to Earl Spencer, the First Lord, after his daring pursuit of a French line-of-battle ship, the *Droits de l'Homme*, into the dangerous waters of Audierne Bay, in Brittany—a dead lee shore—where the enemy was forced ashore and totally wrecked (14 January 1797), and where Pellew's frigate, the *Indefatigable*, narrowly escaped sharing the same fate.

I fear your lordship will think me rather imprudent on this occasion, but what can be done if an enemy's coast is always to frighten us and give them protection as safely as their ports? If Lord Hawke had no fears from a lee shore with a large fleet under his charge, could I for a moment think of two inconsiderable frigates?[16]

In the same way the 'living tradition' was passed on from Hawke to Locker, and from Locker in turn to the greatest of them all; for one of Hawke's young officers, in the crucial campaign of 1759, had been Lieutenant William Locker of the *Sapphire* frigate; and one of Locker's lieutenants, towards the close of Hawke's life, was Horatio Nelson. It was to Locker, his old captain, that Nelson long afterwards, when he had become famous, wrote, 'To you, my dear friend, I owe much of my success. It was you who taught me,—"Lay a Frenchman close and you will beat him".'

CHAPTER 6

THE YOUNG GENTLEMEN

WILLIAM COBBETT once related how in his boyhood he went, in the autumn of 1782, to visit an uncle who lived in the vicinity of Portsmouth. From the top of Portsdown Hill this youngster from an inland village beheld, for the first time in his life, the sea—and, not only the sea, but the Channel squadron riding at anchor at Spithead; and he observed, that no sooner did he behold this inspiring spectacle, than, like so many of his generation, he was filled with longing to be a sailor. In the event, in Cobbett's case this hope was not to be fulfilled: but, for many another, the dream, in truth, came true. It is interesting and perhaps not unprofitable to recall the circumstances under which certain of our future commanders heard and responded to the call of the sea.

At Burnham Thorpe parsonage, during the Christmas holidays of 1770–1, William and Horatio, the young sons of the rector, the Rev. Edmund Nelson, read in the local newspaper that the *Raisonnable*, 64, owing to the threat of war with Spain, was shortly to be recommissioned. The younger of the two boys, Horatio, thereupon begged his brother to write to their father at Bath, telling him that he would like to go to sea with the *Raisonnable*'s captain, their uncle Maurice Suckling. The rector's letter evoked from Captain Suckling the response: 'What has poor Horatio done, who is so weak, that he above the rest should be sent to rough it out at sea? But let him come; and the first time we go into action, a cannon-ball may knock off his head, and provide for him at once.' Early one cold, dark morning in March the rector's servant arrived at North Walsham, where the boys were at school, with the long-awaited summons for Horatio to join his ship. The latter set off with his father to London, where he was put into the Chatham stage. The *Raisonnable* was lying in the Medway; and when at last Horatio

found his way on board he discovered that his uncle was not in the ship, nor
had anyone been apprised of the boy's coming. For the remainder of the day,
lonely and forlorn, Horatio paced the deck, without being noticed by
anyone. Such was the inauspicious introduction to the Service of the greatest
fighting admiral in the annals of the sea.

Thomas Byam Martin was seven when he first visited Portsmouth, where
his father was Commissioner. He recalls that when they arrived at Gosport,
where the Commissioner's barge was waiting to ferry them across the
harbour to the dockyard, his gaze lighted on several sail of the line which
occupied moorings immediately fronting the beach. The spectacle came as a
revelation to him, and he stood there spellbound. 'I was so riveted to the
spot,' he declared, 'so perfectly motionless when I got out of the carriage, so
absorbed in wonder, that I should have been there the whole day if they had
not sent one of the boat's crew to fetch me down.' In crossing the harbour
they passed close under the stern of the *Royal George*, flagship of Sir Edward
Hawke at Quiberon Bay. It was the first time he ever floated on salt water,
he relates; the first hundred-gun ship he ever saw. 'Ye gods! what a
sight—what a sensation! I feel it now as I write, and if I live to the age of
Methuselah it will remain unimpaired, and even fresh to the last moment. It
is impossible to forget the breathless astonishment and delight with which
my eyes were fixed upon this ship. Nothing so exquisitely touching has ever
occurred to me since to produce the same frantic joy. He goes on to say, the
Commissioner's coxswain broke in upon these reflections. 'I see, sir,' said
Allen, 'you are already determined to be a sailor!'

Old John Allen, 'a fine sample of a sailor of the old school: a manly, fine-
looking fellow', never spoke a truer word, Byam Martin comments; for
from that moment, and for ever after, the little boy's mind was fully made
up: he was determined to go to sea. Inside the dockyard he found himself
surrounded by the liveliest, most fascinating scenes imaginable. 'Everything
seemed to be in motion, and the clatter of the shipwrights' hammers was a
music quite in harmony with the notions I had picked up in my voyage
across the harbour. . . . The busy, bustling scene often comes to my
recollection like the renewal of a pleasant dream. There were the officers of
the ships flying from place to place to hasten off stores; the ships loosing their
sails to go out of harbour—signals up, guns firing; and there was, alas! the
torturing sight of little midshipmen, scarcely bigger than myself, swelled
into all the importance of men in authority. This vanity was more than the
flesh and blood of boy could stand. I was at once a prey to the most envious
feelings, and altogether so unsettled at the sight of these consequential
officers as to be utterly unfit for anything. Who will be surprised, after all

this, when I say that the school-master made but an unsatisfactory report of my application to book business?"[1]

The future Commander James Anthony Gardner was a very young boy when, in a home port, he was settled on board the *Boreas* and *Conqueror* with his father, who was master in the first and fourth lieutenant in the second. (From the age of five, indeed, he had been borne on the ships' books as his father's servant.) Gardner goes on to say that he had nothing to do with the midshipmen, as he lived in the gunroom of the *Boreas* and the wardroom of the *Conqueror*. But when he actually entered the Service, he observes, 'I took my degrees (not as a doctor of Oxford, thank God!) but as a midshipman in the cockpit of H.M. ship *Panther*, with some of the best fellows that ever graced the British Navy'. Gardner had eleven shillings given him by some friends in Gosport before leaving, and he says he thought his fortune was made.

On my introduction to my new shipmates I was shown down to the starboard wing berth. I had not long been seated before a rugged-muzzled midshipman came in, and having eyed me for a short time, he sang out with a voice of thunder: 'Blister my tripes—where the hell did you come from? I suppose you want to stick your grinders (for it was near dinner-time) into some of our à la mode beef?'; and without waiting for a reply he sat down and sang a song that I shall remember as long as I live. The first verse, being the most moral, I shall give:

> A Duchess from Germany
>   Has lately made her will;
> Her body she's left to be buried
>   Her soul to the devil in hell.

This gentleman's name was Watson, and notwithstanding the song and his blunt manner of speaking, he proved to be a very good fellow, and was the life and soul of the mess.

I must now describe our starboard wing berth and compare it with the manners and customs of the present day. In this ship our mess-place had canvas screens scrubbed white, wainscot tables, well polished, Windsor chairs, and a pantry fitted in the wing to store our crockery and dinner traps with safety. The holystones and hand-organs [the small holystones], in requisition twice a week, made our orlop deck as white as the boards of any crack drawing-room, the strictest attention being paid to cleanliness; and everything had the appearance of Spartan simplicity. We used to sit down to a piece of salt beef, with sour krout, and dine gloriously with our pint of black-strap [a coarse red wine] after, ready at all calls, and as fit for battle as for muster.[2]

The Midshipmen's berth; oil painting by Augustus Earle, early nineteenth century.

Gardner goes on to lament the later introduction of 'luxury' into the midshipmen's quarters, 'the cockpit abandoned, and my lords and gentlemen ushered into the gunroom fitted up in luxurious style, with window curtains, blinds, buffets, wine coolers, silver forks, and many other appendages unknown in the good old times'. However, it would seem that these refinements were by no means general when young Marryat entered the Service some twenty-five years later. In his earliest novel, *Frank Mildmay*, a work which is to a great extent autobiographical, the latter vividly records his first impressions of the midshipmen's berth. 'I followed my new friend down the ladder, under the half deck, where sat a woman, selling bread and butter and red herrings to the sailors; she had also cherries and clotted cream, and a cask of strong beer, which seemed to be in great demand. We passed her, and descended another ladder, which brought us to the 'tween decks, and into the steerage, in the forepart of which, on the larboard side, abreast of the mainmast, was my future residence—a small hole, which they called a berth; it was ten feet long by six, and about five feet four inches high; a small aperture, about nine inches square, admitted a very scanty portion of what we most needed, namely, fresh air and daylight. A deal table occupied a considerable extent of this small apartment, and on it stood a brass candlestick, with a dip candle, and a wick like a full blown carnation. The table cloth was spread and stains of port wine and gravy too visibly indicated the near approach of Sunday. The black servant was preparing for dinner, and I was shown the seat I was to occupy. "Good heaven!" thought I, as I squeezed myself between the ship's side and the mess-table, "and is this to be my future residence?—better go back to school; there, at least, is fresh air and clean linen."'

One of Marryat's messmates briefly catalogued the appointments of the midshipmen's berth as follows: 'One battered, spoutless, handleless japanned tin mug that did not contain water, for it leaked; some tin mugs; seven or eight pewter plates; an excellent old iron tureen which contained our cocoa in the morning, our pea soup at noon and performed the character of wash basin whenever the midshipmen's fag condescended to cleanse his hands. It is a fact that when we sailed from England, of crockery we had not a single article. We had no other provisions than the ship's allowance. Bread, it is well remarked, is the staff of life; but', the writer added drily, 'it is not quite so pleasant to find it life itself, and to have the powers of locomotion.'

The early impressions of Admiral the Hon. Sir George Elliot were more favourable.

'These were happy days,' he remarked, 'though not luxurious ones. When I first went to sea, midshipmen had no servants, they cooked for themselves, made and washed their own things, but kept up a tolerable appearance; we had little beyond the ship's allowance of provision, and only a tin pot or two to drink out of. . . . I never slept on shore as a midshipman except between paying off the *Goliath* and commissioning the *Elephant* early in 1800; and I had not probably been in port, on an average, a fortnight in the year, unless attacking or defending some place. . . . I can safely say, that out of the five years I actually served as a midshipman, I had not one unhappy day, and no power could have persuaded me to quit the service.'[3]

Throughout the greater part of the era under survey the 'young gentlemen' would enter the Service either under the patronage of the captain or some other officer, or by warrant from the Admiralty. The former would be rated 'Captain's Servant', 'Master's Servant', etc.; the latter, from 1733 on, would pass through the Naval Academy (situated in Portsmouth Dockyard), before going to sea. Then in 1794, by an Order in Council, all Officers' Servants were officially abolished. Their place would be taken by 'Volunteers of the First Class'—who were, however, really no more than Officers' Servants under a new name. In both cases they were youngsters placed on the quarter-deck and preparing to attain, in due course, to commissioned rank. They were obliged to serve (in theory, at any rate) for six years and be twenty years of age before they could pass for lieutenant.

The junior 'young gentlemen' messed in the gunroom under the fatherly eye of the gunner; the older ones in the cockpit on the orlop deck. 'We lived', Lovell related, 'on the lower deck, and in fine weather had daylight, which was better in many respects than the old midshipmen's berths in the cockpit.'[4]

Midshipman carrying a sextant in his left hand; pencil and watercolour sketch by Thomas Rowlandson.

Again and again the irrepressible spirits of the midshipmen's berth breaks out in Gardner's *Recollections*. In the *Edgar* the 'young gentlemen' were accustomed to battle for the possession of the poop while their seniors were at dinner in the wardroom. One side defended the poop and the other tried to storm it. 'In one of these attacks', observed Gardner, 'I succeeded in getting on the poop, when Kiel (who I have mentioned before) attacked me with a fixed bayonet and marked me in the thigh (all in good part). I then got hold of a musket, put in a small quantity of powder, and as he advanced, I fired. To my horror and amazement he fell flat on the deck, and when picked up his face was as black as a tinker's, with the blood running down occasioned by some of the grains of powder sticking in. I shall never forget the terror I was in, but thank God he soon got well; only a few blue spots

remained in his phiz, which never left him. This was the only time I ever
fired a musket and probably will be the last. They used to say in the cockpit
he was troubled with St. Anthony's fire (alluding to my name).' There was
the day when the *Berwick* lay off Leghorn, and Gardner and his messmates
went to Pisa to view the carnival with its procession of 600 coaches. 'Pelting
with sugar plums is customary on this occasion,' declared Gardner; 'and one
of our midshipmen pelted Lord Hervey in his coach; and when told it was
the British ambassador, and that he looked very angry, he immediately hove
another volley at Lady Hervey, observing that she looked better tempered
than his Excellency.' On their return to Leghorn after several days' absence,
they dined at one of the hotels in the city, where there was another rumpus.
'We had a strong party of English officers at the dinner, some of whom got
rather merry before the cloth was off the table, and catching hold of the
waiter they rolled him in the cloth with plates and dishes, the fellow roaring
out all the while to no purpose.' One of the midshipmen took a loaf to the
window (they were on the second floor) and dropped it on the head of a
passer-by, 'which floored him', while others pelted legs and wings of fowls
at those looking out of the opposite windows; but to their kind forbearance
everything was taken as a joke and only laughed at. 'Would this have been
the case in England?' the Irishman, Gardner, concluded—'where every hole
and corner has a board threatening prosecution, and if you pass two or three
stopping in the street, their conversation will be about law, hanging, or
trade.'[5]

 While he was in the *Gorgon* Gardner relates that he fell foul of Jerry
Hacker, their purser, 'a most strange and unaccountable character', who
could not bear the sight of a midshipman in the cockpit and used to do
everything in his power to annoy them. Hacker would sometimes sing a
verse of an old song making game of midshipmen. One morning when
Gardner was in the cockpit the purser was quarrelling with some of the
midshipmen and presently struck up his favourite air—

> Ye salt beef squires and quarter deck beaus,
> Who formerly lived upon blacking of shoes:
> With your anchors a-weigh and your topsails a-trip.
> If they call us by name and we don't answer, Sir!
> They start us about till not able to stir;
> A lusty one and lay it well on.
> If you spare them an inch you ought to be damn'd;
> With your anchors a-weigh and your topsails a-trip.

The purser apparently imagined that nobody knew the song but himself. In this, however, he was mistaken; for as soon as he had finished singing the verse quoted above, Gardner instantly struck up another that sems to have settled him.

> Our b—— of a purser, he is very handy,
> He mixes the water along with the brandy;
>   Your anchors a-weigh and your topsails a-trip.
> The bloody old thief he is very cruel;
> Instead of burgoo he gives us water gruel;
>   A lusty one and lay it well on.
> If you spare him an inch you ought to be damn'd,
> With your anchors a-weigh and your topsails a-trip.

After hearing the last verse, Jerry's 'heavenly voice was heard no more', Gardner observed, and 'he looked with an evil eye' upon the young midshipman for the rest of his stay in the ship.[6]

In Captain Boteler's *Recollections* there are the same high spirits and good fellowship, the same rowdy games in the midshipmen's quarters, and (it may be said) the same love of a scrap. Boteler relates that on rejoining his ship at Chatham there was a great row between the midshipmen of the squadron and the dockyard mateys, which generally began at the theatre when 'God save the King' was called for, and all the actors would appear on the stage to sing it. Then it was 'off hats', says Boteler, and if anyone refused, the 'young gentlemen' would storm the gallery, and there was a free fight. 'I remember a mid. of the *Poictiers* going up and throwing a dockyard young fellow right over into the pit. The thing was to get safe to our ships. We had horns and whistles to call for aid if required, and scenes of this description were carried on night after night.'[7]

'We had few or no real quarrels', says another midshipman, W. S. Lovell, 'the four years we sailed together, and, whenever spare time permitted, our evenings were spent in the amusements afforded by the old games of cribbage, loo, draughts, and able wackets, which is a kind of forfeit played with cards, where each player is subject, for every mistake, to one or more blows with a knotted handkerchief on the palm of the hand. . . . We were all kept tight at work, and had at least four hours of sky-parlour (being sent to the main-topmasthead), when our watch was over, for every delinquency.'[8]

One of Lovell's messmates was the Hon. Henry Dawson, who was accustomed to keep the unfortunate midshipman he was due to relieve waiting for at least half an hour beyond his time on deck. On these occasions the lieutenant of the watch would send down an old quartermaster, Ned Cowen, who had gone round the world with Captain Cook, to arouse the sluggard. Whenever old Ned presented himself at the Hon. H. Dawson's hammock, he used to signify his mission with the customary summons—

'Come, Mr. Dawson, past one bell [the half-hour after the watch had been called], turn out, show a leg, or I am ordered to bring you up on the quarter-deck, hammock and all; take my advice, bring a good, thick greatcoat with you; it is a wet night, and the masthead waiting for you—the old story, you know!'[9]

In the London report of the old *Sussex Advertiser*, in the aftermath of Trafalgar, there is an illuminating account of a scrimmage one night in town involving one of these youngsters. The mid. was strolling down Whitehall when he was accosted and 'sauced' by a young person, delicately referred to as a *wh—e*. In a brisk and matter-of-fact way he turned and chastised the offender . . . whereupon (according to the report) 'he was set upon by her attendant Bully'. The passers-by joyfully formed a ring and action was joined. 'The little Fellow, who was every inch a British Tar', set to and 'soundly thrashed the Bully'; while the crowd cheered him on with enthusiastic cries of 'Well done, young Sprigs of Laurel!' and 'The Navy of Old England for ever!'

Happy days!

It was not unusual for a captain to take a close and continuous interest in the 'young gentlemen' under his charge. Such a man was Commander Manley Dixon of the *Orestes* who, according to Gardner, was a very smart officer, and did everything in his power to teach the midshipmen their duty. 'We used to take helm and lead, and reef the main topsail; also pull in the boats upon particular occasions, such as going along shore in the night after smugglers, &c.' The same writer remarks that Captain Calder of the *Barfleur* would always bring the nobility that visited the ship to see the midshipmen's berths, and used to say: 'This is the place where all the admirals and captains in the service are tried every day, and where no one escapes being hauled over the coals.' Young George Elliot also remembered with gratitude the attentions of the captain and other officers in his first ship. 'I had certainly met with no hardships, according to our ideas, but with constant kindness and friendship, not only from my captain but other officers; one of whom, Lieutenant (afterwards Sir Wentworth) Loring, took a sort of charge of me, kept my books, and made me read in his cabin. Our friendship lasted throughout that worthy man's life. I had gone to sea so young, was so fond of it, and so constantly at sea, that I soon became a thorough seaman in all its branches.'

How an unlucky midshipman would occasionally experience the rough side of his captain's tongue is vividly recounted by Gardner. He relates that when belonging to a guard-ship commanded by Sir Roger Curtis, while lying at Spithead, the main topsail was ordered to be loosed, to swing the ship the right way. The midshipman in question, nicknamed Tommy Bowline, was the first to go aloft and was highly complimented by Curtis for his activity, in these words: 'You are a fine fellow, Mr. Stevens; a most active officer, Mr. Stevens; you are a wonder, Mr. Stevens.' Now it unfortunately happened that Tommy was left behind by the other midshipmen and was last on the yard. Observing this, Curtis called out, 'I recall all my compliments, Mr. Stevens; you are a damned lubber, Mr. Stevens; a blockhead, Mr. Stevens; come down, Mr. Stevens.' This, says Gardner, poor Tommy never heard the last of.[10]

Not a few of these midshipmen had the cares and responsibility of manhood thrust on their shoulders when they were still but children.[11] Bernard Coleridge was only eleven when he entered the Navy in June 1804 as a volunteer of the first class. Well before the age at which prep. schoolboys at the present day are preparing for Common Entrance, he was learning to be a seaman and an officer. From the masthead of the *Impétueux* the youngster would gaze with shining eyes at the vista of masts and spars in Brest roads; in bad weather he would pace the quarter-deck with his hat drawn down over his ears, longing for a warm greatcoat; for weeks on end he had to subsist on 'salt beef, biscuit, stinking water, and brandy'. He was no more than thirteen when one day he fell from aloft and was instantly killed.

In his reminiscences Hay relates that it was a rule on board the *Culloden* in 1804 that every midshipman should send in daily to the captain on a slip of paper a statement of the course and distance made good since the noon of the day before, also the ship's present latitude and longitude, both by observation and by dead reckoning, together with the bearings and distance of the point of land it was intended first to make. The slips, says Hay, were generally handed to the wardroom sentry, who sent them into the captain by one of the boys.

Finally the day approached of passing for lieutenant (an ordeal that brought with it the discomfiting knowledge that all the exertions of the past six years were at stake), when the midshipman found himself in the presence of the three captains who were to decide whether he were fit to hold the King's commission. The candidate's logs and certificates would be examined and approved, his time calculated and allowed to be correct; after which followed various questions on navigation and seamanship. He was carefully examined in the different sailings, working tides, day's work, and double altitudes; and was expected to give some account of the different methods of finding the longitude by a chronometer and lunar observations. In practical seamanship he was expected to be able to take a ship from one place to another, under every disadvantage of wind, tides, etc., and also to give an account how he would proceed in the event of danger and distress, from the loss of masts, rigging, etc. The summons to pass for lieutenant came quite unexpectedly for John Boteler, who was totally unprepared for the examination and, not unnaturally, entertained the liveliest apprehensions.

> While on deck there were our own pendant on board, the *Gloucester*, followed by a telegraph of 772, 'Send Mr (spelling pendant) BOTELER on board to pass.' I was fairly taken aback; I never dreamed of an opportunity, had looked into no book of navigation, nor had I my logs written up. There was no help for it. I went down to the first lieutenant with the telegraph in my hand. 'Why, this is you, sir.' 'Yes, sir.' 'Well, set off at once.' 'May I go down to clean myself?' 'Yes, but be sharp about it,' and in a few minutes I was off to the *Gloucester*, dived into the gunroom, and with John Hamilton Moore and Robinson's *Elements* before me, tried to look at some problem or other, but deuce a bit, they all swam before me, and what made it worse, the entry of a mid. who had missed stays, saying, 'if it were not for going to the devil he would jump overboard.'[12]

There is a lively and revealing account of the examination in question in Vice-Admiral W. S. Lovell's *Personal Narrative of Events from 1799 to 1815*.

> In May 1805 I removed to the *Neptune*, 98, Captain Thomas Fremantle, a clever, brave, and smart officer, who sent me home to pass my examination at Somerset House, in August, which I did, before old Captain Sir Alexander Snap Hammond, whose character for turning mids back frightened me not a little. The one examined before me not having been sent, as from Oxford or Cambridge, to rusticate in green fields and sylvan groves, but condemned to study six months longer in a mid's berth on the briny element in order to finish his nautical education, and eat peas pudding, burgoo and molasses, salt junk, lobscourse, sea-pie, and study Hamilton Moore. Having waited a short time, and got rather better of some odd qualms and palpitations which the unfortunate candidate turned back before me had created, I was ordered to find the time of high water at Plymouth, work an azimuth amplitude, double altitude, bearings and distances, &c., which being performed, I was desired to stand up, and consider myself on the quarter-deck of a man-of-war at

Spithead—'unmoor'—'get underway'—'stand out to sea'—'make and shorten sail'—'reef'—'return into port'—'unrig the foremast and bowsprit, and rig them again.' I got into a scrape after reefing for not overhauling the reef tackles when hoisting the sails. However, they passed me, and desired me to come again the next day to receive my passing certificate. I made the captains the best bow I could, and, without staying to look behind me, bolted out of the room, and was surrounded in a moment by other poor fellows, who were anxiously waiting their turn to be called in for examination, who asked what questions had been put to me, and the answers I made, &c.[13]

It was by no means an unheard-of thing for youngsters who were still at school or even in the nursery to be borne upon the ship's books. False certificates of age were normally winked at. Peter Parker (grandson of Nelson's patron) passed for lieutenant at the age of sixteen, being officially reported as 'upwards of twenty-one'. Nelson himself was certified as over twenty when he was actually under nineteen. In the same way Nelson got his stepson, Josiah Nisbet, promoted to commander by flouting the regulations. It is related by George Elliot that, in 1800, when he and a number of other youngsters went to pass for lieutenants' commissions: 'Our examinations before the old Commissioners of the Navy were not severe; but we were called on to produce certificates that we were all twenty-one years of age—I was sixteen and four days. The old porter in the hall furnished them at 5s. apiece, which, no doubt, the old Commissioners knew; for, on our return with them, they remarked that the ink had not dried in twenty-one years.'[14]

CHAPTER 7

THE MANNING OF
THE FLEET

THE peace-time strength of the Royal Navy was no more than a fraction of what it became in time of war. With the cessation of hostilities the great majority of the seamen returned to their former employment, mainly in the merchant marine or fishing fleets, or else some ancillary occupation. It was not, in fact, until the middle of the nineteenth century that seamen were recruited on a continuous service basis.

Moreover, throughout the period under review the Navy's demands rose higher and higher. In 1756 some 50,000 men sufficed for the needs of the Fleet. The following year the number was increased to 55,000; in 1759, to 60,000; in 1760, to 70,000. Just before the outbreak of hostilities with the American colonists the total strength of the Navy stood at 18,000. In 1776 it was increased to 28,000; in 1779, to 70,000; in 1781, to 90,000; in 1783, to 110,000. But in 1784 it had fallen to 26,000, and more than 80,000 men were paid off and turned adrift. In 1792, on the eve of the long-drawn-out Revolutionary and Napoleonic Wars, the total personnel of the Navy amounted to only 16,000 men. In 1802 it stood at the unprecedented figure of 135,000. During the Napoleonic War it was to rise higher still. By 1812 it had reached a total of 145,000.

In time of peace most of the ships were laid up in the naval ports with skeleton crews on board. The outbreak of hostilities invariably found most of the Fleet paralysed for lack of men; and it became necessary to draw heavily on the total maritime reserves of the realm in the shape of merchant seamen, fishermen, bargemen, boatmen, lightermen, and all other persons 'using the sea'. The absence of any effective, organized system of recruitment was a perennial and serious weakness. Though from time to time suggestions were made by various writers, from Defoe in the seventeenth century to Marryat in the nineteenth, for manning the Fleet, the Admiralty continued to rely for the most part on the time-honoured expedients of bounties and impressment.

Prime seamen constituted the effective nucleus of the crews; of which, perhaps, about one-fifth were volunteers. It is always to be remembered that there were generally large numbers of these volunteers among the new intake, with whatever motive they may have entered. Men would not infrequently volunteer (and draw the bounty) when the circumstances of time and place were such that if they did not there was little or no chance of their escaping impressment. There must also have been occasions when a surge of patriotic fervour was engendered by some band striking up martial music or the inspiriting strains of 'Rule, Britannia' or 'Heart of Oak' bawled out in full-throated chorus in a tavern, and men would eagerly volunteer in a moment of enthusiasm they might afterwards regret.

'We find that seamen enter with great alacrity,' declared the Portsmouth correspondent of the *Naval Chronicle* in February 1803, 'on board two commissioned frigates, the *Amphion* and *Alcmene*, in the harbour.' And in April: 'Men enter very fast, and, on average, there are twelve volunteers to one impressed man; a circumstance never known in any former period of raising men for the navy.' It is stated that at Plymouth the previous December the *Belleisle* had nearly completed her complement, 'which are all prime volunteer able and ordinary seamen'; and, two months later, that 'great exertions are making here to procure volunteer seamen'.

Boys usually entered the Service through the Marine Society and other such organizations. In peace-time the majority of these boys went into the merchant service; in war-time, into the Navy. They grew up to manhood in the Service and often remained in it throughout their working lives. Knowing no other life than that of the Navy, they were not disposed to go elsewhere. The Marine Society also provided clothes for adult volunteers for the Navy. From about the beginning of the Revolutionary and Napoleonic Wars 'Landmen' became an official rating.

Certain cities and corporations, as well as the government, offered bounties for enlistment. At the time of the 'Spanish Armament' in 1790, for example, Edinburgh and Montrose offered a bounty of 42s. a head for prime seamen, London 40s., Aberdeen 21s., and Bristol 20s.; while the government offered 30s. But the expedient was only partly successful.

The rest of the intake would be conscripts of all sorts and conditions. Press gangs swept the streets and alleys of the principal ports and coastal towns and boarded the homecoming trades, or merchant fleets, as well as colliers and

Collier discharging; engraving from Shipping and Craft—fifty plates *by E. W. Cooke, 1829.*

fishing vessels. From these two main sources—the mercantile marine and the fisheries—came the pool of trained seamen from which, in war-time, were drawn most of the crews for the Navy. The majority as well as the best of the pressed men came out of the merchant vessels—for the most part those homeward-bound—in the Channel and North Sea.

There were the large vessels under charter to the East India Company, always strongly manned, engaged in the British traffic with China and India. Very much smaller, but several times more numerous, were the ships employed in the West India traffic, which was rightly valued as an admirable school of seamanship. At the turn of the century there were between 700 and 800 ships engaged in commerce with the United States and British North America. There were about 800 ships, averaging 150 tons, plying to the Baltic and the north; another 400, rather smaller, to the Peninsula, and 200 more, of roughly the same size, to the Mediterranean.

A very large number of merchantmen, most of them fairly small, were employed in the coasting trade: the hard school in which so many skilled and experienced mariners, from the time of Chaucer's Shipman onward, had graduated. A most important branch of this traffic, not only from the commercial, but also from the naval, angle, was the coal trade. It was the coal trade which supplied the shipping which plied to the Baltic. Most of the vessels employed in the Greenland fishery and the Archangel trade were

Brixham harbour; aquatint by W. Daniell, 1825.

colliers, or manned with sailors bred up in the coal trade. The coal trade was a prolific breeding-ground of prime seamen. 'Almost every man', declared Edington, 'that treads the deck of a collier is a complete seaman, inured to hardships, and fully acquainted with the duties of his station.'[1] In war-time the coal trade was the mainstay of the expanded Navy. No protections were then granted except to masters, mates, carpenters, and apprentices. From the colliers had come one of the finest seamen of the Old Navy, Captain James Cook.

The Newfoundland cod fishery was regarded by contemporary statesmen and economists as being of fundamental importance to our naval supremacy and prosperity. It annually employed very large numbers of deep-sea fishermen, recruited principally from our western ports. Another important nursery of deep-watermen was the Arctic and South Sea fishery. The east coast ports still sent out their contingent, as of old, to the Iceland fishery.

The numerous inshore fisheries were for the most part worked by small, undecked craft from a multitude of fishing ports, large and small, situated all round the coasts of the British Isles. The East Anglian and other ports yearly assisted at the famous autumn herring fishery off Yarmouth. The Barking smacks, which were among our earliest trawlers, supplied the capital with fish; this being sent up to the market at Billingsgate in small boats. The fishermen of Ramsgate worked the banks off the Netherlands coast, the men of Rye and Hastings the flat-fish grounds in Rye Bay and the adjacent waters. Already a flourishing fishing centre, Brixham was during the 1770s to inaugurate the trawling industry which brought to its inhabitants nearly a century and a half of abounding prosperity. By 1785 there were nearly 80 smacks working out of Brixham. Under the lee of the Skerries, off Start Point, there was an apparently limitless supply of sole. Presently the trawlers sailed further afield. By the close of the Napoleonic War there were from 60 to 70 Brixham smacks working the southern part of the North Sea and landing their catches at Ramsgate to be hurried off to the London market in light vans. Herring, mackerel, and pilchard driving was extensively carried on in the West Country.

Mention must also be made of the illicit but lucrative smuggling industry, which flourished on many parts of the English coast, but more especially in the southern counties, which lay conveniently close to the Continent. (According to Edgar March, the historian of the British fisheries, by the middle of the eighteenth century 'it was a moot point whether many a fisherman on the South Coast was a smuggler in odd moments, or a smuggler who went fishing in his spare time'.) In 1735 a letter appeared in the *Gentleman's Magazine* stating that 'in several parts of Kent the farmers are obliged to raise wages, and yet are distressed for want of hands to get in their harvest, which is attributed to the great numbers who employ themselves in smuggling along the coast'. The smugglers, many of whom were daring and resourceful seamen, were engaged in a perennial battle of wits with the revenue authorities both by land and sea. By the Navy they were usually regarded with suspicion and dislike.

'This smuggling has converted those employed in it,' wrote Vernon in 1745, 'first from honest industrious fishermen, to lazy, drunken, and profligate smugglers, and now to dangerous spies on all our proceedings, for the enemy's daily information.' Shortly before the younger Pitt dealt a damaging blow at this traffic by reducing the high excise duties, smuggling had increased to prodigious proportions, and the industry was organized as never before. The profits were enormous. The 'freetrader' generally recouped himself if he saved but one cargo out of three. Whole fleets of luggers and other small craft, and whole armies of landsmen, were employed by sea and land in this lucrative traffic. However, the smuggling interest duly contributed its quota—unwillingly withal—to the Navy in time of war.

All told, the total pool of seamen available for sea service of one kind or another—the Navy, the merchant marine in all its branches, the deep-sea and inshore fisheries, and all ancillary occupations—may be safely reckoned at well over 300,000 men; but a certain number of these, it must be remembered, were foreigners.

As the Navy continued to expand, the supply of prime seamen was no longer adequate; and a considerable number of landsmen were swept up by the all-embracing net of the press gang, which gradually extended the range of its activities up and down the coasts of the United Kingdom. In London, according to Hutchinson, 'the streets, and especially the waterside streets, were infested with gangs. At times it was unsafe for any able-bodied man to venture abroad unless he had on him an undeniable protection or wore a dress that unmistakably proclaimed the gentleman.'[2]

Strictly speaking, only seafaring men could lawfully be taken by the press gang, and there was an Act which exempted from the press every male under eighteen and over fifty-five. There were a good many other exemptions, which included the masters of merchantmen and certain of their officers (provided that the ship were of 50 tons burthen or over), and pilots as well, unless and until they ran the vessel aground. Harvesters, and sometimes fishermen, were also on occasion entitled to exemption. But in any serious crisis the law was simply ignored, and then would be enacted scenes such as Rowlandson depicted and Smollett described. As an American visitor to this country observed, 'Englishmen would rise in arms, should the military impress for the army, citizens of every rank, from the fields, the streets, and public roads; but, one particular class of men seem to be abandoned by society, and relinquished to perpetual imprisonment, and a slavery, which, though honourable, cuts them off from most things which men hold dear.'[3]

The marked prejudice against service in the Navy that formerly existed in certain of our fishing ports may not infrequently be traced back to distant memories of the press. In this connection 'The Press'd Man's Lamentation' is worth recalling:

> Now the bloody war's beginning,
>   Many thousands will be slain,
> And it is more than ten to one
>   If any of us return again.
>
> To hear the cries in any City
>   Likewise in any seaport town,
> 'Twill make your heart to bleed with pity,
>   For to hear the press'd men moan.[4]

Occasionally the men would put up a stubborn fight, and sometimes the gangs were beaten off. Certain stretches of the coast were notoriously too strong for the gangs to tackle; others were too difficult: for instance, the Cornish peninsula was largely forbidden ground to the press gang. Portland, again, offered unrivalled facilities for successful evasion. To escape capture, seamen would sometimes disguise themselves as labourers, stablemen, etc.; and their employers would assist them to evade the press by concealing them in their houses, and even in their bed-chambers, 'After a seaman', Pitt observed in the House of Commons in 1755, 'by hard service for many years at sea, has earned and saved as much as may establish him in a quiet retreat at land, he does not know but that in six months, or a less time, he may be torn from his wife and family, and forced again to undergo all the fatigues and perils of a common seaman, without any certainty of ever being released, whilst he is fit for serving in that situation.'

It is not very easy to assess the quality of the pressed men in the Navy during the War of 1739–48 and the Seven Years War. The uncomprising verdict of Captain Edward Thompson has often been quoted: 'In a man of

Jack in the Bilboes; mezzotint by G. Ward after G. Morland.

war you have the collected filth of gaols.' Elsewhere the same authority
referred to the arrival at Portsmouth in 1755 of the *Stirling Castle* with nearly
half her crew 'the pressed refuse of gaols and scum of streets'. The official
correspondence, perhaps, does not go as far as this: but it is sufficiently
forthright. Thus in 1743, during the previous war, Hawke had observed to
the Admiralty that the ship's company of the *Berwick* was largely composed
of 'very little, weakly, puny fellows, that have never been at sea, and can be
of little or no service'; and later he remarked that, 'A great number of them
are lately come from the East Indies, and others are raw men picked up by
the press-gangs in London.' Keppel had written in similar vein to Anson in
December 1747. 'All my *Maidstones* are not come, but all the worst,
worthless rascals are. I shall be prettily made up to begin in a new ship.'

In all probability many of the men swept into the bag by the great press of
1755 were of poor quality. Even so, a high percentage of those impressed
must have been experienced seamen. 'Most of the men', wrote Hawke, then
in command of the Channel squadron, on 3 October, 'have been pressed
after long voyages.' No gaol-birds or corner-boys, these, but seamen. There
is the significant testimony of Captain the Hon. Augustus Hervey, who in
the spring of 1757, refers in his private journal to the *Royal George, Ramillies,
Royal Sovereign*, and *Neptune*, as 'these four prime manned ships', having 'the
best seamen in England', and to the *Torbay's* complement of '680 fine men'.
Such words as these must be set against the sweeping generalization of
Captain Thompson. On the whole, judging from the fine performance of so
many ships' companies in the campaign of 1759, a reasonable conclusion
would be that a large admixture of prime seamen constituted the effective
nucleus of the crews.

Our maritime resources were so severely strained, however, in the later
stages of the War of American Independence that the quality of many of the
ships' companies inevitably deteriorated. For twenty years or so afterwards
there was no comparable drain on the pool of seamen. Shortly before the
outbreak of the next war, when the press was operating again in
consequence of the Nootka Sound imbroglio of 1790, known as the 'Spanish
Armament', Gardner paid this tribute to the crew of the *Barfleur*, 98. 'Our
ship's company were never surpassed. We had the pickings of the East India
men, and our waisters could take helm and lead, and certainly we could have
beaten with ease any two ships of a foreign power of our rate.'[5]

Against the intake of volunteers and pressed men must be set the large and
continuing loss of men through desertion. It is significant that a very high
proportion of those were not the raw and inexperienced hands, but prime
seamen. The large-scale desertion of patients from the naval hospitals

presented a major problem to the authorities. A letter from Vice-Admiral Sir James Douglas, dated 14 May 1777, may be quoted here:

> The desertion of seamen from Haslar Hospital having been lately very great, and it being observed there are several places in the wall round the hospital at which it appears they can get over, particularly where some nails are stuck in, and trees growing near the surgeons' garden which I have ordered to be taken down as they all tended to facilitate their escape, and it being a practice among the men that want to be discharged to wear long beards, and make themselves look worse than they really are . . . and it is absolutely necessary that a captain should visit the hospital every week and I intend that the said visitation should be made every forenoon.[6]

The machinery of impressment was materially improved, on the eve of the Revolutionary War, through the inauguration of the Impress Service. For this the Comptroller, Sir Thomas Middleton, had been mainly responsible. For the future individual captains were no longer saddled with the onerous duty of finding and pressing their own crews, which was taken over by the new organization. The Impress Service operated on a very large scale, with offices and rendezvous in all likely ports and towns throughout the country. A large supply of warrants was constantly held in readiness against the hour of need. The catch would be quickly transported in the local tenders round to the receiving ship.

In the latter half of February 1793 the press was out in London River; and large numbers of seamen were taken out of the incoming merchantmen and colliers. It was the first of many such visitations as the trading fleets came home. Towards the end of April, in 'the hottest press ever remembered', nearly all the ships in the Thames were boarded and stripped of their hands. The drain of personnel from the merchantmen was so heavy and so sustained that by the following January *The Times* observed: 'Sailors are so scarce that upwards of sixty sail of merchants' ships bound to the West Indies and other places, are detained in the river, with their ladings on board; seven outward-bound East Indiamen are likewise detained at Gravesend for want of sailors to man them.'

On the breakdown of the short-lived Peace of Amiens in the early spring of 1803, the press went into action with unparalleled speed, secrecy, and efficiency. In the Thames close on a thousand seamen were taken in a single night. A large haul was made at Portsmouth. On the night of 9 March several detachments of Royal Marines marched through Plymouth, raided the quays and gin-shops, and boarded ships in the Catwater and the Pool. 'A great number of prime seamen were taken out,' recorded the *Naval*

Chronicle, 'and sent on board the Admiral's ship. They also pressed landmen of all descriptions; and the town looked as if in a state of siege. . . . One gang entered the Dock theatre, and cleared the whole gallery except the women.' Once again frigates and smaller cruisers scoured the Channel, boarding merchantmen and fishing vessels and pressing part of their crews. Again to quote the *Naval Chronicle*: 'While the six East Indiamen were lying to off the Eddystone, for the easterly wind, on Monday last [10 April], the English cruisers in the Channel, manned and armed, boarded them all, and made a fair sweep of nearly 300 prime seamen for the service of the fleets; the crews of the Indiamen, till boarded, had not the most distant idea of an approaching rupture with France.'

   A graphic account of the press in operation in the town of Waterford is given by Commander Cathcart, who had recently brought his ship, the sloop *Renard*, over from Plymouth. The officers were made welcome and lavishly entertained by the local gentry; but already the sands were running out, and one day Cathcart received orders from the Admiralty to press for seamen.

> I received the warrants early Sunday morning, and kept the whole a profound secret. The vessels all lay in tiers off the quay of Waterford, which is like the pier at Weymouth, only half a mile in extent, with a gang-board from the inner vessel to the shore. At eleven I landed the marines under their sergeants with orders to post a sentinel at each gang-board. The seamen gave the alarm from one vessel to the other and tried to escape, but were, to their astonishment, saluted with a charged bayonet by the marine at the gang-board and driven back. In four hours with three boats I had 140 men pressed. I was employed the next three days examining affidavits, liberating first mates, apprentices, sick and maimed men; so that out of one hundred and forty I could only keep sixty-five men fit for the service. I now live entirely on board, never being on shore except in the forenoon. I am then pelted and hissed. The expression is, 'A groan for the kidnapper'.[7]

   Robert Hay, anxious to return to his home in Scotland, was making for the wharfs by the Pool of London to procure a passage to Leith, when he was accosted by a wily seaman on Tower Hill and delivered into the hands of the press-gang. The latter promptly dragged him before the lieutenant at the rendezvous and thence to the receiving ship, the *Enterprise*, off Tower Hill. Hay was presently taken down to the great cabin, which he recalls was lined with green-topped tables piled with papers; there he was interrogated by the senior officer.

   'Well, young man, I understand you are a carpenter by trade.'

'Yes, sir.'

'And you have been at sea?'

'One voyage, sir.'

'Are you willing to join the King's Service?'

'No, sir.'

'Why?'

'Because I get much better wages in the merchant service and should I be unable to agree with the Captain I am at liberty to leave him at the end of the voyage.'

The officer said no more, but made a significant gesture with his hand: whereupon Hay was roughly grasped by two marines and hurried along towards the main hatchway with the cry, '*A pressed man to go below!*', and there and then thrust down among five or six score fellow unfortunates and immured in the 'confined and unwholesome dungeon' of a press room.[8]

Perhaps the most degrading experience of all to befall a newly pressed man was when he was herded into a guard-ship or tender. Some idea of the appalling conditions which awaited him there may be gained from a vivid passage in the reminiscences of Jack Nasty-Face, referring to the great press in the spring of 1805. It was no wonder that Lind described the guard-ships as 'seminaries of contagion' which were responsible for many a deadly epidemic.

> After having been examined by the doctor, and reported sea-worthy, I was ordered down to the hold, where I remained all night with my companions in wretchedness, and the rats running over us in numbers. When released, we were ordered into the Admiral's tender, which was to convey us to the Nore. Here we were called over by name, nearly two hundred, including a number of the 'Lord Mayor's Men', a term given to those who enter to relieve themselves from public disgrace, and who are sent on board by any of the City magistrates for a street frolic or night charge. . . . Upon getting on board this vessel, we were ordered down in the hold, and the gratings put over us; as well as a guard of Marines placed round the hatchway, with their muskets loaded and fixed bayonets, as though we had been culprits of the first degree, or capital convicts. In this place we spent the day and following night huddled together; for there was not room to sit or stand separate; indeed, we were in a pitiable plight, for numbers of them were sea-sick, some retching, others were smoking, whilst many were so overcome by the stench, that they fainted for want of air. As soon as the officer on deck understood that the men below were overcome with foul air, he ordered the hatches to be taken off, when daylight broke in upon us; and a wretched appearance we cut, for scarcely any of us were free from filth and vermin.[9]

The activities of the press were to some degree supplemented by the operation of Pitt's two Quota Acts of March and April 1795 in accordance with which the various counties, cities, and towns of Great Britain were required to furnish an additional quota—roughly in proportion to their population—for the King's service. The new intake, which included some very dubious material, duly received the bounty. Most of them were rated Landmen and given the kind of work for which they were suited. As might be expected, the Quota system laid itself open to all manner of abuses. According to a contemporary authority, Captain Brenton, 'The quota-bounty given in 1795, 1796, and 1797, we conceive to have been the most ill-advised fatal measure ever adopted by the government for manning the Fleet. The seamen who voluntarily entered in 1793, and fought some of the most glorious of our battles, received the comparatively small bounty of £5. These brave fellows saw men, totally ignorant of the profession, the very refuse and outcasts of society, flying from justice and the vengeance of the law, come on board with bounty to the amount of £70. One of these objects, on coming on board a ship of war with £70 bounty, was seized by a boatswain's mate, who, holding him up with one hand by the waistband of his trousers, humorously exclaimed, 'Here's a fellow that cost a guinea a pound.'

> Them was the chaps as played hell with the Fleet! Every grass-combing beggar as chose to bear up for the bounty had nothing to do but dock the tails of his togs and take to the tender. They used to ship in shoals: they were drafted by forties and fifties to each ship in the fleet. They were hardly up the side, hardly mustered abaft before there was 'Send for the barber', 'Shave their pates', and send them forward to the head to be scrubbed and sluished from clue to earing afore ye could venture to berth with them below. Then stand clear of their shore-going rigs! Every finger was fairly a fish-hook: neither chest nor bed nor blanket nor bag escaped their sleight-of-hand thievery. They pluck you—aye, as clean as a poulterer, and bone your very eyebrows whilst staring you full in the face.[10]

The proportion of landsmen among the crews of Nelson's ships in the campaign of 1805 has, perhaps, been exaggerated. Much later in the war (1812) a chaplain, the Reverend Edward Mangin, paid tribute to the quality of the newly joined ship's company on board the *Gloucester*.

'The newcomers', observed Mangin, '. . . were drafts from the *Namur* and *Dreadnought* [these were receiving ships]: many of them thoroughbred seamen, and the whole as fine an assemblage of men as could be seen. I stood on the Poop, and viewed them as they passed muster on the Quarter-deck to be entered on the ship's books.' The chaplain counted nearly 400 men above the ordinary size and in the prime of life.[11]

But such was the scarcity of seamen during the Revolutionary and Napoleonic Wars that eventually all sorts and conditions of men were gathered in, as the bottom of the barrel was scraped by the press. Vagrants, debtors, fugitives from justice, felons even, were often to be met with on the lower deck; the worst elements of which were once referred to by Collingwood as 'the refuse of the gallows and the purgings of a gaol'. Those of the landsmen who could not well be trained as seamen were employed as swabbers, scavengers, etc., in the waist. Since the crews of merchantmen were racially very mixed, and it was from merchant shipping that the Navy was principally recruited, it followed that many different nationalities were represented in the Service.

It would appear that the press was generally regarded as a great but necessary evil. At least there was never anything in the nature of large-scale agitation for its abolition. If trade was to continue, our merchant shipping had to be protected; and to furnish that protection, the Fleet had to be manned. The whole problem was, in fact, thus pithily summed up: 'You may talk o' the hardships of pressing—your man-hunting—and the likes of such lubberly prate; but if there's no ent'ring, how the h—l can you help it? Men-o'-war must be manned. . . .'[12] *Men-o'-war must be manned.* That was the crux of the matter.

There was as yet no uniform for the men, but the dress which had gradually become customary among them consisted of white trousers, blue jacket, and tarpaulin hat. These clothes could be drawn from the purser's stores, and were supplied free to those new hands who were drafted on board without decent clothes to wear; after the first month, however, clothes obtained from the purser's stores had to be paid for. Straw hats became common from the first years of the nineteenth century. Pigtails were still frequently worn on the lower deck, though abandoned by the officers. The men at quarters would wear their black silk handkerchiefs tied round their heads. The time-honoured belief that these handkerchiefs were introduced into the Navy as a mark of mourning for Nelson is without foundation; they were in fact used by our seamen many years before Trafalgar.

According to the anonymous 'Jack Nasty-Face', the crew were divided into two watches, starboard and larboard. When one was on deck the other was below. For instance, the starboard watch would come on duty at eight o'clock at night, the first watch. Every half-hour was a bell, as the hour-glass was turned, and the messenger sent to strike the bell. It now became the duty

Sailors holystoning decks; early nineteenth-century German engraving.

of the officer of the watch to have the log-line run out, to ascertain how
many knots the vessel was making, which was entered in the log-book, with
any other occurrence which might take place during the watch. At twelve
o'clock, or eight bells, the bosun's mate would cry, 'Larboard watch, a-
hoy'. This was called the middle watch, and when they came on deck the
starboard watch would go below to their hammocks, until eight bells,
which was four o'clock in the morning. The starboard watch would then
come on deck again, pull off their shoes and stockings, roll up their trousers
to above the knee, and start 'holystoning' the deck. This continued until
about four bells, or six o'clock. They then began to wash and swab the decks
until seven bells, and at eight bells the bosun's mate would pipe to breakfast.

This meal usually consisted of 'burgoo', or porridge, made of coarse
oatmeal and water; others might have 'Scotch coffee', which was burnt
bread boiled in water, and sweetened with sugar. Each mess generally
consisted of eight men, whose berth was between two of the guns, on the
lower deck, where a board was hung, which swung with the rolling of the
ship, and answered for a table.

At half-past eight, or one bell in the forenoon watch, the larboard watch
would go on deck, while the starboard remained below. Once again the
'holystones', or 'hand-bibles', as they were called by the crew, were brought
into use, and the lower deck was scoured and washed. While this was going
on, the cooks from each mess were engaged in cleaning the utensils, and

getting ready for dinner; at the same time the watch were working the ship, and doing whatever was necessary on deck.

At eight bells, or twelve o'clock, hands were piped to dinner; and at one bell, to the tune of 'Nancy Dawson' or some such lively air, the grog was served out. It was the duty of the cook from each mess to fetch and serve it out to his messmates, of which every one was allowed a pint—that is, one gill of rum and three of water, to which was added lemon-juice sweetened with sugar. The grog also served as a kind of currency: for it was grog, not money, which paid debts in a man-of-war.

At two bells, or one o'clock in the afternoon watch, the starboard watch would go on deck, and remained working the ship, pointing the ropes, or doing any duty that might be called for, until eight bells, when the bosun's mate would pipe to supper. This consisted of biscuit, and cheese and butter, together with half a pint of wine, or a pint of grog, to each man.

At one bell, or half-past four, which was called one bell in the first dog-watch, the larboard watch came on duty, and remained until four bells, or six o'clock, when it was relieved by the starboard watch, during what was called the second dog-watch, which lasted until eight o'clock at night. To explain this, it must be understood that these four hours, from four to eight o'clock, were divided into two watches with a view to making the other watches come regular and alternate.[13]

In port the seamen were accustomed to supplement the ship's allowance with fresh supplies brought out to them by the local dealers. A ship would be scarcely anchored at Spithead before she was surrounded by a fleet of wherries, laden with legs of mutton, pounds of butter, quartern loaves, beef sausages, casks of porter, vegetables, and other delicacies, all jostling and manœuvring to obtain the preference. Some of these bumboat-men and bumboat-women were well-known characters. Such a one was Mrs. Cary of Portsmouth, who, when the *Ville de Paris* arrived off Spithead for a refit in July 1804, was there in her boat to meet the flagship, and presently sent up a letter to Cornwallis couched in these terms: 'Mrs. Cary presents her respects to Admiral. She is alongside the *Ville de Paris* with a bottle of *Gin*, a Brown loaf, a pot of Fresh Butter, a Basket of Garden stuff and a pint of rich cream. If the Commander-in-Chief will not receive her and Party, she will immediately dash off to some of the young Captains.'

In Marryat's *Peter Simple* there is a lively description of a ship in harbour being paid off before going to sea.

The ship was now in a state of confusion and uproar; there were Jews trying to sell clothes, or to obtain money for clothes which they had sold; bumboat-men and bumboat-women showing their long bills, and demanding or coaxing for payment; other people from the shore, with hundreds of small debts; and the sailors' wives, sticking close to them, and disputing every bill presented, as an extortion or a robbery. There was such bawling and threatening, laughing and crying—for the women were all to quit the ship before sunset—at one moment a Jew was upset, and all his hamper clothes tossed into the hold; at another, a sailor was seen hunting everywhere for a Jew who had cheated him—all squabbling or skylarking, and many of them very drunk. . . . About five o'clock the orders were given for the ship to be cleared. All disputed points were settled by the sergeant of marines with a party, who divided their antagonists from the Jews; and every description of persons not belonging to the ship, whether male or female, were dismissed over the side. The hammocks were piped down, those who were intoxicated were put to bed, and the ship was once more quiet. Nobody was punished for having been tipsy, as pay-day is considered, on board a man-of-war, as the winding-up of all incorrect behaviour, and from that day the sailors turn over a new leaf; for, although some latitude is permitted, and the seamen are seldom flogged in harbour, yet the moment that the anchor is at the bows, strict discipline is exacted, and intoxication must no longer hope to be forgiven.

CHAPTER 8

DISCIPLINE AND MORALE

I N 1731 there appeared the first issue of King's Regulations and Admiralty Instructions. Hitherto every commander-in-chief had issued his own code of instructions to the squadron under his command. For the future K.R. and A.I. were to be the permanent disciplinary code of the Fleet.

In 1755 the corps of marines passed under Admiralty control and was organized in three divisions, which were stationed respectively at Chatham, Portsmouth, and Plymouth. As the years went by they came to be regarded by the authorities as the king-pins of naval discipline and established their reputation for unswerving loyalty and complete trustworthiness in the troubled decade of the 1790s; it was in recognition of their loyal services that in 1802 they were given the appellation of 'Royal Marines'. 'I never knew an appeal made to them for honour, courage, or loyalty', wrote St. Vincent, who was mainly responsible for this measure, 'that they did not more than realize my expectations. If ever the real hour of danger should come to England, they will be found the country's sheet-anchor.'

The origin of 'Divisions' may be traced back as early as 1755. In that year orders were issued by Vice-Admiral Thomas Smith, then commanding the squadron in the Downs, to all his captains, '*For the more effectual keeping clean the men belonging to his Majesty's ship under your command which must greatly conduce to their health*'—

> Divide the midshipmen and those acting as such into as many parties as you have lieutenants. Put one of those parties under the direction of each of the lieutenants. Divide the rest your ship's company . . . into as many parties as you have lieutenants, and put one of those parties under charge of each lieutenant. Each lieutenant to take an account of the clothing and bedding of

each man in his party, and report the same to you, keeping an account of the same himself.

Each lieutenant to subdivide his party of men into as many parties as there are midshipmen allotted to him, giving an inventory to each midshipman of the clothes and bedding belonging to each man whom he has put into the said midshipman's party.

Each midshipman to muster the clothes and bedding of each man under his direction twice a week, and take care that the men are always kept tight and shifted as often as mustered; and if at any time any of their clothes and bedding are missing, it is to be reported to the lieutenant whose direction they are under. . . .

And that the men's hammacoes [hammocks] may be constantly kept clean and the men are not exposed to lie in them before they are effectually dry, you are to order your boatswain to keep such a number of hammacoes always slung as are equal to one-twentieth part of your ship's company, to be delivered to the men whose hammacoes are sufficiently dry and delivered to others for the same purpose.[1]

It was one of the shrewdest and most influential disciplinarians of his day, Richard Kempenfelt, who, in the first phase of the American War, was responsible for the general introduction of 'Divisions' in the Service. In a long letter to Sir Charles Middleton, the Comptroller of the Navy, Kempenfelt outlined his project.

The only way to keep large bodies of men in order is by dividing and subdividing of them, with officers over each, to inspect into and regulate their conduct, to discipline and form them. Let the ship's company be divided into as many companies as there are lieutenants—except the first lieutenant, whose care should extend over the whole. Each lieutenant's company should be formed of the men who are under his command at quarters for action. These companies should be reviewed every day by their lieutenants, when the men are to appear tight and clean. He is to see that the raw men are daily exercised at arms, and the sails and rigging. The captain should review them himself at least once a week. When it can be done, the men should always have the full time for their meals and for repose, and certain portions of time in the week allotted for washing and mending; but at all other times they should be kept constantly employed; and whatever they are exercised about, be particularly careful that they do it with attention and alertness, and perfect. Labour to bring them to a habit of this, and suffer nothing to be done negligently and awkwardly. The adage that idleness is the root of evil is with no people more strongly verified than with sailors and soldiers. In what order is a military corps kept on shore, when well officered! Certainly the situation of a ship's crew is more favourable to sustain order and regularity than that of a corps ashore, confined within narrow limits, without tippling houses to debauch in, and under the constant eye of their officers. But if six, seven, or eight hundred men are left in a mess together, without divisions, and the officers assigned no particular charge over any part of them, who only give orders from the quarter-deck or gangways— such a crew must remain a disorderly mob, business will be done awkwardly or tumultuously, without order or despatch, and the raw men put into no train of improvement. The officers, having no particular charge appointed them, the conduct and behaviour of the men are not inspected into; they know nothing of their proceedings; and the people, thus left to themselves, become sottish, slovenly and lazy, form cabals, and spirit each other up to insolence and mutiny.[2]

Though there can be no doubt that in certain ships and under certain commanders discipline could be brutal to the point of inhumanity, it is quite possible that the harshness of the system generally, during the earlier part of the eighteenth century, has been much exaggerated. On board many of our ships, in the campaign of 1759, men were seldom flogged. In the *Juno* frigate, for example, there were about half a dozen floggings in the early months of the year, and two in November: that was the whole list. During both these periods the ship was at anchor, first in English waters, and latterly in Quiberon Bay. No flogging was inflicted while the *Juno* was at sea. The punishment in each case, as noted in the ship's log, was twelve lashes; and this was for the kind of offence which in the Navy today would in all likelihood mean cells. There was admittedly a lot more flogging on board the *Hercules*: but this does not necessarily reflect upon the captain—there were bad crews as well as bad commanders.

It is always desirable to keep these matters in proper perspective, and to remember that, in the period under review, corporal punishment was a normal practice, on land as well as at sea. For instance, in southern England a favourite sentence for petty larceny was for the offender to be whipped till his (or her) back 'be bloody'. Youngsters in domestic service were not infrequently whipped. Similarly in the English governing class it was quite usual for young girls as well as their brothers to be soundly flogged with the birch-rod.

Certainly there was a marked increase in severity throughout the Service as the century advanced: particularly after the outbreak, in 1793, of the Revolutionary War. As Commander Owen has observed, 'A normal sentence awarded by court martial for a serious offence would be two or three hundred lashes with a cat-of-nine tails under George III, whereas the punishment for the same offence under Anne would be fifty lashes.'³

The forms of corporal punishment commonly in use were 'gagging', 'starting', 'running the gauntlet', and flogging. Of these, flogging with the cat-of-nine tails—a whip with nine lashes made of knotted cords—was by far the severest.

For 'answering back', 'gagging' was a common penalty. The procedure was as follows: the culprit was seated with both his legs in irons and his hands bound behind his back; his jaws were then forced open, and an iron bar was placed in his mouth just as a bit is placed in a horse's mouth. 'Starting', or beating by a bosun's mate with a cane or rope's end, was such an everyday occurrence in many ships that no mention was made of it in the log. 'Running the gauntlet' was a punishment commonly inflicted for petty theft. The culprit, stripped to the waist, was made to sit in a tub which was hauled on a grating around the deck, to be belaboured in turn by the bosun and his mates with a cat-o'-nine tails, and by each member of the crew with a knotted rope yarn. 'This punishment is inflicted by the Captain's orders,' says Jack Nasty-Face, 'without the formal inquiry by a court martial.'

Flogging, also according to Jack Nasty Face, would be ordered by the Captain for anything that he or one of his officers might consider a crime. 'The prisoner is made to strip to the waist; he is then seized by his wrists and knees to a grating or ladder; the Boatswain's Mate is then ordered to cut him with the cat-o'-nine tails; and after six or twelve lashes are given another Boatswain's Mate is called to continue the exercise; and so they go on, until the Captain gives the word to stop.'⁴ (In point of fact the usual sentence was a dozen, occasionally two dozen, lashes.) The Boatswain's Mates were trained to flog effectively by being made to practise on a cask, under the superintendence of the Boatswain.

For the most serious offences the terrible punishment known as 'flogging through the fleet' was often awarded, of which Jack Nasty-Face furnishes a detailed description. By the men this was regarded as almost the equivalent of a death sentence; and sometimes, indeed, actually resulted in the death of the victim.

Whilst lying at Spithead, in the year 1809 or 1810, four impressed seamen attempted to make their escape from a frigate then lying there: one of their shipmates, a Dutchman to whom they had entrusted the secret, betrayed their intention, and informed the commanding officer of their designs. They were tried by a court-martial, and sentenced to receive three hundred lashes each, through the fleet. On the first day after the trial that the weather was moderate enough to permit, the signal was made for a boat from each ship, with a guard of Marines, to attend the punishment. The man is placed in a launch, *i.e.* the largest ship's boat, under the care of the Master-at-Arms and a doctor. There is a capstan bar rigged fore and aft, to which this poor fellow is lashed by his wrists; and for fear of hurting him—humane creatures—there is a stocking put over each, to prevent him from tearing the flesh off in his agonies. When all is ready, the prisoner is stript and seized to the capstan bar. Punishment commences by the officer, after reading the sentence of the court-martial, ordering the Boatswain's Mates to do their duty. The cat-o'-nine tails is applied to the bare back, and at about every six lashes a fresh Boatswain's Mate is ordered to relieve the executioner of this duty, until the prisoner has received, perhaps, twenty-five lashes. He is then cast loose, and allowed to sit down with a blanket rolled round him, is conveyed to the next ship, escorted by this vast number of armed boats, accompanied by that doleful music, 'The Rogues' March'. In this manner he is conveyed from ship to ship, receiving alongside of each a similar number of stripes with the cat, until the sentence is completed. It often, nay generally, happens that nature is unable to sustain it, and the poor fellow faints and sinks under it, although every kind method is made use of to enable him to bear it, by pouring wine down his throat. The doctor will then feel his pulse, and often pronounces that the man is unable to bear more. He is then taken, most usually insensible, to what is termed the 'sick bay'; and, if he recovers, he is told he will have to receive the remainder of his punishment. When there are many ships in the fleet at the time of the court-martial, this ceremony, if the prisoner can sustain it, will last nearly half the day.[5]

Flogging round the fleet was the usual sentence for desertion. It has been justified on the grounds that the manning of the Navy was a matter of life and death for the nation: it has been condemned on the grounds that as a deterrent it was a failure. Desertion in fact continued to be one of the most serious problems that the Navy had to face.

All this was strictly according to regulation. Not so were such appalling cases of abuse of power by sadistic tyrants like Pigot of the *Hermione*. Pigot (whose maddened crew at last rose and murdered him, along with his officers) was accustomed, among other things, to flog the last man down from aloft. It would appear that some of the complaints against individual officers which found utterance during the mutinous outbreaks of 1797 were by no means unfounded. 'The ill-usage we have on board this ship', the crew of the *Winchelsea* had protested to the Admiralty early in the Revolutionary War, 'forced us to fly to Your Lordships the same as a child to its father.' 'Our first Lieutenant,' ran a similar complaint, 'he is a most Cruel and Barberous man, Beating some at times untill they are not able to stand, and not allowing them the satisfaction to cry out.' For an offence which he did not commit—and could not possibly have committed—John Wetherell received four dozen lashes; he relates that, immediately after the punishment, he was ordered back to his duties—'the shirt on my back was like a butcher's apron'.[6] Both Jack Nasty-Face and Wetherell belonged to the lower deck; but it is worth noticing that their testimony is largely borne out by Captain Boteler in his *Recollections*.

> Our captain was a Tartar, severe in punishments. At night he would call a man down from the yards and give him two dozen, and he was hard upon the midshipmen. One, a Mr. Smith, he declared grinned at him looking up from the maindeck. It was a natural way he had of baring his teeth, and for this he disrated the poor fellow, putting him in the foretop for three months; and another mid. he served in the same way, disrating him and putting him in the maintop to do all duties with the men.[7]

Sometimes, but not very often, a guilty officer would be court-martialled and sentenced; but there can be small doubt that the majority of such abuses went unpunished.

On the other hand, the influence of such humane and enlightened commanders as Boscawen, Hawke, Howe, Duncan, St. Vincent, Nelson, and Collingwood was gradually effecting a transformation. Boscawen and Hawke, as we shall presently see, did much to promote the welfare of their people. Howe as a young post-captain had initiated the custom of granting leave to his ship's company watch by watch and took the greatest care of his sick and wounded. Old Duncan was immensely and deservedly popular with his crews. St. Vincent was as zealous for the health and welfare of his men as he was for discipline and order. Nelson's influence over officers and men alike was almost magical. 'He had', writes Hannay, 'an extraordinary faculty for inspiring the men under his command, first with confidence in himself, and then with a desire to emulate him. The real Nelson Touch was the torch of fire with which he lit up the souls of men.' In the early months of 1797 the *Theseus*, Captain John Aylmer, had been, according to St. Vincent, 'an abomination'. But the latter had at last got Aylmer to transfer to the *Captain*; and one night, early in June, a paper was dropped on the quarter-deck of the *Theseus*, now the flagship of Rear-Admiral Sir Horatio Nelson:

> Success attend Admiral Nelson! God bless Captain Miller! We thank them for the Officers they have placed over us. We are happy and contented, and will shed every drop of blood in our veins, and the name of *Theseus* shall be immortalized as high as the *Captain*'s.

Collingwood, who was renowned throughout the Navy as a disciplinarian, came nearly to abolishing flogging in the ships under his command. He would not permit his officers to use coarse or abusive language when addressing the men; and he laid the foundations of a new and better tradition of relationship between the lower and quarter-deck. 'No swearing,' observes Hay, 'no threatening or bullying, no starting was to be heard or seen. Boatswain's mates or ship's corporals dared not to be seen with a rattan or rope's end in hand; nor do I recollect of a single instance of a man being flogged while he remained on board. Was discipline neglected then? By no means. There was not a better disciplined crew in the fleet.'[8]

To individual commanders there was no lack of good testimony from those who served under them, volunteers and pressed men alike. C. R. Pemberton, 'Pel Verjuice', who was a volunteer, had nothing but praise for the discipline maintained on board the *Alceste*, Captain Murray Maxwell.

> Whenever Captain Murray manœuvred his ship the whole of the vast machine moved like clockwork, without jar or impediment. With him she was a feather in a cup of oil, floating and bounding so easily and smoothly. Why was this? True, he was one of the most skilful and cool-headed seamen that ever commanded a ship, as the thousands who knew him will allow. . . . [His men] were willing, because they found he wished to be, would be, just; they put forth their strength, skill and cheerful alacrity because he was merciful and considerate in his discipline; he never irritated them by caprice; there was no *vexatious niggling* in anything he ordered to be done. Half the ships in the fleet during the last war contained crews that only required a spark to start them into open mutiny; the combustion was daily accumulated under their toil from the caprice of officers and their *vexatious niggling discipline*.[9]

The lower deck does not appear to have expressed any general disapprobation of severe discipline as such—provided only that discipline were just and reasonable. A strict commander was not necessarily considered a tyrant. In his reminiscences Béchervaise makes this point quite clear. 'I would always', the old Jerseyman declared, 'choose a ship in which every duty was attended to strictly, in preference to one in which a man did almost as he liked. Indeed, I've frequently heard old seamen say (when two ships were in commission and both wanting hands), 'I'll go with Captain ———: he's a taut one, but he is Captain of his own ship.'

A by no means unimportant factor in the relationship between officers and men at this time was that of common territorial ties. Nelson, Collingwood, Hardy, Saumarez, and Pellew could reckon upon a substantial following of volunteers from Norfolk, Northumberland, Dorset, Guernsey, and Cornwall respectively; and there were numerous other local attachments. Many of the Hoods' people hailed from the West Country. The family influence of the Pakenhams attracted numbers of Irishmen. 'In consequence of the great war establishment', observes Dr. Mathew in *The Naval Heritage*, 'naval officers who had links with a countryside would often place the sons of neighbouring farmers or gamekeepers or bailiffs on board the line-of-battleships. This, with Nelson's example, fostered the growth of that penetrating individual care for the members of the ship's company which was to prove so clear a characteristic of the naval captain.' Another significant factor in the gradually improving situation was the influence for good of the 'blue lights', as they were called—commanders of firm Evangelical convictions, who were prepared to put their precepts into practice.

Although it was not until late in the nineteenth century that the cat was finally abolished in the Service (strictly speaking, it was only suspended), the ordering of tyrannical and excessive punishments was gradually discontinued. The punishment of running the gauntlet was abolished in 1806 and that of starting three years later. In Captain Cumby's private order book of 1811 it was explicitly ruled that, 'The highly improper practice of what is called starting the men is most peremptorily forbidden'.

It was something more than punishment, or the threat of punishment, that spurred on such crews as those that manned Nelson's *Agamemnon* and Cochrane's *Impérieuse*. On the eve of Copenhagen, Nelson himself, it is recorded, 'was struck with admiration at the superior discipline and seamanship, that were observable on board the *Amazon*'. On board Saumarez's flagship, the *Caesar*, before the second action of Algeciras, the men were so eager to get the half-disabled ship ready for battle again that they not only toiled from dawn to dusk, but worked *watch and watch* throughout the night; and notwithstanding that a good many of the people had to be sent on shore for stores, there was not a single case of drunkenness or absence from duty. On board the *Impétueux*, on the stormy station off Brest, the mess-decks of a Saturday night resounded with the full-throated chorus of 'Rule Britannia', and the seamen danced on the moonlit deck. 'The *Prompte*'s crew', declared Richardson, 'was like a family united, and would, both officers and men, risk their lives to assist each other.' Robert Wilson—no volunteer, but a pressed man—came to develop an intense pride in his ship, the *Unité*, and in the qualities of his officers. Pemberton, too, dearly loved the ship in which he served—'my beloved and beautiful home, the *Alceste*, the happiest home I ever knew'.

When drums beat to quarters to the familiar double-double-double beat of 'Heart of Oak', the crews would hail the prospect of a fight with the keenest relish and satisfaction. 'When everything was cleared', remarked one of the seamen of the *Goliath* before the battle of St. Vincent, 'the ports open, the matches lighted, the guns run out, then we gave them three such cheers as are only to be heard in a British man-of-war.' Earlier in the Revolutionary War, Gardner testifies to the strong impression that their businesslike preparations made on a certain Spanish officer who visited his ship, the *Berwick*, 74, when she was cleared for action. 'The officer seemed astonished when he saw our men at quarters,' Gardner observed, 'their black silk handkerchiefs tied round their heads, their shirt sleeves tucked up, the crows and hand-spikes in their hands and the boarders all ready with their cutlasses and tomahawks, that he told Sir John Collins that they put him in mind of so many devils.'[10]

In *Frank Mildmay* Marryat has sketched for us an unforgettable description of a smart frigate's crew at quarters, recalling the 'noble tier of guns in a line gently curving out towards the centre; the tackle laid out across the deck; the shots and wads prepared in ample store (round shot and canister), the powder boys each with his box full, seated on it, with perfect apparent indifference to the approaching conflict. The captains of guns, with their priming boxes buckled round their waists; the locks fixed upon the guns; the lanyards laid around them; the officers, with their swords drawn, standing by their respective divisions.'

Before the Nile, the squadron which sailed in relentless pursuit of Napoleon and Brueys was strung up to the highest pitch of keenness and expectancy. The crews were continually drilled and exercised for the coming battle; every man was ready to start to his post at a moment's notice; the decks of all the ships were kept cleared for action night and day. 'The officers and crews in the several ships are all the highest spirits,' Saumarez declared, 'and I never remember going into action with more certain hopes of success.'

'My station', recounted an eye-witness on board the *Goliath*, 'was in the powder magazine with the gunners. As we entered the bay, we stripped to our trousers, opened our ports, cleared, and every ship we passed gave them a broadside and three cheers.'[11]

There were similar scenes of joyful expectancy and enthusiasm in Nelson's fleet before Trafalgar. One of the marine officers of the *Belleisle* has related how he was awakened that morning by the cheering of the seamen and their pounding up the hatchways to get a view of the Combined Fleet. He describes the scene on the gun-decks as the men stood at quarters: 'Some were stripped to the waist; some had bared their necks and arms; others had tied a handkerchief round their heads; and all seemed eagerly to await the order to engage.' On board the *Ajax*, according to another officer of marines, 'The men were variously occupied: some were sharpening their cutlasses, others polishing the guns, as though an inspection were about to take place instead of a mortal combat, whilst three or four, as if in mere bravado, were dancing a hornpipe; but all seemed deeply anxious to come to close quarters with the enemy, many of which had been on former occasions engaged by our vessels.'[12]

The prospect of prize money bulked large in the imagination of the Old Navy, quarter-deck and lower deck alike. Though the spoil was always very inequitably divided, all felt they had a stake in the great lottery of war. 'If these French gentry do not escape me this time, they will pay for the house and furniture too,' wrote Boscawen to his wife in May 1756, 'besides something to save hereafter for all our dear children.' 'You can't think how keen our men are,' he observed in a later letter; 'the hope of prize money makes them happy [and] a signal for a sail brings them all on deck.' Occasionally a seaman got such a haul of prize money that he would buy his discharge from the Service. Much smaller sums would at least secure for him several days, and even weeks, of glorious debauchery.

The abiding attraction of prize money is well brought out in many a contemporary ballad. After Kempenfelt's victory over de Guichen in 1781, Gardner, then a pupil at the Naval Academy, happened to be standing on Gosport beach when some of the French prisoners taken in the engagement were landed under escort of the military, accompanied by a naval lieutenant and several midshipmen; and a crowd of women came running out of a neighbouring alley chorusing:

> Don't you see the ships a-coming?
>   Don't you see them in full sail?
> Don't you see the ships a-coming
>   With the prizes at their tail?
> Oh! my little rolling sailor,
>   Oh! my little rolling he;
> I do love a jolly sailor,
>   Blithe and merry might he be.
>
> Sailors, they get all the money,
>   Soldiers they get none but brass;
> I do love a jolly sailor,

> Soldiers they may kiss my ——
> Oh! my little rolling sailor,
>   Oh! my little rolling he;
> I do love a jolly sailor,
>   Soldiers may be damned for me.[13]

The more spectacular hauls were sometimes made the occasion of a naval triumph. Anson's victory over the French in 1747 was celebrated by a grand military procession through the streets of London, with the wagon-loads of captured treasure as the principal show-piece; the houses were illuminated and there were bonfires in every street. The capture of the Spanish *Hermione* by a couple of British cruisers outside Cadiz, in 1762, brought in a haul of about half a million pounds. According to Beatson:

> The treasure was conveyed from Portsmouth to London in twenty waggons, escorted by a party of sailors. The waggons were decorated with the British colours flying, having those of Spain underneath them. . . . On their coming to London, they were joined by a troop of light dragoons, with a band of music, consisting of kettle-drums, French-horns, trumpets and hautboys: and in this manner did they march on through the city to the Tower, amid the acclamations of a prodigious concourse of people.[14]

After the storming of Havana, also in 1762, the Admiral received nearly £122,700 as his share of the prize money, while each seaman secured £3 14s. 10d.

Captain William Parker of the *Amazon* frigate kept a journal in which he was accustomed carefully to record the various amounts of prize money to which he was entitled. 'When he finally paid off the *Amazon* in 1812 he had received no less than £40,000 in prize, which was not bad going for a man then just under thirty years of age. . . . A considerable number of promising young officers were lost to the Navy because, having made a quick fortune in prize money, they retired from the Service to live ashore on their gains.'[15]

Prize money brought many a fortunate commander-in-chief a splendid fortune. Anson and Saunders amassed enormous sums of prize money. Boscawen, Hawke, Pocock, and Rodney were among those who also did very well for themselves. Keith secured very large sums indeed in the Mediterranean, at the Cape, and in the Dutch East Indies, out of which he purchased his two Scottish estates. The younger Sir Hyde Parker gained about £200,000 in the West Indies. Rainier and Pellew are each believed to have made £300,000 during their careers. In the words of David Hannay, 'When a man got a few pounds, just enough to keep him drunk for a fortnight, the lieutenant gained a few score, the captain a few hundreds, the admiral gained thousands, for he shared in all the prizes taken on his station, whether he had been present at the capture or not. It is therefore easy to see what an important matter prize money was to a flag-officer. To get a rich station, and to keep it free from the intrusion of a superior, was the ideal of luck.'

Prize money was regrettably responsible for much dissension and ill-feeling in the Service. Nelson's quarrel with St. Vincent on this issue is sufficiently well known; but there were countless other disputes of the same character of which little is heard or remembered. As has already been said, a number of promising young captains, having made a fortune through prize money, forthwith quitted the Service. Others abandoned the station to which they had been posted and went cruising after rich prizes. Innumerable abuses centred round the payment and distribution of prize money. Nevertheless, there can be small doubt that the pros greatly outweighed the cons in the matter. 'Whatever may be the ideas of modern statesmen,' Cochrane declared 'prize money formed then, as it will ever form, the principal motive of seamen to encounter the perils of war.' Human nature being what it is, the Navy would have been materially weakened once deprived of this powerful incentive. The case for prize money was convincingly pleaded by James Stephen:

> Let us give full credit to our gallant officers, for that disinterested patriotism, and that love of glory, which ought to be the main springs of military character, and which they certainly possess in a most eminent degree. But it would be romantic and absurd, to suppose that they do not feel the value of that additional encouragement, which his Majesty and the legislature hold out to them, in giving them the benefit of the captures they make. What else is to enable the veteran naval officer, to enjoy in the evening of his life, the comforts of an easy income; the father to provide for his children; or the husband for an affectionate wife, who, from the risques he runs in the service of his country, is peculiarly liable to survive him? By what other means, can a victorious admiral, when raised, as a reward of his illustrious actions, to civil and hereditary honours, hope to support his well earned rank, and provide for an ennobled posterity? The pension he may obtain will be temporary, and scarcely adequate even to his own support, in his new and elevated station. It is from the enemies of his country, therefore, that he hopes to wrest the means of comfortably sustaining those honours, which he has gained at their expense.
>
> As to the common seamen and mariners, the natural motives of dislike to the naval service, are in their breasts far more effectually combated by the hope of prize money, than by all the other inducements that are or can be proposed to

them. The nautical character is peculiarly of a kind to be influenced by such dazzling but precarious prospects. They reason, however, and calculate on the chances and the value of success; witness the proverbial remark, that a Spanish war is the best means of manning our navy.[16]

For those few, who, surviving the hazards of battle and tempest, rose to the summit of their profession, there was the compelling lure of honour and glory. The fame which Nelson had always so ardently desired was his in full measure following the action of 14 February 1797. For the future his name was a household word among his fellow-countrymen—in his own lifetime, indeed, he had become a legend. After Algeciras, as his sister-in-law observed, Saumarez was now 'the theme of every conversation, the toast of every table, the hero of every woman, the boast of every Englishman'. It is said that in his years of retirement St. Vincent invariably wore the star of the Order of the Bath; and to a small boy who one day asked him what it was and where he found it, the old Admiral replied, 'I found it upon the sea; and if you become a sailor, and search diligently, perhaps you may find just such another.'

CHAPTER 9

HYGIENE AND SUPPLY

'HYGIENE and supply', the late Sir Herbert Richmond declared, 'are fundamental elements affecting both strategy and tactics.' In the Royal Navy, during the period under survey, the proportion of deaths due to sickness was far in excess of the number of those who died in battle. It is clear from a study of the evidence that one of the principal factors which limited the sea-keeping of ships and squadrons was this prevalence of disease. The evil was rampant, not only on unhealthy foreign stations, but also in temperate climates and in home waters.

In the fever-ridden anchorage of Porto Bello, and next off Vera Cruz and Havana, disease carried off between 4,000 and 5,000 men (including the Commander-in-Chief, Admiral Hosier, and eight of his captains) in the ill-starred campaign of 1726–7. The deadly tropical fever dealt another terrible stroke against a powerful British squadron in the same region in 1741. It was to commemorate the latter campaign that the doleful ballad of 'Admiral Hosier's Ghost' was composed.

During Anson's great voyage of 1740–4 his squadron suffered appalling losses through disease; and a large number of those who survived owed their lives to the vigilance and forethought of their commander rather than to any medical provision made by the authorities.

'I find', wrote Hawke in September 1755, 'the ships' companies falling down so fast in fevers that I am afraid I shall not be able to keep out long.' On board the *Grafton*, 70, during a cruise which lasted from 12 May to early September 1755, 21 men died at sea and 112 sick were landed at Halifax—many of whom appear to have died also. 'In 1755', Captain Edward Thompson related, '. . . when she had been on no long cruise, and had been exposed only to the hardships of a few months of service in the

Song sheet of 'Admiral Hosier's Ghost'; engraving by C. Mosley, 1740. 'Think what thousands fell in vain, Wasted with disease and anguish, Not in glorious battle slain.'

Channel, the *Stirling Castle*, 64, Captain Samuel Cornish, arrived in Portsmouth with four hundred and eighty men, of whom two hundred and twenty-five were the pressed refuse of gaols and scum of the streets. She was full of fever and other sicknesses, and when the diseased had been sent ashore, but one hundred and sixty remained for duty.' Less than three months later, when, having filled up her complement in England, the

Stirling Castle had proceeded to New York, Thompson wrote, 'We have now one hundred and fifty-nine people ill in fluxes, scurvies, and fevers.'

The number of seamen and marines killed in action during the Seven Years War was rather more than 1,500; but no less than 133,708 are said to have died of sickness or deserted. (These figures are taken from the *Annual Register* for 1763. Though they are certainly exaggerated, the losses due to disease and desertion must nevertheless have been enormous.) 'Of the thousands and tens of thousands that perished in our late contests with France and Spain,' wrote Dr. Johnson some years later, 'a very small part ever felt the stroke of an enemy; the rest languished in tents and ships, amidst damps and putrefaction. . . . By incommodious encampments and unwholesome stations, where courage is useless, and enterprise impracticable, fleets are silently dispeopled and armies sluggishly melted away.'

Scurvy was still the scourge of the Navy. Down to the latter half of the eighteenth century little progress had been made in combating the disease. This was mainly due to the apathy of the authorities, for the causes had long been known.

'Captain Graves of H.M.S. *Barfleur*', wrote Anson on 13 August 1758, 'having acquainted to me, by letter of this date, that, altho' he has already sent sixty men home to the hospitals, since he left Plymouth, he has now one hundred and thirty-nine men sick on board, seventy-four of whom are so far gone in the scurvy, that the surgeon is of opinion that they will die, if not speedily sent on shore, and that there are besides, Fourty men on board who have scorbutish eruptions upon them, though they are not yet included in the surgeon's sick list: I have thought it absolutely necessary for me to send the ship to Portsmouth, for the recovery of the sick men, as well as for the preservation of the rest of the crew.' 'I am to acquaint you,' Anson informed the Secretary of the Admiralty a fortnight later, 'for the information of the Lords Commissioners of the Admiralty, that it is absolutely necessary for me to send the *Union* to Portsmouth, and the *Norfolk* and *Fougueux* to Plymouth, the former having one hundred and sixty-eight, the second one hundred and forty, and the other one hundred and twenty men on board, chiefly with fevers and the scurvy. You will see, by the inclosed state and condition of the squadron, that many of the other ships are sickly, and indeed some of their men are so dangerously ill, that I have thought proper to send near one hundred and forty of them to the hospitals at Portsmouth and Plymouth, by the three ships above mentioned.' 'I find a letter in town from my Lord,' wrote Lady Anson about the same time, 'who confirms that his squadron is in general very bad with the scurvy, so that he has been obliged to send in three large ships, with a great number of sick men, collected out of the fleet; most, if not all of them, would have been dead and thrown overboard in the course of ten days: he has kept his own ship healthy by dint of expense, he says; I imagine in greens and fresh provisions from Plymouth.'

Two other deadly diseases which periodically ravaged our squadrons were typhus and yellow fever—otherwise 'Yellow Jack'. The first was associated with foul clothes, overcrowded ships, dirt, and malnutrition. It was at its worst during the rapid expansion of the Service in the American and Revolutionary Wars. Many an outbreak of typhus might be traced to the infected clothing of the newly pressed men, a few sickly recruits drafted to a ship resulting in an epidemic among a previously healthy ship's company. The grossly overcrowded man-of-war was a prolific breeding-ground of typhus, which reached its peak towards the turn of the century and thereafter gradually declined. The second was an acute infectious fever of a malarial type, spread by a certain mosquito, which was common in tropical climates, especially in low-lying, marshy regions. It was the particular scourge of the West India and West Africa stations, and was rampant in the years 1793–1805.

In 1749 a celebrated London physician, Dr. Richard Mead, produced his *A Discourse on Scurvy*, which treated mainly of that disease as it was observed on board Anson's squadron during his voyage round the world. In the following decade James Lind, one of the most knowledgeable of the naval surgeons of his day, published, whilst engaged in private practice in Edinburgh, two highly important works, *A Treatise on the Scurvy* (1753) and *An Essay on Preserving the Health of Seamen in the Royal Navy* (1757). In the first of these works, which he dedicated to Anson, Lind suggested vegetables, fresh fruit, and lemon juice as anti-scorbutics. The publication of this book marked a milestone in the progress of naval hygiene. '*A Treatise on the Scurvy*', writes Dr. Roddis of the United States Navy, 'is one of the great classics of medicine. . . . As has been pointed out, many others had used the citrus fruit juices, both as a preventative measure and in the treatment of scurvy, but it was Lind who most clearly and convincingly proved their value.'[1] More than forty years, however, were to pass before Lind's recommendations about the use of lemon juice as an anti-scorbutic were officially adopted.

Bad ventilation was a prolific source of weakness. It was related by the surgeon of the *Cambridge* that during a cruise in the Bay of Biscay in 1758 the weather was so wet and stormy as to prevent the gunports on the middle deck being opened to ventilate the ship. 'The consequence was a putrid fever,' observed the writer, 'which spread rapidly amongst the seamen and marines, so that in six weeks we had 300 men upon the sick-list—almost half the complement.'[2]

The introduction in the middle of the century of artificial ventilation between decks was a revolutionary improvement brought about largely through the strong advocacy and great professional prestige of Dr. Mead. Frequent mention is now made in captains' logs of the ventilators at work, notably in the early campaigns of the Seven Years War.

One of the earliest and most painstaking pioneers in the field of naval hygiene was Lord Howe, who 'gave it as part of his instructions to wash the upper decks every day, the lower decks twice a week, and the orlop once a week at least. He also ordered that every washing, smoking, mustering of clothes, and other means for the health of the ship, should be marked in the log-book, and the reason to be assigned there if they were omitted at the regular times.' Another was Captain the Hon. Augustus Keppel. 'The *Torbay*, Captain Keppel, was kept so healthy during a cruise of four months that she did not lose a single man, by the following precautions:— (1) The men and their clothes were mustered twice a week. (2) The hammocks were sent on deck every morning, and the ports hauled up; the lower deck scraped and washed every day in fine weather; the beams dried by burning, in matchtubs partly filled with sand, dry wood sprinkled with powdered resin. (3) Portable ventilators were constantly in use, and water was let into the ship and pumped out again daily. (4) The beams were occasionally washed with warm vinegar.'[3]

Both Boscawen and Hawke were renowned for their persistent efforts to improve the health and comfort of the seamen under their command. It was Boscawen who was responsible for introducing Hales's ventilators, first, in his flagship, the *Namur*, in 1747, and in later years in the Navy generally. The inscription on the Admiral's monument justly testifies to his 'concern for the interest, and unwearied attention to the health, of all under his command'. The care of the sick and the supply of medical necessaries were somewhat improved as a result of Hawke's protests in 1755.

Sir Charles Saunders, who commanded the squadron which co-operated with the military expedition against Quebec in 1759—by far the most important and most successful amphibious operation of the century—was justly commended by Lind for his constant concern for the health and well-being of the seamen of his flagship, the *Neptune*.

> I enquired particularly into the condition of the sick-apartment in the *Neptune*, while she was at sea; and found it was on the lower gun-deck, and was both spacious and neat. In it were cut two scuttles for the admission of fresh air, and

these were at all times kept open. The adjoining ports were also thrown up, when it could be safely done, though the fresh air, admitted by the two scuttles, was sufficient to keep the place at all times sweet, and free from any bad smell. It was washed twice a week with warm vinegar, besides being duly cleaned out every day. Sir Charles Saunders, who commanded the fleet, was on board this ship, and spared no method to have the apartment for the sick, the whole ship, together with the men, kept wholesome and clean.[4]

Another and very important figure was Captain Cook. As a result of his meticulous attention to the health of his men, Cook, on his second voyage to the Pacific in 1772–5—after remaining at sea for longer than anyone else in history—had lost only one man through sickness. 'The method which he discovered', observed one of his officers, Lieutenant King, 'and so successfully pursued, of preserving the health of seamen, forms a new era in navigation, and will transmit his name to future ages amongst the friends and benefactors of mankind.'[5]

The sickness which seriously handicapped the Navy in the earlier years of the War of American Independence may be accounted partly responsible for the reverses which this country then sustained. In Kempenfelt's correspondence there are numerous references to the inadequacy of the victualling and the consequent ravages of scurvy. When Geary commanded the Channel fleet in the summer of 1780 he had to return to port after cruising for only a few weeks. In August of that year about 2,400 men were down with scurvy. Kempenfelt's recommendation was that the fleet, when cruising before Brest, should every month or so put into Torbay for a few days. 'This', he observed, 'should keep the scurvy off; their provisions and water up; whilst you do this, you might cruize the whole year; for, except for the scurvy, the men keep freer from diseases at sea than in port, as they have neither women nor spirits, the chief causes of their diseases.' Kempenfelt went on to say; 'I should prefer Torbay for the recovery of scorbutics to either Portsmouth or Plymouth, for a small squadron where, at this season of the year, they might be lodged under tents, the communications with the shore quick and easy, and plenty of every kind of refreshment.' Early in July 1781 the Channel fleet, now under Darby, was forced up Channel to Torbay; thence he sailed for Spithead to obtain provisions and new drafts to replace the sick. 'I can't help observing to your lordship', he informed Sandwich, 'the sour krout is mostly expended, the beer at an end, and the scurvy making strong strides; many ships have been but short times in port, so that if these ships are kept out long they will be rendered useless for want of men.'

The year 1780, which witnessed an immense expansion of the Service, was also—and for that very reason—the worst year of the entire war for epidemics and sickness in general. The incidence of scurvy remained fairly constant; but virulent outbreaks of typhus and typhoid continued to ravage the Channel fleet, principally as a result of infection caught from the new drafts. In his *The Health of Seamen* Lind referred to a guardship, into which the newly pressed men were taken, as 'a seminary of contagion to the whole fleet'. He went on to say that he had known a thousand men confined together in one guardship, some hundreds of whom had neither beds nor change of linen; and that he had seen many of them admitted to Haslar Hospital in the same clothes and shirts they had been wearing when pressed several months earlier. In such circumstances it was impossible to prevent the outbreak or spread of disease, for 'the fatal mischief lurked in their tainted apparel, and rags; and by these was conveyed into other ships'.[6]

About this time another and far more influential doctor appeared on the scene. This was Dr. (afterwards Sir) Gilbert Blane, who was of opinion that 'more may be done towards the preservation of the health and lives of seamen than is commonly imagined; and it is a matter not only of humanity and duty but of interest and policy'. Blane, who accompanied Rodney to the West Indies in 1780 as the Admiral's private doctor, was strongly critical of the medical neglect and apathy which he witnessed on every side.

'I perceived the most anxious and laudable pains taken to husband and preserve from decay all manner of stores, such as ropes, blocks, spars, gunpowder, and arms. But however precious these may be as the indispensable weapons of war, it will not be disputed that human hands are equally so. Yet, although there was the additional motive of humanity, it does not appear that this branch of duty has been studied with the like degree of anxiety as that which regards the inanimate materials of war. It must also be obvious to naval officers that it is on the numbers and vigour of the hands that their own success and reputation must depend in the conflict with the elements, and in the hour of battle.'[7]

Nevertheless, in the final phase of the American War effective steps were being taken to raise the standard of medicine and hygiene in the Service. At Lind's suggestion the Admiralty instituted receiving ships into which all newly pressed men were taken to be thoroughly cleansed and issued with new clothes. This did much to reduce the spread of typhus and typhoid.

The most effectual preservative against this infection, during a press, would, perhaps, be to appoint a ship for receiving all ragged and suspected persons, before they are admitted into the receiving guard-ship. This ship should be furnished with slops, shirts, bedding, and all the necessary articles of seaman's apparel; with soap, tubs, and proper conveniences for bathing, and with a room upon deck for fumigating of clothes. Every suspected person, whether imprest at sea, or on shore, should be first put on board of her; their stay in her, however, should be short, as soon as they are stripped of their rags, well washed and cleaned, they should be supplied with new clothes and bedding, and sent on board the receiving guardships. Such of their apparel as appears tolerably good ought to be cleaned, or, if necessary, fumigated with brimstone and returned to them; but it will be absolutely necessary to destroy all filthy rags, and all such clothes as are brought from Newgate or other prisons.[8]

On his return to the West Indies in 1781 Rodney secured the appointment of Gilbert Blane as Physician of the Fleet. Blane was not only a very skilful physician, but also a first-class administrator. Enjoying the firm support of his Admiral, he made a number of recommendations for improving the general health of the fleet, which were embodied in an official report and eventually carried into effect. He laid particular stress on preventive measures.

I hardly ever knew a ship's company become sickly which was well regulated in point of cleanliness and dryness. It is the custom in some ships to divide the crew into squads or divisions under the inspection of respective officers, who make a weekly review of their persons and clothing, and are answerable for the cleanliness and regularity of their several allotments. This ought to be an indispensable duty in ships of two or three decks; and when it has been practised, and at the same time ventilation, cleanliness, and dryness below and between decks have been attended to, I have never known seamen more unhealthy than any other men. The neglect of such attentions is a never-failing cause of sickness. . . . It would certainly be for the benefit of the service that a uniform should be established for the common men as well as for the officers. This would oblige them at all times to have in their possession a quantity of decent apparel, subject to the inspection of their superiors. . . . The greatest evil connected with clothing is the infection generated by wearing it too long without shifting, for the jail, hospital, or ship fever seems to be more owing to this than to close air.[9]

The reforms recommended by Blane concerned such vital matters as these, also regulations for the prevention of scurvy, a more adequate supply of medical necessities, the avoidance of 'filth, crowding, and mixture of diseases' in naval hospitals ashore, and the provision of hospital ships. Special attention was paid to the provisioning of ships on foreign stations, with the result that scurvy was slowly but surely eradicated from the Royal Navy and mercantile marine. In consequence of these medical and sanitary reforms advocated by Blane, the health of the squadron was greatly improved during the latter part of Rodney's command, and, whereas in the year ending on 13 October 1781 one man out of every seven had perished from disease on the West India station, in the year ending on 16 July 1782 the loss had been reduced to only one in twenty. In 1785 there appeared the first edition of Blane's classic work, *Observations on the Diseases Incident to Seamen*.

The reforms continued in the Channel fleet in the next war. There was still, indeed, much to be done. Even as late as 1799, when the Channel fleet lay in Torbay, the sick had to be carried in open carts to Dartmouth where the accommodation was in any case inadequate. It was for this reason that temporary sick quarters were presently provided in Tor Quay. Despite the heavy demands made on officers and men by St. Vincent's policy of close blockade, the squadron enjoyed excellent health; and on their return to port only 16 sick were landed out of 23,000 men.. 'Of all the services I lay claim to,' St. Vincent wrote in later years, 'the preservation of the health of our fleets is my proudest boast.'

The commissioners of the Sick and Hurt Board, upon whom fell the main responsibility for the medical service of the Fleet, on the whole discharged their duties conscientiously and well. The Commissioners were usually doctors, some of them highly distinguished ones. Both Blane and Baird, in their time, served on the Board. Blane during his term of office continued to promote the improvement of the diet and hygiene of the seamen. Baird was an indefatigable visitor of ships and hospitals (it was largely due to his representations that pig-sties were eventually shifted from the vicinity of the sick berths).

That disease was kept within tolerable limits in the Channel squadron was mainly owing to the admirable work of Drs. Blane and Trotter and the improved standards of hygiene at sea established under Howe, Bridport, and St. Vincent. Thomas Trotter, who rose from surgeon's mate to be Physician of the Fleet (1794–1802), was responsible for the introduction of inoculation against smallpox. Trotter also did much to raise professional standards in the naval medical service, to overhaul the discipline and administration of Haslar Hospital, and generally to improve the diet of the lower deck. Many of the admirals and captains had a particular concern for the welfare of their men. Captains of the fleet would from time to time inspect the hospitals ashore. Individual commanders would act on their own responsibility. Stoves and better systems of ventilation were installed; on the lower and orlop decks dry scrubbing with sand and holystones was substituted for washing; the supply of medicines was much improved; and a more adequate provision of fresh meat, vegetables, and fruit was ordered. Last but not least, the status and emoluments of the surgeons were materially improved. Though down to the close of the Napoleonic War there was never a sufficient number either of surgeons or of office workers in the naval medical service, the period was one of sustained progress.

Much of the sickness which decimated the Service is to be attributed to the inadequacy and poor quality of the provisions supplied to the Navy. Many a commander-in-chief had occasion to complain of insufficient and bad supplies. Incompetence, neglect, and at times corruption, on the part of those responsible for the victualling of the Service lay at the bottom of those evils. Contemporary pamphlets contain such illuminating items as the following:

> That seamen in the King's Ships have made buttons for their Jackets and Trowsers with the Cheese they were served with, having preferred it, by reason of its tough and durable quality, to buttons made of common metal; and that Carpenters in the Navy-Service have Trucks to their Ships' flagstaffs with whole Cheeses, which have stood the weather equally with any timber. . . . That their bread has been so full of large black-headed maggots and that they have so nauseated the thoughts of it, as to be obliged to shut their eyes to confine that sense from being offended before they could bring their minds into a resolution of consuming it. That their beer has stunk as abominably as the foul stagnant water which is pumped out of many cellars in London at midnight hour; and that they were under a necessity of shutting their eyes, and stopping their breath by holding of their noses before they could conquer their aversion, so as to prevail upon themselves in their extreme necessities to drink it. . . . That the pork, which the Fleet under the command of the late Admiral Boscawen was served with, was so rotten, that when boiled it wasted away to mere rags and crumbs, so that it could be eaten with a spoon, and that when the liquor it had been boiled in was drawn off, it flowed out of the cock of the ship's boiler like curds and whey: it was also so nauseous that it made the men sick who did eat of it; and therefore resolving to fast rather than eat any more of it, they have thrown it privately out of their ship's port-holes to prevent being discovered by the officers of their ship.[10]

The author of the observations quoted above was William Thompson, who was systematically victimized and vilified and at last driven out of the public service on account of the embarrassment he had caused to those in authority by these revelations. In a later work he goes on to illustrate with telling effect the intimate connection, in naval warfare, between hygiene and supply, on the one hand, and strategy and tactics, on the other.

But one instance of the corrupt victualling of the Royal Navy, occur'd whilst I was there, and this too extraordinary to be forgot, was the late *Admiral Martin*'s bringing into *Plymouth* Hospital and Sick Quarters, such an incredible number of sick men, as can best be verified by the books of the sick and dead List, if not falsified, at his return from a six weeks cruize, to intercept Mons. *D'Anville*, who then commanded the *Brest* squadron. The sickness by the report of the Admiral, and unanimous opinion of all, both officers and common men, was owing to the badness of their provisions; if so, it will be easy for a common capacity to determine what must have become of Admiral *Martin*'s whole squadron, if Mons. *D'Anville* had given him battle.[11]

Shortly before the outbreak of the Seven Years War, Hawke embarked on a protracted struggle with the victualling department regarding the quality of the beer supplied to his squadron. Anson had experienced the same difficulty in the War of 1739–48. Since water had to be stored in casks it could not be kept sweet for any length of time. Ships then took to sea nearly as much beer as they did water: consequently a supply of good beer was of prime importance if a squadron was to keep the sea.

'The beer which came off in the two tenders from Plymouth', Hawke observed in the autumn of 1755, 'was very bad: so that I was obliged to direct it to be expended immediately; and if what is now coming should prove to be the same, the squadron will be greatly distressed, as good beer is the best preservative of health among new-raised men. Notwithstanding the promise of the contractors for slops to supply better, I find what were issued to the ships at their coming out to be of the same quality with those complained of: and yet our wants oblige us to make use of them, which I beg their Lordships will please to give directions for effectually remedying hereafter.'

In the crucial year of the Seven Years War, 1759, Hawke's insistence on the regular and adequate provision of beef, pork, beer, and other supplies for his squadron proved a factor of prime importance in the close investment of Brest. These suppliers were not secured without a struggle.

'The squadron will soon want butter & cheese,' Hawke wrote on regaining his station after a series of westerly gales on 21 June, 'which must be sent to the rendezvous.' 'I have not yet received the supplies of butter and cheese, beef, pork, &c.,' he informed the Admiralty some four weeks later, 'insomuch that I cannot help regretting the want of a commanding officer at Plymouth to see all orders executed with the expedition and punctuality necessary.' 'I am extremely glad', he wrote soon afterwards, 'to find their Lordships have ordered bullocks and sheep for the preservation of the sick. I hope such numbers will be sent as that the ships' companies may have a share,

to prevent their falling down in scorbutic disorders.' Again and again he had
reason to complain about the quality of the beer supplied to him from
Plymouth. 'The greatest part of the beer from Plymouth brewhouse has
been condemned already. As the Portsmouth, Dover, and London beer held
good to the last,' he protested on 28 August, 'I look on it as a demonstration
that the badness of the Plymouth beer was owing entirely to a want of the
due proportion of malt and hops.'[12]

Hawke's remonstrances had not been unavailing. The Admiralty gave
orders for live cattle and sheep to be regularly transported to the fleet off
Ushant, not only for the use of the sick, but also for that of the ships'
companies in turn. Cabbages, turnips, carrots, potatoes, and onions were
also to be provided. As to the beer, 'Their Lordships have ordered you all the
beer from the eastward that can be provided', the Secretary of the Admiralty
told Hawke on 22 August, 'and they have ordered all there is both at
London, and Portsmouth, to be sent out to you, and have directed every
means to be used to supply the ships under your command with what is
good.'[13]

The difficulty of victualling the fleet increased with the approach of
autumn. 'I have at length distributed the provisions,' observed Hawke on 10
September, 'but taking beer & water out of these small vessels if the weather
be westerly takes up a vast deal of time, & is not to be done if it blows fresh.'

Lind pays a handsome tribute to Hawke, whose insistence on high
standards of hygiene and supply was reflected in the admirable health of his
squadron in the crucial campaign of 1759.

> In the grand fleet of England, commanded by Sir Edward Hawke, who, on the
> 20th November, defeated the French under Mons. Conflans, they enjoyed a
> most perfect and unparalleled state of health. This fleet is supposed, at most
> times, to have consisted of above twenty ships of the line, and ten or more
> frigates, in which were embarked about 14,000 men. On the day of action,
> many of those ships and men had been above six months from Spithead;
> notwithstanding which, there was not then among them twenty sick in all.
> Out of 880 men in the *Royal George* (Sir Edward Hawke's ship) there was but
> one man who was incapable of duty. In the *Union* (Sir Charles Hardy's ship) of
> 770, they had likewise but one unfit for service; and on board the *Mars*,
> commanded by Commodore Young, though a new ship of 64 guns, there was
> not a sick person. It was hardly ever known before, that ships could cruise in
> the Bay of Biscay, much above three or four months at a time, without having
> their men afflicted with scurvy. An exemption from which was entirely owing
> to this fleet having been well supplied with fresh meat and greens.[14]

There was a corollary to this. The heavy weather of November 1759 continued intermittently throughout December. Though the fleet was safely anchored in Quiberon Bay, communications with England were for long interrupted, and supplies of fresh provisions were scanty and irregular. It was in consequence of these privations that the following rhyme went the rounds of the fleet.

> Ere Hawke did bang
> Monsieur Conflans,
> You sent us beef and beer.
> Now Monsieur's beat,
> We've nought to eat,
> Since you have nought to fear.

In successive dispatches to the Admiralty, Hawke referred with increasing urgency to the pressing need of supplies of all kinds. There had been no such scarcity during all the time his squadron was blockading Brest, though the men were mistaken in supposing that it was due to official indifference.

Though individual captains and ships' surgeons saw to it that their crews were adequately supplied with fresh fruit and vegetables, the lack of sufficient supplies and the consequent increase in sickness was one of the chief causes of the weakness of several British squadrons in the War of American Independence. Despite Blane's recommendation in 1781 for a regular supply of lemons nothing had been done and scurvy continued to be the scourge of many ships' companies.

A striking example of the influence of hygiene and supply upon naval strategy was seen in the campaign of 1779. The Bourbon Powers prepared to invade the British Isles. Our Channel fleet under Sir Charles Hardy numbered only thirty-five of the line against d'Orvilliers's sixty-six. But the Combined Fleet, despite its overwhelming numbers, was seriously weakened by disease and lack of provisions; and this proved a major factor in the campaign. Their death-roll was very heavy, and in the end d'Orvilliers had to return to Brest, where he landed 7,000 sick, without having achieved anything.

Victualling presented grave problems in the West Indies. Owing to the lack of storehouses the provisions were stored in hulks and deteriorated in consequence; and certain types of provisions which were suitable for home waters were by no means suitable for the tropics. Rodney's flag-captain in the *Sandwich* complained to Sir Charles Middleton:

> I am amazed at their not having storehouses to put the provisions in. They would not only save the enormous expense of shipping, but the provisions also;

for the bread is full of vermin and the other provisions destroyed by the heat of the hold. . . . I am likewise to acquaint you that the large quantities of butter and oatmeal sent to the West Indies is so much money lost; the butter is not wanted and the oatmeal hardly made use of. . . . I cannot conceive why in the West Indies the men cannot be allowed sugar, coffee, and chocolate in lieu of the oatmeal.[15]

It is worth noticing that complaints about the victualling and insufficiency of medical supplies were included in every one of the seamen's petitions in the naval mutinies of 1797; and improvements in these regards were among the concessions that were made to the insurgents. Even more effective, however, were the representations of Blane and Trotter, coupled with the sustained endeavours of individual commanders like Howe, Bridport, Jervis, Duncan, Nelson, and Keith.

It was due in large measure to Blane's powerful support that, in 1795, the general use of lemon juice as a specific was enjoined by the Admiralty: with effects that were almost magical. When in 1797 Lord Spencer visited Haslar, there was not a single case of scurvy then in the hospital; and by the end of the war scurvy had very nearly disappeared from the Channel fleet. Dr. Andrew Baird (who played something of the same role under St. Vincent's command as Blane had under Rodney's) was also a strong advocate of the provision of lemon juice as an antiscorbutic. In 1799 lemon juice was issued to all ships both at home and on foreign stations.

Trotter during these years usually lived on board the hospital ship *Charon*. His first demands were for large quantities of fresh vegetables and an increased supply of lemon juice. Grappling with an outbreak of scurvy in the squadron in the spring of 1795, he observed, 'The reader may smile at the idea of a Physician of the Fleet attending the stalls at a vegetable market, or perambulating the country to calculate the produce; but it never appeared to me below the dignity of the profession; nor did I consider it a mean task to serve the salad with my own hands from the *Charon*'s quarterdeck.'[16] Late in the following year Trotter declared, 'The late occurrences in the Channel Fleet have sufficiently established the fact that scurvy can always be prevented by fresh vegetables and cured effectually by the lemon or the preserved juice of the fruit'. It was largely due to the efforts of Trotter that the victualling of the Channel squadron had so far improved that, in August 1799, he could declare that 'liberal supplies of cabbages, onions, turnips and carrots are now sent to sea'. Towards the end of the Napoleonic War canned meat was issued to the sick in the same squadron with very beneficial results. About the same time tea was commonly supplied for breakfast. It would seem that Trotter would have liked to see cocoa, too, issued to the Channel squadron.

In the Mediterranean, the welfare of his ships' companies was Jervis's constant preoccupation. Hitherto, by a judicious system of victualling, he had successfully ensured a continual supply of fresh provisions for the squadron. 'From the failure of the supplies of live cattle since the enemy has been in the possession of Leghorn,' he observed, 'I have been under great apprehensions of a return to the scurvy.' Despite difficulties that might well have appeared overwhelming he persevered in his unremitting and, in the main, successful exertions to keep the crews healthy. 'I am confirmed in an opinion that I have long entertained', he noted on another occasion, 'that, next to fresh animal food, onions and lemons are the best antiscorbutics and antiseptics'; and he added that, 'no price is too great to preserve the health of the fleet'. 'Our fleet is in excellent order,' declared Collingwood later, 'well provided with everything; in which our Admiral, Sir John Jervis, takes wonderful pains, and the consequence is we are remarkably healthy after being twenty-eight weeks at sea.'

It was the greatly improved victualling of the Service that, in fact, enabled the large squadrons of the Revolutionary and Napoleonic Wars to remain on their stations through the long years of the blockade of the enemy's coasts.

CHAPTER 10

'FAIR PORTSMOUTH TOWN'

OUR three naval bases—Portsmouth, Chatham, and Plymouth—
were all situated in the south of England, whence most of the
personnel of the Service, then and for generations afterwards, were drawn.
Its unique strategical location had made Portsmouth—to quote the words of
a contemporary authority—'the grand naval arsenal of England' and 'the
rendezvous and headquarters of the British Navy'.

The town, which stands on a narrow peninsula, was then encircled by
formidable ramparts guarded by batteries, and also enclosed by a deep and
wide ditch. On these ramparts the inhabitants of Portsmouth were
accustomed to promenade of a fine evening to listen to the military bands
and to observe the mass of shipping at Spithead and in the harbour. Several
miles to the northward, behind the town, rose the smooth grey undulations
of Portsdown Hill.

Portsmouth was bisected by its long High Street, in which were situated
most of the principal inns, shops, banks, libraries, and offices of the various
naval departments. The George, to which the senior officers of the Navy
usually resorted and where Nelson spent his last hours in England, stood on
the south side of the High Street almost opposite the port admiral's office.
The Fountain, a hostelry chiefly favoured by the lieutenants, lay further
down the street. Portsmouth theatre, of which mention is made in Marryat's
naval novels and other contemporary works, was situated at the upper end
of the High Street. Meredith the tailor (father of the great Victorian
novelist), who was the leading naval outfitter of his day, resided at No. 73,
opposite the Parade Coffee House; in this house Hardy and a number of
other officers used to lodge when in Portsmouth. Opposite the Fountain,
at No. 85, was the establishment of one Morgan, displaying a sign which

notified the passer-by: *Sailors rigged complete from stem to stern.*

Between the High Street and the shingle beach, divided from the rest of the town by a drawbridge, was Portsmouth Point, 'the Wapping of Portsmouth', a picturesque, heterogeneous assemblage of taverns, liquor-shops, eating-houses, cook-shops, tailors, drapers, pawnbrokers, watch-jobbers, and trinket-merchants, backed by a warren of mean streets and alleys. It was a place throbbing with life and excitement. An enormous business was done there in war-time. At the sally port on the east side there was a constant coming and going of barges, launches, gigs, and jolly boats on duty. The stairs and streets leading off the sally port were filled with a jostling throng of men-of-war's men in their familiar dress—blue jackets and trousers in winter, striped Guernsey frocks and white trousers in summer. Such was the Point, the Mecca of all returned seamen.[1] When crews were paid off, relates an eye-witness of those days, 'the scenes of debauchery and brutal violence, gave to this part of Portsmouth its fearful name'. Of the notorious Blue Anchor he writes:

> As a lad I have been into these defiled rooms to deliver messages and parcels to the captains' coxswains, and I have been paid bills from the apron of the landlady, held over her arm, and filled with the coinage of every part of Europe; while the complaints were eternal to the authorities of sailors who, in

a few hours in the buildings in the rear (a species of store divided into sleeping rooms) had lost the whole of their pay and prize money, and from the constant influx of customers detection was impossible. In the first floor of the house was a regular built and formed turf cock-pit, where persons addicted to this species of cruelty nightly congregated, and large sums of money were lost and won.[2]

In Portsmouth Point, next to the coach office,[3] stood the famous hostelry fronted by two large blue posts, much frequented by the 'young gentlemen' of the Service. This, as the coachmen informed Marryat's Peter Simple at the end of their drive down from London, was 'the Blue Postesses, where the midshipmen leave their chestesses, call for tea and toastesses, and sometimes forget to pay for their breakfastesses'. Here, of a raw winter's day, the youngsters would crowd round a blazing fire in the snug coffee-room on the right-hand side of the entrance, briskly demanding 'Tea for two and toast for six'. Of hostelries there was a wide choice at the Point—these for the most part called after well-known fighting ships or famous victories. In the Neptune and Mars; in Bathing House Square were the Quebec and the Roving Sailor; and in Capstan Square, besides the Blue Posts, there was the Lord Hood. A turning off the main street, on the left-hand side, led down to the sally port.

The West Prospect of Portsmouth; engraving from Views of Towns *by Nathaniel and Samuel Buck, 1726–52.*

To the eastward of the dockyard, gradually extending over an expanse of ground that was formerly a common, was the town of Portsea. In its teeming streets and alleys dwelt the families of many of the men who manned the wooden walls, as well as those of the thousands of dockyard 'mateys' who built and maintained them. It was to Portsea that Gardner went one day with his friend Hungerford (first of the *Brunswick*) to dine with Wills, the master of the same ship. The latter had on his door a large brass plate with 'Methusalah Wills' engraved thereon in capital letters. Hungerford told the story that old Wills had the following inscription on the plate:

> Methusalah Wills Esquire,
> Master in the Royal Navie,
> Passed for a first-rate of 110 guns,
> Him and his wife lives here.[4]

Across The Hard from Portsmouth Point was the main entrance to the dockyard. Thence the visitor was conducted through two great gates and along the carriage road skirting the wharves, past the mast-houses and mast-pond, the rope-houses, the Commissioner's House, the mould and sail lofts, the offices, workshops, and store-houses, the officers' quarters, the boat-houses, docks, and building slips, the mills, and the anchor-forge. The dockyard lay on the eastern side of the broad, bottle-shaped harbour, which was, according to Henry Slight,

> the finest in the world, possessing every possible advantage without one single disadvantage; capacious enough to receive the whole British Navy; sheltered by high lands and towns from every wind; affording most excellent anchorage, with a depth of water, at any time of tide, for a first-rate ship to enter, or ride in security within; surrounded by arsenals and docks of magnificent extent, and guarded on every side with fortifications, in all the pomp and majesty of war. The entrance between the Round Tower and Blockhouse Fort is not wider than the Thames at London-bridge; but immediately behind these it expands, passing in a kind of lake, on the Gosport side, past Haslar Hospital, as high as the village of Stoke (Haslar Lake), and on the Portsmouth side, into the Camber and Mill-dam.[5]

Haslar Hospital was built on a mud-girt peninsula on the western shore of the entrance to Portsmouth Harbour. It was thought that the encircling morass would make desertion difficult and hazardous. The original design had envisaged a building quadrangular in form. The work was begun in 1746. the front block was completed by 1754, and the wings were added by 1762. The building was four storeys high; the front block was 567 feet in length, and the wings 553. In the earlier stages of construction convalescents were accommodated in wooden sheds erected alongside the hospital. Then, as the work proceeded, the completed part was progressively occupied by patients. The hospital was built of red brick baked from the local clay with white stone facings. It was notable for being the largest building constructed of brick in the kingdom. With open colonnades (which could be enclosed to provide extra accommodation) running the whole length of the front and wings, it occupied three sides of a quadrangle. The remaining, or south-western, side was left vacant until 1796, when it was closed by high iron railings. The problem of desertion, however, continued for many years to exercise the authorities, notwithstanding the railings, the barring of windows with heavy iron gratings, and the locking of all doors at sunset. A favourite mode of escape was by way of the main drain of the hospital and out into Haslar Creek. Another major problem was the inadequate water supply. The original well was open and unlined, the water being pumped from it by a pumping machine to which four horses were yoked. Later, a number of additional wells were sunk in various parts of the hospital grounds.

'The sick', a visiting doctor related, 'are brought in boats, and, conveniently, received on shore at a landing-place at the hospital. This great building, fitted for the accommodation of two thousand patients, together with houses for officers and the medical attendants, a chapel, a laboratory, a variety of offices, and thirty-eight acres of good pasture land, belonging to the institution, is enclosed within a high brick wall, with iron gates, and a porter's lodge at the entrance, which no stranger is permitted to pass, without the leave of one of the resident lieutenants.'[6]

The history of Portsmouth during the period under review reflected for the most part that of the Navy. The fortunes of the town were inseparably linked with those of the Service. Portsmouth and the fleet anchorage at Spithead were the setting or background to so many important naval occasions, with the populace as interested spectators or participants.

Portsmouth shared in the enthusiasm which attended the return in 1744 of Anson's *Centurion*, after the great voyage of circumnavigation, to Spithead, with spoils valued at £1¼ million; and the arrival, eighteen years later, of the *Hermione*'s treasure captured by a couple of British cruisers off Cadiz.

In the 'Year of Victories', 1759, Saunders's fleet, which formed part of the most formidable armament that had ever crossed the Atlantic for the final and conclusive campaign against French North America, was fitted out at Portsmouth. It was to Portsmouth that Wolfe's body was returned, in the

Admiral Augustus Keppel;
oil painting by Joshua Reynolds, 1779

autumn of the same year, in the *Royal William*, and brought ashore to the accompaniment of minute guns.

In the early spring of 1778 George III came down to Portsmouth to review the fleet at Spithead. His arrival was greeted by a royal salute from all the ships and forts, and he was enthusiastically cheered by the dockyard 'mateys'. The King was rowed through the fleet, followed by all the flag officers and captains in their barges, with each ship cheering as he passed, past thousands of boats crowded with spectators. He presently went on board Admiral Keppel's flagship, the *Prince George*, 98, where he visited the men at their quarters and held a reception for the officers of the fleet. On his return that evening all the houses in Portsmouth and Gosport were illuminated in his honour. Finally he visited the dockyard and the Naval Academy.

Portsmouth, like the Channel squadron, was moved to furious indignation by the court-martial, in 1780, of Admiral Keppel, following the indecisive action off Ushant the year before and the public quarrel between Keppel and Palliser. Keppel's friends and political allies, including a good many noblemen and M.P.s (Fox, Burke, and Sheridan were among the latter), crowded into Portsmouth for the trial, which was held at the Governor's House. Every day the Admiral's partisans, together with the townsmen of Portsmouth, packed the court, to applaud every point made in Keppel's favour and to hiss whenever the evidence went against him. Not a few of the witnesses were effectively intimidated. The dice, in fact, were loaded against Palliser. The case dragged on for five weeks amid scenes of wild excitement. The reports of the trial occupied the newspapers to the exclusion of other news. The verdict, which had long been a foregone conclusion, was delivered on 11 February. The court found that the charge was 'malicious and ill-founded' and that Keppel had behaved as 'a judicious, brave, and experienced officer'. On his acquittal a signal gun was fired to dispatch the news to Spithead, on which the ships saluted and cheered. When he emerged from the court the Admiral was chaired through the streets of Portsmouth to the strains of 'See the Conquering Hero Comes'. A grand ball was given that night in Keppel's honour by the admirals and captains of the fleet at the Assembly Rooms, and the whole town was illuminated.

In ordinary workaday times the dull grey streets of Portsmouth did not offer much excitement. The housewives swept and scrubbed and cooked for their large families; and on Sundays, dressed in their best, strolled on the ramparts. There was the regular arrival and departure of the London coach to look forward to; the periodical appearance of a street musician or travelling peep-show; and (of purely vicarious interest in the case of the great majority of the inhabitants) the announcement of an approaching function in the Assembly Rooms. Except for an occasional affray, conflagration, burglary, drowning, or other fatality, that was about all. Sometimes the jangle of the muffin-man's bell could be heard in some distant lane, gradually drawing nearer. Sometimes a tinker made his rounds of the town. The common cries of Portsmouth were very similar to those of the metropolis: 'Hot cross buns!' 'Water-cresses!' 'Milk-o!' 'Cherry ripe!' 'Sweet blooming lavender!' and so on. There were, however, a couple of quite distinctive ones. Water (always a scarce commodity in Portsmouth) at a halfpenny a bucket was cried through every street; umbrellas, carried around in a large hand-cart, were hawked throughout the town.

With the outbreak of the Revolutionary War in 1793 the place came to life again. Not since the 'Spanish Armament' of 1790 had there been such scenes of bustle and excitement as those which accompanied the assembly of the large trading fleets awaiting convoy at Spithead. Once again the streets, shops, markets, and taverns of Portsmouth were thronged with seamen and passengers, as well as with all the wagons, carts, and hand-barrows loaded with baggage and provisions. During the war the dockyard was the scene of furious and unremitting industry, employing no less than 1,500 shipwrights, 250 sawyers, 200 smiths, 200 riggers, and 350 hands in the rope-yard, as well as various labourers and other workmen.

On 13 June 1794 Portsmouth heard the joyful news of the Glorious First—the first fleet action of the war. Howe brought his battle-scarred squadron and his prizes into the anchorage and landed at the sally port to the triumphal strains of Handel's music and the thunder of artillery. He was escorted through the streets of Portsmouth to the Governor's House by a wildly enthusiastic concourse of townsmen. On the 26th the King and his daughters drove down to Portsmouth. They dined with Howe on board the flagship. The King presented the victor with a sword set with diamonds, and boarded the French prizes.

Dr. George Pinckard, writing of Portsmouth in the following year, describes 'the crowd and confusion of the picture' which attended the embarkation of Grey's expedition for the West Indies: 'such as multitudes passing into and overflowing the shops; people running against or tumbling over each other upon the streets; loud disputes and quarrelling; the sadness of parting; greetings of friends unexpectedly met and as suddenly about to separate; sailors quitting their trolls; drunkards reeling; boatmen wrangling; boats overloaded or upset; the tide beating in heavy spray upon the shore; persons running or hurrying in every direction for something new or something forgot; some cursing the boatman for not pushing off with more speed, and others beseeching and imploring them to stop a minute longer.'

The rent of houses and lodgings, as well as the price of provisions and other necessities, rose high above their ordinary peace-time level. During this time all the hotels, lodging-houses, and apartments in the town were packed with temporary inhabitants. All the butchers' and bakers' shops were cleared of provisions. The streets were thronged with redcoats, besides crowds of men-of-war's men and merchant seamen.

'Such was the state in which we left Portsmouth', Pinckard relates, 'after a residence of three weeks, during which time we had regarded it was a dull, inanimate place; but the change was sudden and will be only transient; the hurry and tumult will vanish with the sailing of the fleet, and the town will relapse into its tranquil sameness until the recurrence of a similar occasion.'[7]

Perhaps the most dramatic event in the history of Portsmouth was the mutiny of the Channel fleet, which broke out, on the morning of 17 April 1797, at Spithead. At sunrise the crew of the flagship *Queen Charlotte* suddenly manned the shrouds and gave three defiant cheers, their example being followed by the crews of the surrounding ships. During the next few days the seamen refused point-blank to weigh anchor until their grievances had been redressed, 'except the enemy are at sea and a convoy wanted'.

The storm had long been gathering up. By the spring of 1797 the discontent on the lower deck had reached a crisis. A whole succession of anonymous petitions had been ignored by the authorities, as had also several warnings they had received from officers of the Channel fleet. The grievances mentioned above related principally to pay, prize-money, food, clothing, leave, and discipline.

Mutiny of the Nore; Richard Parker handing the mutineers' terms to Vice-Admiral Buckner on board the Sandwich; *mezzotint, 1797.*

Of all the questions at issue the utter inadequacy of the seamen's pay was by far the most serious and least defensible. Since the days of Charles II it had scarcely risen at all, and compared very badly indeed with the pay of a merchant seaman; nor could the seaman always be sure of receiving even the meagre wages to which he was entitled. As in 1780 Sir Samuel Hood wrote to his brother: 'The poor devils of seamen are so turned from ship to ship, without the smallest consideration to them, that there is not a possibility of doing them justice respecting their wages.'

Spencer hurried down to Portsmouth on the night of the 17th and held long consultations with Bridport and three other admirals, who, supported by many of the captains, urged the immediate concession of the men's demands. Meanwhile it had been resolved by the delegates of the ships' companies assembled in the *Queen Charlotte*, and their decision notified to Spencer and his colleagues that, until there was a full concession of all their demands, 'the grievances of private ships redressed, an act passed, and His Majesty's gracious pardon for the fleet now lying at Spithead be granted, that the fleet will not lift an anchor: and this is the total and final answer'. Spencer at once returned to town, called for a Cabinet council, and then, accompanied by the Prime Minister and the Lord Chancellor, set off for Windsor to secure the King's pardon, which was duly read out on board the fleet two days later. However, the crews were still suspicious, and trouble flared up on 7 May, as a result of which several seamen were mortally wounded. During the next few days a large number of officers were ordered to leave their ships.

The Delegates in Council or Beggars on Horseback; a caricature of the mutineers at Spithead in 1797 by George Cruikshank.

The inhabitants of Portsmouth, assembled in hundreds on the ramparts and beaches to watch the coming and going of the ships' boats and to gaze with awe and apprehension at the red flags floating over the men-of-war anchored at Spithead, could hardly credit the evidence of their senses. 'The horror and confusion of this town are beyond description,' recorded the *Morning Post*; and added later; 'The whole town wears a most gloomy appearance and every countenance betrays the most evident anxiety.'

By this time, however, the 'seamen's bill' had passed through both Houses of Parliament; and Howe was sent down to Portsmouth to settle the business. The King and Spencer, who were responsible for this mission, could not have made a better choice. 'Black Dick', as he was called, had long been the idol of the lower deck; he was trusted by the seamen as was no other flag-officer. On 11 May he was rowed out to St. Helens, where he set to work, with the utmost tact and patience, to convince the crews of the government's good faith.

The final act of reconciliation took place on 15 May, when Howe read out the royal pardon on board the *Royal George*. Three tremendous cheers were given, and the red flag was replaced by the royal standard. All the other ships followed suit. The mutiny was ended. On his return to Portsmouth the old Admiral was carried shoulder-high, through wildly cheering crowds, up to the Governor's House, where the day's jubilations ended with a great banquet given to the delegates by Lord and Lady Howe.

The year 1797 heralded the advent of better times for the lower deck. For a time, it is true, there was a significant number of courts-martial held on officers for ill-using their men; but later, as the situation improved, such cases became rarer and rarer. The contemporary historian, William James, sums up the matter thus:

> The complaints of the Portsmouth mutineers having been, for the most part founded on justice, the sympathy of the nation went with them, and very few persons throughout the kingdom did or could grudge the additional allowances (many of them a mere exchange of the real for the nominal) which the British sailor, after a hard struggle, got permanently secured to him.[8]

On the eve of the resumption of hostilities in the spring of 1803, after barely a twelve-months' uneasy peace, the streets and alleys of Portsmouth again echoed to the ominous tramp of the press-gang. With the Impress Service operating with unexampled speed, secrecy, and efficiency, large numbers of prime seamen were gathered in for the coming war. So hot was the press at Portsmouth that all the colliers then in port were stripped of their crews and unable to put to sea. On 14 March the *Hampshire Telegraph* reported— 'A very hot press commenced on Tuesday night, at this place and the neighbourhood, by which 500 able seamen were obtained. It was chiefly planned and conducted by Captain Bowen, who pressed a great number of seamen and able watermen by the following stratagem; At ten o'clock at night he assembled a party of Marines, with as much noise and parade as possible, to march to quell a pretended riot at Monckton Fort, on the Haslar side of the water. As the news spread, everybody ran to the fort; and when Captain Bowen saw he had attained his object, he silently placed a party at the end of Haslar Bridge, next the Hospital, and took every man that answered his purpose as he returned from the scene of the false alarm. On the same night the boats of the *Loire*, with press warrants signed on the 7th inst., boarded all the ships in the road and harbour of Cowes, and carried away a number of able seamen.' 'It is with the utmost difficulty that people living on the Point can get a boat to take them to Gosport,' recorded the *Naval Chronicle* about this time, 'the terror of a press gang having made such an impression on the minds of the watermen that ply the passage.'

Colonel Landmann, who arrived in Portsmouth in that first spring of the Napoleonic War, many years afterwards recalls in his *Adventures and Recollections* the scenes of unparalleled excitement that attended

> the collecting here of vast fleets of merchant ships, seeking the protection of convoys, whose boats covered the landing-places, and whose thousands of sailors and passengers filled the streets, shops, and markets; the constant rattling of wheelbarrows full of luggage, the hallooing of porters accompanying them; the confusion created by the light carts passing to and fro from the landing-place at the Point engaged in the carriage of live stock, butcher's meat, vegetables, groceries, liquors, crockery, etc.; the crowds of officers of the navy and army about the doors and windows of the Crown and Fountain inns, and near the bank at the corner of the Parade, forming groups, actively discussing the news of the day, whilst others are shaking hands with old friends, just landed from abroad, and occasionally with a staff-officer, the bearer of important dispatches, on his starting for London in a chaise-and-four, in faded uniform, having had no time to procure a plain suit. . . . Along the Point, and at the back of that celebrated thoroughfare, dozens of midshipmen were seen scudding about from drinking-shop to drinking-shop, and into all the dancing-houses, hunting up their boats' crews, and forcibly separating their dearly beloved, but intoxicated sweethearts, in order that all might be right, on the Captain presenting himself, to be pulled to his ship.

The same writer goes on to describe the inspiring spectacle of a regiment about to embark as it marched down Portsmouth High Street from Hilsea Barracks,

> with Colonel Mair riding at their head, the colours unfurled and flapping with the wind, dogs barking, women and children screaming, and a vast concourse following. In the contrary direction came trains of straggling recruits, just landed, some from Gosport, others from the Isle of Wight, or perhaps Southampton, with streaming blue, red, and white ribbons fastened to their

hats, marching off to the depots, as merry as larks; and close on the heels of all followed gangs of *disinterested* Jews, pressing the sale of 'sealing-wax made of brick-dust, and pencils mitout lead', warranted gold watches, at twenty shillings a-piece, gold wedding-rings at four-pence, silver pencil cases and penknives, all as cheap as dirt; lastly came fiddlers, mountebanks, fortune-tellers, pickpockets, and the never-failing two little brothers, offering, for the smallest trifle, to play you a tune on their chins.

As a background to all the hubbub and excitement, was heard the far-off clamour of the dockyard, the creak and splash of oars, the long-drawn-out rattle of waves on the shingle, the cries of sea-birds wheeling and circling above the crowded roof-tops. Landmann continues:

To these may be added the frequent firing of salutes from the ships at Spithead, re-echoed from the saluting-base on shore, then the huzzas of half-drunken sailors, parading through the streets on the tops of hired coaches, shouting and waving their hats and banners, and drinking and cheering at every corner, hailing one another from coach to coach with all the roughness and wit peculiar to their profession, and, in short, striving how to expend large sums of hardly-earned prize-money in the least possible time.[9]

Nelson did not care for the town—'a dirty place', he called it; though nowhere in the kingdom, indeed, was he acclaimed with greater ardour and affection, and Portsmouth's last farewell to Nelson, on 14 September 1805, was one of the most moving and memorable scenes in our history: an American visitor who was present on that occasion observed that the streets of Portsmouth were dirty and the town presented little that was pleasing or interesting 'beyond the means of war, of which', he declared, 'it is little else than a great magazine'. The annals of Portsmouth are indeed crowded with the alarums and excursions of war: of great armaments preparing at Spithead; of famous commanders arriving and departing; of historic courts-martial; of fitting out of fleets and assembling of convoys. The eyes of the crowds strolling on the ramparts were constantly on the great ships anchored at Spithead. The dingy roads were daily a kaleidoscope of smart uniforms. The workaday life of the great naval arsenal was diversified by the periodical incursion of the press-gang, by the return of a victorious squadron with its prizes, by the paying-off of ships, and by such rowdy jollifications as Free Mart Fair.

Such was Portsmouth Town in 'Eighteen-hundred and war-time', when Jane Austen's Fanny Price and her sailor brother, William, came down from Mansfield Park by post-chaise to visit their family.

~~~~~~

CHAPTER 11

ADMIRALTY

THE centre from which the world-wide ramifications of British sea power—squadrons, ships, commanders, ports, arsenals, dockyards, depots, and stores—were controlled was the unpretentious pile erected at the north end of Whitehall, in 1722–5, by Thomas Ripley. For thirty years and more the Admiralty was enclosed by a high brick wall with a single entrance. Adam's screen, facing the entrance from Whitehall, was added in 1760. Originally a large part of the building was reserved for the private apartments of the various members of the Board; then, as the business and numbers of the Admiralty staff continued to increase, further accommodation became necessary; and in 1785–8 a new wing was added, on the south or Horse Guards side, as the private residence of the First Lord and the First Secretary.

A narrow cobbled courtyard led up to the tall portico below which was the entrance hall with its buff-coloured walls, plain pedimented doorways, and oaken doors—all this still much as it was in the days of Nelson. In the centre of the hall hung a handsome brass lamp, dating back to the end of the eighteenth century. The second door on the left gave access to the captains' waiting room, beneath whose fine arched ceiling Nelson's body lay, on the night of 8 January 1806, watched by Dr. Scott, before the burial next day in St. Paul's. According to tradition, it was over the chimney-piece of the Captain's Room that Marryat, in a moment of exasperated boredom, inscribed the following lines:

> In sore affliction, tried by God's commands,
> Of patience, Job, a great exemplar, stands;
> But in these days, a trial more severe
> Had been Job's lot, if God had sent him here.

Facing the head of the principal staircase, lighted by a dome, was the entrance to the Board Room. This was a large and nobly proportioned chamber with dark-oak panelling and a high white ceiling. Along the east wall were three tall windows overlooking some mews. Opposite was a great fireplace flanked by Grinling Gibbons carvings (the grate still bearing the arms of Charles II), and above the chimney-piece was a set of charts wound round rollers. On the north wall were two book-cases; and between them was a globe, surmounted by a wind-dial, whose gilded pointer, geared to a vane erected on the roof of the Admiralty, showed at a glance which way the wind was blowing. Over in the corner stood a fine grandfather clock with a portentous tick, telling both time and date; it had been constructed, late in the reign of William III, by Langley Bradley, who had made the great clock of St. Paul's.

In 1796 a system of semaphore signalling was adopted by the Admiralty for communicating with Portsmouth and Chatham, the signals being passed on by a chain of signal stations erected on hill-tops within sight of each other. In London, the semaphore apparatus was erected on the roof of Admiralty House, the residence of the First Lord. The sites of the signal stations on the Portsmouth line were as follows: Admiralty—Royal Hospital, Chelsea—The Highland, Putney—Netley Heath—Hascombe—Blackdown—Beacon Hill, Harting—Portsdown Hill—The Glacis, Portsmouth; on the Chatham line: Admiralty—36, West Square, Southwark—New Cross Gate, Nunhead—Shooter's Hill—Swanscombe—Gad's Hill, Shorne—Chatham Yard. The system was later extended to Plymouth and Yarmouth. It has been said that in clear weather a signal could be transmitted by this means from Whitehall to Portsmouth in about ten minutes. In fog, of course, the manual telegraph could not operate.[1]

In the middle of this room where so much of England's history was made was a long mahogany table around which the members of the Board would take their seats. Beneath that lofty ceiling, each in his day, Wager, Anson, Hawke, Sandwich, Spencer, St. Vincent, and Barham presided over the deliberations of the Board of Admiralty. Here Anson evolved the great reforms that created the Navy which Jervis and Nelson knew. Here Sandwich held his agreeable dinner parties and considered the probable effects of Keppel's acquittal. Here Spencer heard the shameful news that Admiral Man had quitted his post, that our squadrons at Spithead and the Nore had mutinied, and that Bridport, watching Brest, had let Bruix slip through his fingers—and heard, too, in happier times, the joyful tidings of the Glorious First, St. Vincent, Camperdown, and the Nile. Here 'old

View of the Admiralty, showing telegraph on the roof; engraving published by Ackermann, 1818.

Jarvie', assisted by Troubridge and the faithful Tucker, applied himself to the herculean labour of reforming the dockyards. Here Barham set in train his dispositions for the crucial campaign of 1805 which culminated in the greatest sea-victory of all time.

And here on a November night William Marsden, the Secretary, was sitting late over his papers when suddenly in the small hours there was a rumble of wheels in the courtyard below and the door opened to admit Lieut. Lapenotière of the *Pickle* schooner. 'Sir,' exclaimed the officer, who had come up post-haste from Falmouth with Collingwood's dispatches—'Sir, we have gained a great victory; but we have lost Lord Nelson!'

Throughout the long war against Napoleon the Board of Admiralty was composed of seven members, presided over by the First Lord and assisted by the First and Second Secretaries.

Notwithstanding the enormous expansion of the Navy in the past half-century, the administration of the Service was still carried on under the old system with remarkable efficiency. Though there were to be no major reforms until 1832, the Board managed to adapt itself to changing

The Board Room of the Admiralty; engraving from Ackermann's
Microcosm of London.

circumstances, insisted on securing fair conditions for its staff, and successfully bore the stress and strain imposed by the Revolutionary and Napoleonic Wars.

Sir Evan Nepean, who was appointed in 1793, was succeeded as First Secretary in 1804 by William Marsden, his Second Secretary, who was likewise succeeded as Second Secretary by John Barrow. (The latter was to hold the post, with one brief interval for the next forty years.) These secretaries were able and industrious men who corresponded, not only with serving officers all over the world, but also with the Navy, Victualling, and Sick and Wounded Boards. The usual procedure was that all letters were read, answered, and filed on the day they were received. Despite Lord Barham's complaint of 'everything being left to the memory and discretion of the clerks', it would seem that the latter managed tolerably well.[2]

The correspondence carried on with ships and establishments all over the world was immense. To the Admiralty came dispatches from the principal stations of the British Navy both near and far; marine intelligence from Lloyd's; reports from British secret agents in neutral, and even enemy, ports. Between the Admiralty and admirals and captains flowed an unending stream of correspondence; requests for supplies, and assurances that such would be sent; letters concerning convoys, troop transports, and naval stores. Day by day the work of dating, annotating, filing, and docketing continued; of perusing captains' and masters' journals, and then stowing them away; of checking and copying; of totting and casting. All this enormous mass of paper-work, now stored in the Public Record Office, bears witness to the admirable efficiency of the administrative machine under whose direction the Royal Navy achieved and maintained the Empire of the Ocean.

The most notable First Lord at the outset of the Georgian era was Lord Torrington (formerly Sir George Byng), the victor of the action off Cape Passaro in 1718, who had crowned a long and successful career by becoming First Lord on the accession of George II. Another important figure was Sir Charles Wager, who, like Torrington, had shown himself to be a brave and capable sea-officer. In the War of Spanish Succession he commanded on the West India station, and made his name famous by his daring attack on the Spanish treasure ships in 1708 (it was Wager who was credited with the saying, 'A man who would not fight for a galleon would fight for nothing'). He became First Lord in Walpole's ministry after serving for sixteen years as a junior member of the Board. During the years that followed, the Board was predominantly civilian and the standard of naval administration depended on the First Lord and the First Naval Lord. Wager was generally liked and trusted. He was one of the few men who could handle Vernon, who had long served under him and whom he had appointed to the crucial West Indies command. He secured firmer control over the Navy Board. On the other hand, there can be no doubt that on the outbreak of the War of Jenkins' Ear the Navy was found to be dangerously weak in ships, stores, and equipment.

Wager's fortunes were inseparably linked with those of Walpole. When Walpole resigned, his First Lord resigned also. After a brief period of weakness when the Earl of Winchilsea succeeded Wager, Bedford, Sandwich, and Anson took office.

The appointment of Anson to the Board of Admiralty in 1745 marked an era in naval administration. It would be difficult, indeed, to exaggerate the debt which the Georgian Navy owed to this great officer. In 1751 he became First Lord and continued to hold that office, with but one brief interval, until 1762. He was unquestionably the ablest, strongest, and most responsible administrator since Pepys. The revision of the method of promotion to flag rank; the introduction of a new code of articles of war; the establishment of a uniform for the officers of the Service; the reorganization of the corps of marines, were all due to Anson. Another important reform for which he was responsible was a measure providing for the punctual payment of the men and allowing them to assign part of their pay to their families. He overhauled the dockyards and other shore establishments of the Navy, and materially improved the whole administration of supply. Even though these reforms cannot be said to have extirpated the variegated and deep-rooted abuses of the dockyards, they nevertheless did much to put down idleness, incompetence, waste, and embezzlement. It was from Anson that some of the finest officers of their day had procured preferment. Boscawen, Rodney, and Howe were his selections. Jervis received both his nomination and his commission from Anson.

Hawke, one of the foremost fighting admirals in our history, was by no means equally successful as First Lord. Though it is true that he managed to obtain rather more adequate supplies during the locust years of peace than heretofore, and both supported and encouraged Captain Cook, he was manifestly unable to arrest the rot which had set in. In the 1760s the Navy suffered a serious decline in strength and efficiency.

The belief that Sandwich was responsible for a perfect orgy of corruption and incompetence and for the weakness of the Navy in the War of American Independence has long since been dispelled. A different story is told by the Admiralty papers of the period. The truth is that Sandwich was a first-rate man of business, who had already been First Lord twice before and twice Secretary of State. He had been the friend and colleague of Anson, and he worked amicably with Rodney. 'No man in the Administration', wrote Horace Walpole, 'was so much master of business, so quick, or so shrewd.' Wraxall likewise testified that Sandwich was 'universally admitted to possess eminent talents, great application to the duties of his office, thorough acquaintance with public business'. He added, that in all his official functions 'he displayed perspicuity as well as despatch'. In 1749, when he first took his seat at the Board of Admiralty, one of his earliest measures had been to institute a strict and searching visitation of the dockyards and other naval establishments. In later years he caused such visitations to be frequently made: as a result of which many abuses were brought to light and corrected. Among the most important of the other achievements of Sandwich's administration were the 'coppering' of the entire Navy of Great Britain, 'from a first rate to the smallest cutter', with the exception of a few ships that were not yet returned from foreign stations, and the introduction of the carronade. He also did much to remedy the deficiency of timber and of naval stores generally. On the debit side of the account must be set the furious quarrel which well nigh rent the corps of officers asunder under the

Sandwich regime. After Keppel's court-martial the resentment of Whig officers focused upon the First Lord. It was openly avowed that 'out Twitcher must'.[3]

The early years of Spencer's term of office as First Lord were by no means so successful as the later ones. He was young, capable, energetic, and conscientious; he brought new standards of method and punctuality to the administration of the Admiralty; but he lacked ministerial experience and knew little of naval affairs; he was, besides, arbitrary and incautious, and over-confident in his own powers; he had recently managed to fall out with Sir Charles Middleton, for many years the real power behind the throne at the Admiralty—with the result that the latter at last resigned; and he had driven into retirement several of our most distinguished commanders. By the time of the mutinies, however, he may be said to have found his feet at the Admiralty; and if the crisis was unfortunately handled in its initial stages much of the credit for the ultimate settlement of the affair belongs to Spencer. He later became one of the ablest and most successful First Lords who ever presided over the Board of Admiralty. No one before or since has held that office for a comparable period in war-time (1794–1801). The debt owed to Spencer by his country can scarcely be set too high. It was he who successfully chose for their high commands Jervis, Duncan, and Nelson: with each of whom he kept up an intimate and regular correspondence.

In February 1801 Pitt resigned on the Catholic issue and was succeeded by Addington. St. Vincent became First Lord of the Admiralty in the new ministry. One of his first measures in that office was to hasten the departure to the Baltic of Sir Hyde Parker and his fleet, to deal with the situation created by the Armed Neutrality. Parker had recently married a very young wife and was apparently waiting for a farewell ball which the lady was giving at Yarmouth on 13 March. The 'prog' which St. Vincent addressed to the laggard Admiral was a model of its kind; and the fleet weighed and sailed. Following the battle of Copenhagen, in which Sir Hyde had not distinguished himself, he was presently relieved of his command and replaced by Nelson.

On the temporary cessation of hostilities in the spring of 1802, St. Vincent addressed himself to the reform of the dockyards. 'Nothing short of a radical sweep in the dockyards can cure the enormous evils and corruptions in them', he had told Spencer a year before; 'and this cannot be attempted till we have peace.' Despite strong opposition he insisted that a Parliamentary Commission should inquire into conditions in the dockyards; and he virtually forced this measure on the Cabinet. In each of the dockyards visited grave abuses were brought to light. St. Vincent in consequence had the timber inspectors replaced by new men and ordered 'all oak delivered on contract' to be strictly scrutinized. The effect of these measures was to arouse the violent hostility of the contractors; and the ensuing reprisals brought about a timber crisis of the first magnitude. There can be no question that St. Vincent's well-intentioned but inopportune reforms seriously weakened the Navy. When the short-lived Peace of Amiens broke up in the spring of 1803, the dockyards lacked the necessary materials for repairing vessels worn out by long years of service. 'The deficiencies', declared Barrow, 'in every species of naval stores in the dockyards were quite alarming.'[4] At the same time the lack of co-operation between the Navy Board and the Board of Admiralty nearly brought the machinery of naval administration to a complete standstill. St. Vincent had thus antagonized the dockyards and estranged the Navy Board: all of which contributed in no small measure to the fall of Addington's ministry in 1804.

During the great invasion scare which followed swiftly upon the renewal of hostilities with France, St. Vincent put his trust in the defensive dispositions which had stood the test of time, and refused to be stampeded by popular clamour into constructing a multitude of small craft (as he said), 'to calm the fears of old ladies both in and out', at the expense of the battle fleet on which the safety of the realm really depended. 'I do not say, my Lords,' he observed gruffly in the House of Lords, 'that the French will not come. I only say they will not come by sea.' In the event St. Vincent's confidence in our defensive strategy was completely justified.

When Pitt returned to office in May 1804 he chose Melville as his First Lord. The latter at once abandoned his predecessor's reforms and successfully appeased the contractors; with the result that he obtained sufficient oak to repair, in the course of the next eighteen months or so, thirty-nine of the line—roughly one-third of the total British battle fleet. But early in 1805 the Commission of Naval Inquiry issued its Tenth Report, showing that Melville had been guilty of 'gross irregularities' while Treasurer during Pitt's previous term of office. After this exposure Melville was replaced in April by Admiral Sir Charles Middleton, who took the title of Lord Barham.

Barham was then nearly eighty years of age. Pitt had in fact secured his appointment in the face of strong opposition. But Barham soon showed that he was much more than a mere stop-gap. The new First Lord was an administrator and strategist of the first order.

Under his direction the staff work of the Admiralty was to attain an unexampled level of efficiency. It was Barham's policy to divest himself of routine responsibilities and to delegate these duties to subordinates, while

Charles Middleton, Lord Barham; engraving after the portrait by
Isaac Pocock.

reserving to himself the higher direction of the war at sea. He clearly defined
the duties of the Naval Lords (who were now for the first time called Sea
Lords). This new allocation of specific duties was an emergency measure
that was destined to endure, and was incorporated in the structure of the
Admiralty when reorganized in 1832. Barham may indeed be regarded as
one of the creators of the modern Admiralty. His grasp and understanding of
the strategic problems confronting the Admiralty were probably
unequalled—as was also the promptitude with which he acted. His
disposition of our squadrons and detached divisions effectively exploited the
strategic advantages which the blockading force must necessarily possess
over the blockaded. Moreover, it is always to be borne in mind that even in
the crisis of the naval campaign of 1805 the problem of trade protection was
exercising the Admiralty to a far greater degree than the threat of invasion. It

was of crucial importance to the national economy that commerce should be kept flowing; and Barham saw to it that it was kept flowing.

The second Lord Melville, who was appointed First Lord in 1812, presided over the Admiralty, except for one brief interval, for no less than fifteen years. He was one of those Tory magnates who, on the death of Lord Liverpool, declined to serve under Canning and resigned. In 1828 he was reappointed to the Admiralty by the Duke of Wellington, notwithstanding certain sharp exchanges which had passed between the two long before in the Peninsular War. Melville as First Lord, perhaps, has been somewhat underrated. He had co-operated well with Keith in the closing stages of the Napoleonic War, had put the naval case effectively to Wellington, and appears to have been reasonably successful as an administrator during his long term of office.

CHAPTER 12

'THE DANGERS OF THE SEA'

THE crucial importance of seamanship as a factor in operations at sea can be gauged from the significant fact that, during the period under survey, by far the greater part of the losses suffered by the Navy were due, not to enemy action, but to 'the dangers of the sea'.

The gravest disasters of all were those caused by severe weather, like the Great Storm of 1703, the West Indian hurricane of 1780, and the terrific gale off Newfoundland, in 1782, which sank so many of the prizes taken at The Saints. They were likewise caused by errors of judgement such as those made by Sir Clowdisley Shovell in 1707, by the master of the *Ramillies* in 1760, and by Rear-Admiral Robert Reynolds in 1811. Above all, it was the exigencies of the arduous blockading service which exposed our warships, more especially the smaller cruisers, to every hazard of rocks, shoals, tides, and weather.

'It is not fighting, my dear William,' Codrington had informed his brother shortly after Trafalgar, when a succession of heavy gales had buffeted the battered fleet, 'which is the severest part of *our* life; it is the having to contend with the sudden changes of season, the war of elements, the dangers of a lee shore, and so forth, which produce *no food for honour or glory* beyond the internal satisfaction of doing a duty *we* know to be most important, although passed by others unknown and unnoticed.'[1]

A point worth noting is that most of the losses occurred in coastal waters. For instance, in the War of 1739–48 comparatively few of our vessels foundered in the open sea. The majority of them were wrecked on the rocks and sands of the English Channel, and off the West Indian islands (the hurricane of 20 October 1744 accounted for several). The pattern was repeated in the Seven Years War. There were similar losses in the Channel

A shipwreck on the coast of Sussex in November 1829; contemporary watercolour sketch.

and in the Caribbean. In the campaign of 1759 the *Achilles* frigate struck on the Goué Vas rock near Quiberon Point and was badly damaged; however, she was eventually got safely to England. Two of the heaviest losses of the war were those of the *Resolution* and *Essex* in Quiberon Bay shortly after, and of the *Ramillies* off the Bolt early in 1760. Several men-of-war were lost in a hurricane in the East Indies in 1761.

In the War of American Independence, though there were a good many losses as usual in the West Indies (in the hurricane of 5 October 1780 over a dozen of our ships were lost, including a 74 and several frigates), a fair number at various points on the east coast of North America, and a few in the Channel and in the East Indies, the heaviest toll levied by 'the dangers of the sea' at a single stroke was in the violent gale of 1782, already mentioned, in the vicinity of the Grand Banks.

In the long struggle of 1793–1815 the statistics are illuminating to a remarkable degree. It has been calculated that, during the Revolutionary and Napoleonic Wars, no less than two hundred and fifty-four warships of all types were driven ashore, or on to rocks and shoals, and wrecked; and another seventy-five foundered. On the other hand, during the same period, losses attributed to the 'violence of the enemy' amounted to only one 74, one 54, and eight frigates. The heaviest total of losses occurred on the Atlantic coast of France; after that came the hurricane-stricken zone of the Caribbean.

In the days of sail the entrance to the English Channel was, without doubt, one of the most hazardous landfalls in the world. No part of the coasts of the British Isles was more subject to sudden changes. Since a fair wind up Channel—that is, at south-west—was always liable to fly to the northward, should such a change occur vessels standing along the south side would find themselves immediately on a dead lee shore. On the French side of the Channel, too, from Ushant to Alderney, there were numerous islands, rocks, and outlying dangers; and along this shore, and among the islands and rocks, the flood-tide, at a distance from some thirty miles off the land, set to the south-east, while the ebb did not set north-west, but west: with the result that vessels driven on this coast with north-westerly gales would not have the tide to help them off, and would be most liable to be driven on shore. On the other hand, vessels coming into the soundings on a more northerly parallel were confronted by equal, if not greater, dangers. Some twenty miles to the westward of Land's End lie the rock-girt Isles of Scilly. According to an old Scillonian tradition the islands have witnessed the loss of as many good ships as there are rocks in the archipelago; and the number of these rocks must total several hundred. Away beyond the Scillies lie the iron-bound shores of Cornwall and south-west Wales, fringed by dangerous rocks and islets like the Seven Stones, Wolf, Longships, Stags, Brisons, Shutter, Skokholm, and the Smalls. Moreover, after strong or long-continued south-westerly or westerly winds have prevailed in the vicinity of the Bay of Biscay, it would appear that a set or current frequently sets obliquely across the western approach to the Channel. This may well sweep a vessel towards, or northward of, the Isles of Scilly.

'For when you come near the soundings,' Joshua Kelly noted in his *The Modern Navigator's Compleat Tutor*, 'and till you bring Ushant south of you, on the E.S.E. course, *you will hardly hold your latitude*.' 'It is a circumstance well known to seamen,' Rennell declared, 'that ships, in coming from the Atlantic, and steering a course for the British Channel, in a parallel somewhat to the *south* of the Scilly Islands; do, notwithstanding often find themselves to the *north* of these islands.'

It was this special difficulty in approaching the Channel, this danger in coming into the soundings, that gave rise to the great importance attached by the old navigators to what they called the three L's—Lead, Latitude, and

Look-out. Because of all the unpredictable factors inherent in dead reckoning, or navigation by account, the hazards in approaching the entrance to the Channel were immensely increased when, as not infrequently occurred, observations became impossible, and the navigator was compelled to fall back on dead reckoning. The disaster which overtook Sir Clowdisley Shovell in 1707, although certainly the most memorable of its kind, was but one among many which must be attributed to the same cause—namely, an error in reckoning due to the variable northerly set across the entrance to the Channel. The danger in approaching the entrance to the Channel is admirably illustrated in the following excerpt from Gardner's *Recollections*.

> We had a most dreadful passage home, blowing a gale of wind the whole time with seldom more sail set than a close-reefed main topsail. . . . However, at last we got to the northward and westward of Scilly, with the wind at S.W.; but it must be understood, to give the devil his due, that we had not an observation for a long time, and our dead reckoning was not to be trusted; but at last we found out by instinct or soundings that we were not in the right place. Now it so happened that we were lying to on the larboard tack, the wind, as I have stated, at S W, under a close reefed main topsail and storm staysails, when in a thundering squall it shifted to N N W and took us slapaback. Over she went, with the upper dead-eyes on the lower rigging in the water, and we thought she would never right, but the old ship came to herself again. After standing to the southward for some time until we thought we had got into 49° 30' by our dead reckoning, which is the latitude of mid-channel, we then altered our course to S E b E ½ E. I had a presentiment that something bad was hanging over us, and I went on the fore topsail yard (I think about 9 at night) to look out ahead, the ship scudding at the rate of eleven knots, . . . [when] after running some time I saw a light right ahead, which I instantly knew to be Scilly light, and I called to Captain Wallis, who immediately hauled the ship off to the southward. If the weather had not cleared after the squall before mentioned we should certainly have made the port where Sir Clowdisley Shovell took in his last moorings.[2]

The fate of the *Ramillies* on 15 February 1760 further exemplified the hazards of making the land at the western entrance of the Channel in bad weather. The evening before, Hawke's former flagship, which had recently been refitted after the campaign of 1759, parted company with Boscawen and the rest of the squadron; and, leaking badly, stood all the night to the eastward. About ten o'clock next morning, in thick sou'-westerly weather, some of the officers thought they saw the land: but the master was of a contrary opinion. The *Ramillies* stood in to make the land, and, about an hour later, her look-outs suddenly sighted the coastline. Actually it was Bigbury Bay; but the master, mistaking Borough Island for Looe Island, supposed that they were still to the westward of Plymouth.

Crowding all the canvas which the ship would carry, the crew of the *Ramillies* endeavoured in vain to double the high rocky promontory of the Bolt which, owing to the master's error, they had taken for Rame Head at the entrance to Plymouth Sound. Though the captain as well as some of his officers had been of opinion that they would not be able to weather the headland, the master was firmly persuaded that they could. Directly he realized his mistake he endeavoured to stay the ship and get into Bigbury Bay: but the heavy westerly swell, added to the dead weight of water lying in her hold, made it impossible. In the end the *Ramillies* fetched up under the precipitous cliffs of the Bolt Tail, where she was dismasted, and, her cables having parted, engulfed in the mountainous seas, and rapidly went to pieces. More than 700 men perished amid the breakers at the foot of the cliffs or were battered to pieces among the rocks.

The loss of the *Ramillies* is to be attributed to the three successive errors of judgement on the part of the master. The first of these occasions was on the morning of the 16th when that officer, unconvinced that they were already near the land, had stood in to make it. If they had only continued on their course they should have had no difficulty in weathering the Bolt and might well have got safely into Torbay. Later on, the master had taken Borough Island, which lies in the depth of Bigbury Bay, for Looe Island, which is on the further side of Plymouth. Thirdly, the master had made the final and fatal error of supposing they could weather the headland.[3]

Another revealing example of the dangers to navigation at the entrance to the Channel under certain weather conditions may be found in the first winter of the Revolutionary War. The Channel squadron was then saved from imminent disaster when, returning to port after several days of sailing by dead reckoning in hazy sou'-westerly weather, James Bowen, the master of the flagship, the *Queen Charlotte*, volunteered to lead the fleet into Torbay.

After a little consideration Howe agreed; but both the Captain of the Fleet and the Flag Captain remonstrated with Bowen on the impossibility of his knowing exactly where they were and on the probability of his making a mistake and losing the whole fleet in Whitsand Bay. Bowen, however, was quite confident that he could manage it; and then, at Howe's desire, he shaped a course for Start Point. The *Phaeton* frigate was directed to keep on the lee bow of the *Queen Charlotte* as far ahead as she could go without losing sight of her. The *Black Joke* was directed to do the same by the *Phaeton*. In this way the squadron stood in to the land. Just before dusk the *Black Joke* was observed to haul short up on the starboard tack, having run very close to the breakers off the Start, and the *Phaeton* to follow her example. The *Queen Charlotte* continued on her course, 'by which she just cleared Start Point so as to keep away for Bury [Berry] Head; and thus the whole fleet were conducted into a snug anchorage in Tor Bay by the confidence and skill of James Bowen, the master.'[4]

A very large number of our ships were continually engaged in blockading the enemy's ports and coasts under conditions which courted disaster. The greatest risks in this dangerous blockade service were necessarily run by the lesser cruisers, which so often were obliged to keep close in with the enemy's coasts, and of which no less than 170 were lost.

The close investment of Brest, which had been initiated by Hawke and afterwards revived by St. Vincent and Cornwallis, made the severest demands on the seamanship of the blockading force. The stormy Brittany coast, in the prevailing westerlies, was a dead lee shore. The main approach to Brest is the Iroise Channel, between the flat, craggy island of Ushant and the long tongue of islets, reefs, and shoals known as the Chausée de Sein. To the northward of the Iroise Channel, about six miles to the westward of St. Mathieu Point, lie the Black Rocks, a chain of rocks, above water and sunken; and five miles to the southward is the Parquette, a half-tide rock, usually marked by breakers when covered. Surrounded by all these dangers the blockading fleet had to contend with the strong tidal streams in the Iroise and in the neighbouring approaches. Both gales and fogs were of common occurrence. Considering the risks that were taken, the wonder is not that there were losses, but that the losses were not far heavier.

The strain imposed by days and nights of fog in the vicinity of the Black Rocks, where so many vessels narrowly escaped disaster, and a number of them actually were wrecked, had to be experienced to be understood. (Not for nothing had the hazardous station in the Iroise become known as 'Siberia'.) The post off Brest was the crucial point in our naval strategy; and the inshore squadron close in with the enemy's principal naval arsenal was essential to the proper holding of it. The difficulty always was to find commanders capable of fulfilling this important duty on the advanced station: contending continually with 'tides and rocks, which', as Collingwood observed, 'have more of danger in them than battle once a week'. 'It is evident', St. Vincent informed Spencer in the summer of 1800, 'that the man who faces a Frenchman or Spaniard with intrepidity does not always encounter rocks and shoals with the same feeling.' It may be suspected that it was the danger

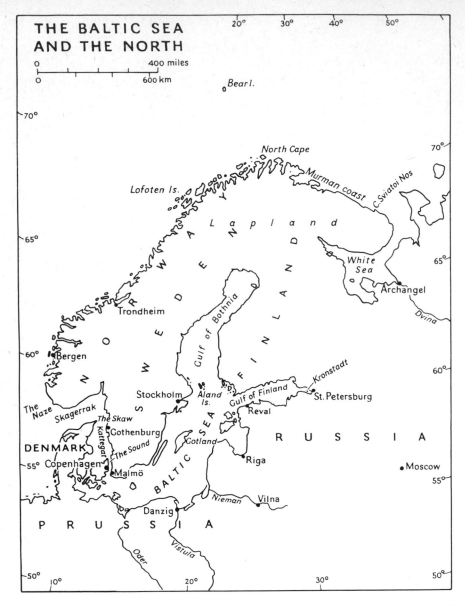

THE BALTIC SEA
AND THE NORTH

and hardships entailed by the close blockade of Brest which was the real
reason for the aversion of so many of our flag-officers and captains for this
strategy.

The intricate shoals and tides off the Dutch and Flemish coasts presented
their own special dangers to the cruisers engaged in blockading the hostile
ports. Should the wind come north-westerly and strong, as Nelson pointed

THE NORTH SEA

out in the summer of 1801, none of the square-rigged vessels blockading
Dunkirk could beat off the shore under low canvas, and would have to trust
to their anchors and cables. It was for this reason that he proposed that the
blockading force on this part of the coast should be permitted to retire into
Margate roads on the appearance of blowing weather, leaving one or two
cutters to keep watch on the motions of the enemy. He similarly
recommended that, since Calais, Boulogne, and Dieppe likewise lay in
bights, and with the wind right in 'hardly any ship can beat out', except in
fine weather, the squadron should withdraw to the Downs, leaving cutters
to watch the hostile ports. The losses among the lesser cruisers would
certainly have been far heavier but for the resource and skill of experienced
old salts like 'old Yawkins', whom Nelson so warmly admired, with their
wonderful knowledge of the intricate navigation of the sands, the tides and
eddies, and the signs of the weather.

The amphibious operations on the north coast of Spain, during the
Peninsular War, were carried on under conditions of considerable difficulty
and danger. In the frequent north-westerly gales of winter the whole
Biscayan coast was a dead lee shore, with strong easterly currents setting
towards the head of the Bay; there was no safe harbour except Pasajes. Even
in summer it was hazardous for ships of the line or even the larger cruisers to
anchor off this coast which was subject to gales and a heavy swell. The
smaller vessels were also exposed to the danger of foundering in a high
breaking sea. Off Cape Ortegal, in the early spring of 1814, two sloops, the
Rover and the *Derwent*, only saved themselves from foundering in a violent
nor'-wester by heaving more than half their guns overboard. The coast
between Bayonne and Pasajes was one of the most dangerous in Europe.

On the distant northern trade-route to Archangel, it was not only enemy
privateers, but also 'the dangers of the sea', which awaited our convoys on
their comings and goings. Under the lowering grey skies of the Arctic,
observations might be impossible for days on end. When standing along the
bleak and barren Murman coast the utmost caution was called for on account
of the strong indraught which set on shore, the frequency of fogs, and the
unreliability of the compass in the vicinity of the land. In these high northern
waters, even in the summer, sleet, snow, and severe gales, with heavy
breaking seas, were often encountered.

Nearer home, 'the dangers of the sea' periodically exacted a grievous toll
in the Baltic. The hazards involved in a late return from that region were a
risk which had to be run in the interests of trade protection; and from time to
time the forfeit was claimed. Thus, in December 1808 the last convoy of the
year left Karlskrona for Great Britain. Standing down the Malmö passage

towards the Sound, the convoy was presently caught in the newly formed ice, while three of the escorting warships were wrecked. Again, in October 1810 our convoys were struck by a heavy gale, in which 150 vessels are said to have been lost. But the heaviest toll of all was that levied in 1811. In November of that year the last homeward convoy was caught by a strong north-westerly gale in which a number of vessels either ran aground or foundered. The following month, when the Baltic squadron sailed for England, the *St. George* and the *Defence* drove on the shoals of Jutland with the loss of all their crews except eighteen survivors, and the *Hero* ran upon the Haak Sand, off the Texel, with the loss of the whole ship's company. The disasters of 1811 cost the Service three fine ships and the lives of 2,000 officers and men.[5] It was the worst catastrophe in our naval annals since the loss of the *Association* and several other ships of Shovell's squadron off the Isles of Scilly in 1707.

CHAPTER 13

LONDON RIVER

I N very early times London owed its exceptional importance to its geographical position as the centre of the lines of communications in the British lowlands. A broad and deep river penetrated sixty miles inland into the heart of the country—at no other point in this island was there to be found such a fortunate combination of communications. As high up the river as the site of the future London Bridge, the Thames was both tidal and navigable, and accessible to sea-going ships. Here was the first crossing of the river, and here the meeting of the principal trackways to the north and south. The broad, sheltered reaches of the Thames were not subject to excessive flooding, nor were they likely to be blocked with ice; the natural scour of the stream was in itself almost sufficient to maintain the depth of the channels. The port was situated in convenient proximity to the Continent, and accessible in all weathers, capacious and secure. Moreover, London was the only instance of a great port which was also a capital city.

In the age of sail, vessels bound to and from the Channel would use the southern approach channels to the north and south of Margate Sand, according to the time of the tide, weather conditions, and size and rig of the vessel. Ships would congregate in the Downs waiting for a favouring wind to round the North Foreland and enter the estuary. The main channel up the Thames estuary from the North Sea and Baltic ports was the King's Channel and the East and West Swin, which were fringed by extensive sandbanks, across which the tides would set strongly; particularly in fresh south-easterly winds in the latter part of the flood, at which time ships would be set to leeward by both tide and sea. Through this cause, and through ships standing in too close to the banks when tacking, and grounding when in stays, the Gunfleet and the neighbouring sands were the scene of many wrecks.

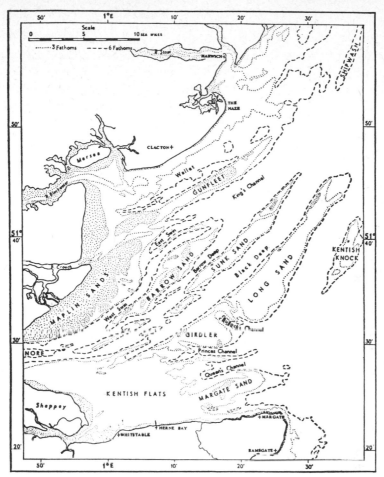

Chart of the outer banks and channels of the Thames Estuary based on the surveys of Captain Bullock, 1832–47.

The Nore was the common point of arrival and departure for vessels proceeding into or out of the Thames. From the Nore, it would depend very much upon the time of tide and force and direction of the wind by which channel a vessel should be taken.

Beyond the Sea Reach, fringed by wide estuarine marshes fronted by shoal flats, lay Gravesend, where vessels would anchor to await a favouring tide to ascend the river, or a favouring wind to put to sea. In Gravesend Reach, which was straight and deep and unimpeded by shifting banks, they would anchor by the score when strong easterly winds prevented them from getting out. All movement above Gravesend, both in and out of the river, was largely governed by the tides.

In the northern approach channels of the estuary colliers from the Tyneside ports, their canvas black with coal dust, would occasionally be seen in considerable numbers. William Hutchinson, a contemporary authority on seamanship and navigation, who had served in one of these colliers in his youth, claimed that mariners brought up in this hard school were 'the most perfect in working and managing their ships in narrow, intricate, and difficult channels, and in tide ways'. In the navigation from Newcastle to London, he declared, most of the passage was among dangerous shoals and intricate channels; and the colliers were so large that to get them safely and expeditiously through these shallow waters, and to make so many voyages in the course of the year, required an exact knowledge of the sands on that part of the coast, and of the tides. Wages were paid by the voyage; and the small crews managed their vessels with admirable skill, turning to windward against westerly winds through narrow and shoal channels.[1] Losses were so few in proportion to the large number of ships employed in the trade that the owners generally preferred to carry the risk themselves and thereby save insurance.

The larger colliers were ship-rigged, those of medium size were barques, and the smaller ones—under 200 tons—were brigs. (Early in the nineteenth century three-masters were gradually being replaced by brigs.) They were apple-bowed and broad-sterned, with deep and narrow squaresails. To make them draw as little water as possible, the deeply laden ships were trimmed near an even keel, and they were lightly rigged to make them easy to handle, with few hands, in working to windward in narrow channels. In fact, says Hutchinson, for sailing by the wind, and turning well to windward, no ships of equal burthen could match them.[2]

Gales and contrary winds were often the cause of large fleets of colliers snowballing and sailing together, each vessel striving to outsail the other, to get first to market with her coals, or for her turn to load at Newcastle, where there were sometimes 200 or 300 ships working to windward, and sailing out of that harbour in one tide. The entrance to the Tyne being so narrow, with the dangerous Sparrowhawk rocks on one side, and the Herd sand on the other, with a shoal bar across, where the sea at times ran very high, the utmost dexterity and resource were demanded. The sight of so many ships, passing and crossing each other in so little time and room, is said to have made a certain French gentleman of rank throw up his hands and exclaim, 'that it was there that France was conquered'—so greatly impressed was he at such an exhibition of consummate seamanship.[3]

On approaching the outer banks of the Thames estuary they would stand as close in with the shore as safety would permit at the first making of the windward tide and stand to the offing during the latter part of it; and by so doing would often beat through the King's Channel against fresh contrary winds that kept other ships wind-bound.

When they turned to windward up the Swin in dark, hazy weather they would know by their soundings that they were in the fairway, and what side of the channel they were on; and by standing right across the main channel they would avoid the danger of falling into swatchways where the tide runs through and where the soundings at the entrance are the same as in the main channel: which is the reason why, with a fair wind and hazy weather, a compass course was not to be relied upon.

> Their management in working these large ships to windward, up most parts of *London* river with their mainsails set is likewise remarkable, and, from their great practice, knowing the depth of water according to the time of tide, and how much the ship will shoot a-head in stays, they stand upon each tack to the greatest nicety close from side to side as far as possible things will admit of to keep in a fair way, and where eddies occasion the true tide to run very narrow, or ships, &c. lie in the way so as not to give room to turn to windward, they very dexterously brail up mainsail and foresail, and drive to windward with the tide under their topsails by such rules as have been described; and in the pool where there is so little room to pass thro' such crowds of ships, their management has afforded me the greatest pleasure, to see when they get near their designed birth, to what a nicety they let go their anchor, veer out the cable to run freely as occasion may require, so as to bring the ship up exactly in time in surprising little room, clear of the other ships, and lay her easily and fairly along side of the tier of ships where they moor, so that, as they say, they can work and lay their ships to a boat's length occasionally. And there is no doubt but that to shorten the voyage, by which the men are paid, occasions this extraordinary industry, and dexterous management, every man for his own interest here exerting himself, encouraging and striving to get before and excel each other, in doing the necessary duty. When it happens that the ships come a-ground, they readily first carry out a catch [kedge] anchor and towline, and if that is deficient, they haul out a bower anchor by it, to heave the ship off.[4]

In Long Reach, above Gravesend, these colliers would often be moored in tiers, each waiting its turn to work up the busy waterway, employing every resource of seamanship to turn their large ships to windward under their grimy topsails—sometimes a stern-board, sometimes a long tack, backing and filling broadside on to the tide, dropping an anchor when necessary, breaking it out again and drifting upwards as soon as an opportunity offered itself. For many miles in either direction the Thames at such times would be crowded with shipping, doggedly working, hour after hour, towards the distant dome of St. Paul's, which loomed to the westward above the river and the marshlands.

'In heaving up their anchor briskly', Hutchinson declared, 'they greatly excell other merchant ships.' He had discovered by experience that seven men from a collier were able to heave up the anchor in a quarter of the time that it used to be done by eighteen men: 'and this difference', he went on to say, 'was entirely owing to their dexterity, learn'd by great practice; they rise with their handspikes, and heave exactly all together with a regular brisk motion, which unites their powers into one. And they are equally brisk and clever in warping, or transporting a ship with ropes, and likewise in handing, reefing and steering, &c.'[5]

A particular tribute was paid, by another contemporary authority, to the fine seamanship of the small collier brigs, which were of but half the tonnage of the large collier ships. The former usually hailed from the lesser coal ports of the north-east coast, such as Sunderland and Blyth. 'On their arrival in Yarmouth roads they meet with a strong gale at south west, quite in their teeth, and if for London, the whole way from the roads is buoyed in by sands, and a very intricate navigation, those also going round the Kent shore are buoyed in by sands. Notwithstanding this, if these small vessels can but carry double reefed topsails, they will tide it away. I have many times stood at the North and South Foreland, and viewed the astonishing seamanship of those Sunderland and Blyth vessels in a gale of wind.'[6]

It was no wonder that, in war-time, the crews of these colliers were regarded as first-rate material for the Navy.

London River was the busiest, most crowded highway in the kingdom. 'The whole River, in a Word, from *London Bridge* to *Blackwall*, is one great *Arsenal*, nothing in the World can be like it,' wrote Defoe, adding that, 'That Part of the River which is properly the Harbour, and where the Ships usually deliver or unload their Cargoes, is called the *Pool*, and begins at the turning of the River out of *Limehouse* Reach, and extends to the *Custom-house* Keys: In this Compass I have had the Curiosity to count the Ships as well as I could, *en passant*, and have found above Two Thousand Sail of all Sorts, not reckoning Barges, Lighters, or Pleasure-Boats, and Yachts; but of vessels that really go to sea.' Except—and that only in lesser degree—in Amsterdam, this was a spectacle without parallel anywhere in Europe. It is recorded that in 1728 no less than 1,839 foreign-going merchant ships entered the Port of London, as well as 6,837 British coasters. The only docks then in existence were those of the King's yard at Deptford and the single dock at Blackwall used by the ships of the East India Company. As to the rest, for unloading the incoming, and loading the outgoing vessels, there were about 140 wherries and 2,000 lighters, barges, billy-boys, and other small craft.

Parallel with the Pool was Wapping High Street, one of the busiest of the riverside thoroughfares, which would usually be thronged with wagons loading and unloading. Wapping was for centuries the abode of the armies of watermen who served the Pool, and the haunt of the sailormen from near and far and the harpies who preyed on them. Hard by the Pool were the banks, offices, warehouses, and other business premises of the City, the centre of the trade and wealth of the kingdom. Two miles to the westward lay Westminster and the Court of St. James. On the north bank of the river, between Parliament Stairs and London Bridge, there were at least thirty places where watermen waited with their craft to carry passengers along or across the Thames.

Despite the ravages of the Plague and the Fire in 1665 and 1666 respectively, the growth of London in power, opulence, and population had continued throughout the seventeenth, and the early part of the eighteenth centuries without a check. Owing to its great wealth, wrote Sir John Reresby, the city after the Fire was 'rebuilded most stately with brick (the greatest part being before nothing but lath and lime) in four or five years' time'.

By the beginning of the eighteenth century London contained well over a tenth of all the inhabitants of England. Her nearest rivals, which were Bristol and Norwich, possessed only a small fraction of her population. Bristol alone was the centre of a trading system altogether independent of London, disposing of the American goods she imported through her carriers and agents. Elsewhere in the kingdom the operations of commerce, both home and overseas, were largely controlled from the capital.

'London, which sucks the vitals of Trade in this Island to itself', as Defoe had declared in his *Tour through Great Britain*, had by now supplanted Amsterdam as the chief centre of the world's commerce. 'The Keys, or Wharfs, next the River, fronting not the Custom House only, but the whole space from the Tower Stairs, or dock, to the Bridge, ought to be taken Notice of as a publick Building, nor are they less an Ornament to the City, as they are a Testimony of the Vast Trade carried on in it, than the Royal Exchange itself.' And besides being an unrivalled entrepôt, London was also a great manufacturing centre, whose innumerable crafts and industries attracted a wide range of commodities from near and far—iron, copper, timber, hides, tallow, wax, paints, indigo, kaolin, hemp, wool, silk, linen, cotton, calico, and other stuffs.

Of the total imports of Great Britain, London's share amounted to
upwards of 80 per cent; and of the total exports, to nearly 74 per cent.
Incomparably the greatest port in the kingdom, London now practically
monopolized the trade with India and China, as well as controlling most of
that with Europe and the Mediterranean, and sharing the American trade
with Bristol and, to a lesser degree, with Liverpool. A high proportion of
the commerce with the Port of London was carried on by the great trading
companies—the East India Company, the Russian Company, the Levant
Company, the South Sea Company, the Hudson's Bay Company.

The swarming coastal traffic of the kingdom was likewise dominated by
London. To the Thames were carried three-quarters of the coals exported
from Newcastle; vast quantities of corn from East Anglia and the southern
counties; herring and cod from Lowestoft and Yarmouth; Norwich
woollens; Cromer lobsters; butter and cheese from Ipswich; oysters from
Queenborough and Faversham; Kentish hops, pippins, runnets, and cherries
by the hoyload; Folkestone mackerel; Purbeck flags and marble, and the
white Portland stone that had been used for the building of the new St.
Paul's; Dorset ale; woollens, serges, and cider from Exeter and Topsham;
Cheddar, and other West Country cheeses; Cornish tin, lead, and copper;
druggets, cantaloons, mixed cloths, and other stuffs from Bristol; Welsh
oats; Cheshire cheese and salt; hides and wool from Cumberland; Scottish
salmon. From innumerable ports, great and small, up and down the coast,
came the unending stream of ships, supplying London with food, fuel, and
raw material.

In this busy coastwise traffic, which, in the days before railways, canals, or
macadamized highways, was of immense economic importance, the largest
type of vessel engaged was the Newcastle collier. The coal industry
throughout the period under review was continually expanding. 'This trade
is so considerable', Defoe observed, 'that it is esteemed the great Nursery for
our best Seamen.'

The incorporation in 1514 of Trinity House 'of Deptford Strond' as a guild
of pilots, entrusted with certain rights and responsibilities, was a landmark in
the history of the Port of London. Similar corporations were set up, in the
reign of Henry VIII, at Newcastle and Hull; but the one at Deptford was
always the most important. As the number and tonnage of vessels entering
and leaving the Thames had increased, so had the number of skilled and
experienced pilots required for the intricate navigation of the river and
estuary. The Corporation of Trinity House, together with the organization
of the pilots of the Cinque Ports, provided a pilotage service that was a factor
of the utmost importance in the expansion of the Port of London.

From the earliest times, it would appear from a statute of 1566, that 'certain steeples, woods, and other marks' had served as navigational aids for mariners sailing for 'the port and river of Thames'. On account of the intricacy of the channels which threaded the extensive network of sands impeding the estuary, sea-marks were a necessity on this part of the coast; and it was the province of the Corporation of Trinity House systematically to construct, erect, and overhaul 'such, and so many beacons, marks, and signs for the sea' in the Thames estuary; the cost of their erection and maintenance being met out of the shipping dues which the Corporation was entitled to levy. 'In these coastes', the Mariner's Mirror truly observed in 1588, 'is very great traffique.' Six years later the rights of beaconage and buoyage, and ballastage in the Thames, were transferred from the Lord High Admiral to Trinity House. In the latter part of the sixteenth century there was a marked improvement in the beaconage and buoyage of the river.

For centuries shipping usually proceeded as far as possible by way of channels nearer the shore, within sight of various sea-marks, such as steeples, woods, and clumps of trees. These were far more important to the mariner, in fact, than the few primitive lights which then existed. The twin spires of Reculver church on the Kentish shore were very highly esteemed 'as marks whereby they avoid certaine sands and shelues [shallows] in the mouth of the Tamis', being visible even with fog overlaying the neighbouring waters. But as the tonnage of vessels frequenting the estuary substantially increased, there was a natural tendency for them to move to deeper and more seaward channels, which were often out of sight of the accustomed marks. Thus to avoid the Kentish Flats large vessels like the East Indiamen were compelled to follow the King's Channel on their way to London from the Downs, necessitating a considerable detour. In the course of the Stuart era Trinity House placed a number of buoys along the main channels as an aid to navigation.

After the Restoration the Corporation of Trinity House continued to advance in authority and status. The commerce of London was materially fostered by the development of an adequate pilotage service and by the marking of the channels in the estuary with buoys and beacons.[7] Trinity House in fact had a much better record with regard to the buoyage and beaconage of the Thames than it had in respect of the provision of lighthouses. How important were the buoys, beacons, and sea-marks to the mariner may be seen from the drastic measures to remove them when there was danger of a hostile descent up the Thames. This occurred several times in the sixteenth and seventeenth centuries.

It was a very old usage that foreign vessels were obliged to take on board

English pilots when bound for the Thames. The object of the custom was to prevent foreigners from becoming too well acquainted with the channels and sands, which it was intended should remain a closely guarded secret. (The successful passage of the Medway by the Dutch, in 1667, had underlined the lesson.) A charter of James II accordingly granted the Corporation full power and authority to forbid any alien or stranger born to sail in any English vessel coming into or going out of the River Thames. For many years to come foreign vessels were prohibited from entering the Thames without an English pilot.[8]

The unique position attained by Trinity House was fortified and extended by the Pilotage Acts passed during the eighteenth and nineteenth centuries. Two supervisors of Pilotage were rendered necessary by the improved and greatly extended system of pilotage now embracing all the coasts of the kingdom. Four Brethren of the Trinity formed the examining Committee for Masters in the Navy and Pilots.

In the final quarter of the eighteenth century an eminent authority on seamanship and coastal navigation, William Hutchinson, thus explained what was expected of a pilot.

> A Pilot's qualifications should as much as possible be every way equal to the dangers and difficulties that attend his navigation, and should know where the shoals extend to a great distance, and where the channels are narrow, intricate, and shallow, where and when exposed to dangerous waves, where life as well as property being at risk. None should be admitted to this important charge, but such as from experience and practice can give a ready verbal account of the course and distance from one place to another, the flowing and setting of the tides, depth of water, land marks, buoys, beacons, lights, &c.[9]

From time to time in particular surveys of the coast and of coastal waters became essential. The lighthouses, light vessels, and every variation of the sands were carefully inspected and reported on by a committee of the Corporation proceeding in the Trinity House yacht. The buoys and beacons marked out the limits of particular sands fringing particular channels and served as a guide to keep vessels in the fairway. The examination and buoyage of new channels, or improving the marks, buoyage, and beaconage of the old, were one of the most important duties of the Corporation. The attempts to improve these aids to the difficult and intricate navigation of the estuary were so many as to tax the resources of every Brother who ever filled the office of Buoy Warden.

In 1774 a survey carried out by Graeme Spence in collaboration with Murdoch Mackenzie resulted in the southern approach route formerly in use past Reculver Cliffs and across the Kentish Flats to the Nore being abandoned for a deeper and more seaward channel which had been revealed by their survey, named Queen's Channel. It was buoyed out by Trinity House in the following year. Towards the end of the century the examination of the northern approach route to the Thames was taken in hand by Spence, who surveyed the passage through the King's Channel and East Swin and thence over the swatch-way into the West Swin. As a result of Spence's work in opening up new approach routes to the Thames, the three main channels leading through the banks were, the North Channel (Swin); a central channel known as the Nub, Nobb, or Knob; and the southern, or Queen's Channel.[10] During the mutiny at the Nore in 1797 the government ordered all the buoys and beacons in the Nub and Queen's Channels to be removed, which effectually cut off the escape of the rebel fleet.

The buoyage of the outer channels proceeded rapidly in the latter part of the Georgian era. The number of buoys and beacons maintained by Trinity House in 1684 was 16, and in 1776 it had only increased to 21; but by 1816 the number had more than trebled, and there were 65 buoys situated between the South Foreland, Orfordness, and Gravesend.

The Buoy Warden (who, with the Rental Warden, ranked next to the Master and his Deputy) was charged with the immediate superintendence of all the buoyage and beaconage. This entailed the examination of all the channels, and the placing and replacing of the buoys and beacons; in the discharge of these particular duties he had to be himself at sea on frequent occasions; the charge of the Corporation's yachts was in his keeping, as well as the lightships, with all their establishments, equipment, and stores, and, of course, the buoys.[11]

To sum up: at the close of the Georgian era the sunken beacons (such as Gunfleet, Whitaker, Shoe) were relatively few: but the buoys placed in the various channels of the estuary were very numerous, to serve the needs of the considerable volume of shipping which already frequented those channels, as well as the far greater volume of traffic which was to ply to and from London River in the ensuing decades.

On the verge of the Revolutionary and Napoleonic Wars, London River was still the main highway of British trade. On these waters plied the busiest and most lucrative traffic in the world. It has been estimated that the average number of entries and departures from the Thames amounted to something between 13,000 and 14,000 annually; two-thirds of which passed through the Channel and the remainder trafficked in the North Sea and the Baltic. London River carried more than half the total commerce of the entire country.

British shipping was now three times more numerous than that of France, her great rival. British registered tonnage, which in 1702 had amounted to rather more than a quarter of a million tons had, by 1773, almost trebled; and by 1793 it had again practically doubled. It continued to expand throughout the Revolutionary and Napoleonic Wars.

If in the latter half of the eighteenth century British trade with Holland and the Peninsula was declining in comparative importance, that of the 'Atlantic triangle' was substantially increasing. The British recovery after the disastrous war of 1778–83 had been rapid and in the ensuing decade of peace our imports and exports rose by more than 50 per cent. With the increasing use of the new machinery British industry was entering on a phase of progressive and unparalleled expansion. 'Our good old island', Aukland had lately remarked to Grenville, 'now possesses an accumulation of prosperity beyond any example in the history of the world.'

Into the Thames estuary came shipping from every part of the globe, carrying cargoes of colonial produce both for home consumption and for the re-export trade, foodstuffs for the rapidly growing population of this country which her own soil could no longer support in full, as well as raw materials for her busy manufactories; East Indiamen bringing tea, spices, pepper, silks, muslins, nankeens, cottons, calicoes, porcelain, saltpetre, and drugs; West Indiamen with sugar, rum, coffee, cocoa, ginger, and tobacco; Yankee packets with rice, corn, tobacco, and raw cotton; sturdily built ships of the Hudson's Bay Company with furs and skins; deep-laden whalers from the Arctic and South Seas with rich cargoes of train-oil; brigs and snows from the Baltic with grain, timber, naval stores, iron, linen, and hemp; wine-ships from the Peninsula, Madeira, and the Canaries; topsail schooners with citrons and other fruits from Smyrna and the ports of Greece.

The West Indian trade, being essentially a seasonal one and employing large fleets, was a major cause of congestion in the Thames. Another trade which tended to congest the river was the timber trade to the Baltic and Norway. At least half the timber fleet, comprising about 400 ships, would arrive with a cargo of logs. These logs, when rafted in the river, would occupy ten times the space of each ship. There was also the arrival, in war-time, of large convoys. But the traffic which caused the greatest congestion of all was the coal trade. The collier fleet had increased enormously during the seventeenth century; and it went on increasing. By 1750 the coal exported to London from the Tyne exceeded half a million tons. By the turn of the century the figure had risen to a million tons. There were times when close on a hundred colliers would be discharging simultaneously in the Pool; since each ship discharged into a dozen lighters, more than a thousand of these craft would be jamming the river at one time. When delayed by gales or foul winds in the Tyne, Humber, or Yarmouth roads, the colliers would come crowding on directly the wind turned fair—sometimes from five to seven hundred of them swarming up the river at a time. On the other hand, there would occasionally be a sudden, rapid clearance when a crowd of merchant vessels would sweep down from London on the ebb, or with a strong westerly wind 'so that they have, what they call fresh-way, and ships come down apace'.[12]

Between Poplar and London Bridge the river was crowded with shipping. 'The whole surface of the Thames', observed Lydia Melford, 'is covered with small vessels, barges, boats, and wherries, passing to and fro, and below the three bridges, such a prodigious forest of masts, for miles together, that you would think all the ships of the universe were here assembled.'[13] Vessels were not infrequently crowded into shoal water so that at low tide they were grounded and suffered more or less serious damage. The larger East Indiamen lay out at Deptford and Blackwall. Along the wharves lining the Pool were coasters in dozens and scores moored in tiers; but the mooring tiers would only accommodate about 600 vessels between London Bridge and Deptford, and the great majority of them perforce discharged and loaded at their moorings in the stream. They discharged into lighters, which then landed the goods at the quays. Export and import trades were jumbled together to their mutual detriment. Sometimes goods had to remain on the quays for days, exposed to all weathers. Wagons, carts, and trolleys conveyed the goods direct to the merchants or to public warehouses situated in the neighbouring streets. The narrow thoroughfares leading off Thames Street were often jammed with traffic and added to the congestion all around the quays.

This part of the city and its environs swarmed with seamen and watermen. Both ashore and afloat there were likely hands for the taking. London River without question represented one of the Navy's most prolific sources of man-power in time of war. From it the press drew some of their most notable hauls. Here were to be found many of the large trading fleets on their return from overseas: East and West Indiamen, the Mediterranean, Peninsular, North Sea, and Baltic convoys, as well as colliers and other coasting vessels, and the local fishing fleets. Periodically the press-gangs combed the teeming streets and lanes of London's 'sailor town' in search of seamen and were seldom disappointed.

The period 1802–15 was marked by an enormous expansion of the dockyard accommodation of the Port of London. Below the Bridge the bends of the river and extensive gravel banks greatly facilitated the construction of

An elevated view of the new dock at Wap

docks. The windings of the Thames enabled entrances to be formed at each end of them. The gravelly subsoil of the area was readily excavated and provided a firm foundation for the walls. The progress of civil engineering had by now made possible the construction of docks on an unprecedented scale.

To provide a spacious new dock system for a highly lucrative trade, the West India merchants in 1795 opened a subscription for funds and in two days raised a capital of £800,000. The West India Docks were opened in 1802 in the presence of a distinguished gathering which included the Prime Minister, Henry Addington. The new system consisted of two docks, parallel to each other—one for imports and the other for exports—formed across the neck of the Isle of Dogs, with entrance locks and basins at each end. The West India Docks occupied an area of 95 acres and provided accommodation for 600 vessels of from 300 to 500 tons. Shipping would enter the locks at the seaward end of the system: lighters would enter at the

other end, and were thereby saved the three miles' passage round the Isle of Dogs. The docks were equipped with cranes and winches for the swifter unloading of cargoes. For the safe storage of vast quantities of valuable goods, a line of warehouses—the finest and largest of their time—were erected, extending for nearly three-quarters of a mile. The docks were surrounded by a high wall, with a guardhouse flanking the entrance.

Towards the end of 1805 the London Dock was constructed at Wapping 'for the greater accommodation and security of shipping, commerce, and revenue within the Port of London'. The new system, which was intended for the reception of wine, brandy, and tobacco, stretched across the first bend of the river below London Bridge. It was therefore within much shorter distance of the City. It was provided with fine brick warehouses, five storeys high, occupying an area of five acres. 'The great tobacco warehouse', wrote McCulloch, 'is the largest, finest, and most convenient building of its sort in the world. It is calculated to contain 24,000 hogsheads of tobacco, and covers the immense space of *five* acres!'[14] Below this warehouse lay a range of spacious vaults for the secure stowage of wine and spirits.

The following year saw the completion of the East India Docks—comprising an import and an export dock, as well as a broad entrance basin connecting the docks with the river—covering in all an area of 31 acres. In this case there was no necessity to erect warehouses in the docks, as the East India Company already possessed large warehouses of its own in the city, to which the goods could be conveyed in closed and locked wagons. The opening of the new East India Dock was reported in the *Globe* on 4 August 1806.

> Yesterday this ceremony so auspicious to the increasing commerce and prosperity of the British Empire, took place according to previous announcement. Several thousand tickets had been distributed on the occasion to the India stock proprietors and their friends by order of the directors, as well as to a very numerous circle of the nobility and gentry in town, who, aware of the splendour and vivacity which distinguish every exhibition connected with the new prosperity of this country, were, of course extremely solicitous to obtain orders for admission to this scene. Shortly before two, the signal of the Royal salute was fired from six pieces of flying artillery, being the regimental guns of the Company's Volunteers, for the destined ships to enter at the time of flood; immediately upon which the elegant little yacht of the Trinity House, decked to her masthead in the naval finery of flags and streamers of all nations, led into the basin in a very elegant style, followed by the 'Admiral Gardner', East Indiaman, with the British anchor at her fore-topmasthead, the Royal Standard at her main, and the Union Flag at her mizen; and displaying from the lower rigging the colours of all nations, the French under all. As she passed in, she answerd the salute of the Artillery by firing her minute guns, while the company's band, on her quarter-deck, played 'Rule, Britannia' with full chorus from the ladies and gentlemen who crowded her decks. Among the accommodations prepared for the greater security and better convenience of their trade, through the medium of this dock, appeared 60 closed carriages, or light wagons, each mounted on four wheels and capable of conveying 50 chests of tea each from the landing to their stores at the India House, which will place the whole trade under the immediate care of their own servants. An elegant dinner was given in the evening by the directors at the London Tavern.

The original route from Poplar to the city, by way of the Ratcliff Highway, was narrow and over-crowded; but after the formation of the East and West India Docks the two Companies began to build a new road—the Commercial Road—to carry the vastly increased traffic.

Tolls were levied in this thoroughfare until the abolition of turnpikes.

On the south side of the river, at the Rotherhithe bend, the Commercial Dock Company, formed in 1807, proceeded to enlarge the old Greenland Dock for the accommodation of shipping laden with timber and grain. In 1813 the Commercial Dock was completed.

Towards the end of the period under review, the St. Katherine Dock, designed by Thomas Telford, consisted of two small docks and a basin, occupying a total area of ten acres. The docks were surrounded by wide and commodious quays and by high warehouses which projected over the quays so that the fronts of the warehouses were flush with the edge of the docks, thereby enabling goods to be transferred directly into any floor of the warehouses. The St. Katherine Dock, which was opened in 1828, was the nearest of any of the docks to the Custom House and other centres of commerce. After the St. Katherine Dock no further docks were opened until the middle of the century.

The new system of docks made it possible for much of the shipping to leave the river and dispensed with the need for immense fleets of lighters. The separation of the shipping and lighter traffic greatly relieved the congestion in the Thames. The provision of warehouses secured costly goods against the operations of the resourceful and ingenious thieves with which the river abounded; moreover, these edifices enabled a system of bonded warehouses to be introduced, under which goods were permitted to remain without payment of duty. This was a development of the greatest importance; for London was now the principal depot for colonial and tropical produce and carried on an immense entrepôt trade.

The docks proved adequate to the needs of London throughout the following half-century. The Thames was patrolled by constables and the docks were guarded by sentries. (A Marine Police Force had been established, in 1798, with its headquarters at Wapping New Stairs.) As a result of all these measures the depredations of the water-thieves, which had previously been on the greatest scale—according to Colquhoun's calculations the losses in 1798 totalled more than £½ million—were for the most part put a stop to. The matter was thus summed up by a contemporary authority:

And among the results were, that watermen were no longer to be observed hanging about as during their discharge; none of those infamous transactions with receivers, which are detailed in the Parliamentary Report before quoted, were then to be found, whereby the before mentioned horrible pillage took place, and all the opulent and inferior receivers of twelve classes, who quickly moved off, and the mates, lumpers, coopers, scuffle-hunters, long-apron men, bum-boat men and women, river pirates, light horsemen, mud-larks, rat-catchers, and other depredators, vulgarly called tag, rag and bobtail, with all their skilful appendages of jiggers, bladders with nozzles, pouches, bags, sacks, pockets, &c., whose departments and uses are so ably defined and described by Colquhoun, were no longer to be seen surrounding them at dusk and at low water.[15]

~~~~~~

CHAPTER 14

LLOYD'S

IN the reign of James II an enterprising coffee-house keeper called Edward Lloyd set to work to collect and post up information for the particular benefit of the shipping interest. By so doing he gradually built up a flourishing business. Six years later, in 1692, Lloyd's Coffee-House in Lombard Street, in the heart of Mercantile London, had become a favourite rendezvous of merchants, shipowners, and shipmasters desirous of obtaining the latest intelligence concerning shipping and foreign trade. References to Lloyd's Coffee-House are to be found in the contemporary issues of the *Tatler* and *Spectator*; Steele mentions as one of the distinctive features of the establishment the pulpit from which auction sales were conducted and shipping news read out; and for a few months in the year 1697–8 the proprietor published a sheet known as *Lloyd's News* which contained shipping and other news. By experimenting with novel methods of signalling and other ingenious devices Lloyd endeavoured to secure for his clients prompt and accurate information of the shipping in the Thames, reports of casualties, and other marine intelligence. After his death, in 1713, the business continued to prosper under his successors. Sam's Coffee-House, which in the opening years of the century had been a rival to Lloyd's, gradually dropped out of the running. The fame and popularity of Lloyd's Coffee-House in Lombard Street steadily increased. Throughout the eighteenth century sales of ships were generally held at Lloyd's, which was now the recognized resort of ship-brokers.

At the outset, and for a good many years after, Lloyd's was not exclusively concerned with underwriting, but with ship-broking and foreign trade generally. It is in fact unknown when underwriting actually began at Lloyd's, but as the century advanced the business done in the crowded

Poster advertising the sale of a ship 'by the candle' on 12 August 1761. In the early eighteenth century the largest part of Lloyd's business was composed of auctions during which bidding continued as long as a selected piece of candle burned.

Coffee-Room became more and more connected with purely maritime affairs, particularly marine insurance. Instead of going from office to office in search of underwriters, those who desired to take out policies against maritime risks found it more convenient to go to a coffee-house where they could expect to meet, not one, but a number of insurers. There were men of substance who were ready to underwrite policies against risks at sea. Merchants who wished to insure their goods knew that at a certain hour they could count on meeting a wide choice of underwriters at Lloyd's. At a somewhat later period the underwriters frequenting the Coffee-House formed themselves into an association known as Lloyd's.

Owing to the steady increase of our overseas trade, the age of Walpole witnessed a progressive expansion in the volume of marine insurance undertaken, and in the number of marine underwriters, in this country. It was to satisfy the demand of the underwriting interest for shipping intelligence that in 1734 there appeared *Lloyd's List*, the precursor of the modern *Lloyd's Register*. The object of *Lloyd's List* was to publish all the arrivals and departures in overseas trade at the principal British ports.

As early as the War of 1739-48 Lloyd's was sometimes able to send the first news of an important victory to the government. Thus the Coffee-House was first in this way with the tidings of Vernon's capture of Porto Bello in 1739 and of Anson's action off Finisterre in 1747. In this way there gradually grew up a close and cordial co-operation between Lloyd's and the Admiralty which has continued down to the present day.

From 1771 onward Lloyd's was governed by a Committee elected by the subscribers. Three years later the corporation of underwriters established itself in the Royal Exchange, where it was to remain for more than a century and a half. The new premises were fitted out as a Coffee-House, but at the expense of the subscribers. By the time of the move the number of the subscribers was steadily increasing, and they were now really in control of Lloyd's. At the turn of the century the elected Committee of Lloyd's received the power of choosing the subscribers of whom it approved and refusing those to whom it objected. For the future the word 'members' was used in place of 'subscribers'. In 1804 official correspondence which had hitherto passed through the hands of the masters of the Coffee-House was transferred to the Secretary of the Committee.

About the same time the first daily record of ships lost and ships safely arrived in port began to be kept. The large volume, bound in green vellum, instituted for this purpose, was familiarly known as 'The Book'. The important news service maintained by Lloyd's was the essential clue to its remarkable popularity among underwriters. As a clearing house of marine intelligence it was, indeed, unique.

Lloyd's Subscription Room at the Royal Exchange; engraving from Ackermann's Microcosm of London.

At other coffee-houses in the City they could no doubt get business accommodation free of rent. They need only frequent the places and spend a little money on food and drink to have a roof over their heads, pen, ink, and paper, a table to sit at and a fire to keep them warm. But at Lloyd's they got, as well, the best available news service about the world's shipping, messages from the Admiralty and from every British port, gossip brought by homeward-bound skippers from every part of the world in which they might be interested, and reports of casualties at the moment when they first reached London. With all these attractions to offer—negligible working expenses, the first cut at the news and the first show of the brokers' risks—it is not surprising that Lloyd's drew the underwriters like a magnet, and proved far too much for the cumbrous heavily capitalized chartered companies. The attractions were all considerable, but the greatest of the three was the news service. It was on that rock that Lloyd's was built.[1]

The increasing wealth and expanding organization of Lloyd's enabled it to stand the strain of the long years of war with France in the latter half of the eighteenth century. It is hardly too much to say that, without such an organization, the continued expansion of British trade and shipping in those years would have been impossible. In the same way the French wars gave a tremendous impetus to the business done at Lloyd's.

Shortly after the move to the Royal Exchange the War of American Independence broke out. The revolt of the American colonies later merged in a general maritime war in which this country found itself confronted by a formidable coalition. The struggle has been well described as 'the greatest ordeal in the history of marine underwriting'. The subscribers were subjected to losses which strained their resources to the limit. In August 1780 the greater part of the combined East and West Indies convoy, outward bound, was taken by the enemy. The loss was estimated at approximately £1½ million. Coming as it did on top of earlier losses, it was the heaviest single stroke at British trade since the loss of the Smyrna convoy in 1692. A large number of underwriters failed. Even long after, in the Napoleonic War, the disaster of 1780 was still remembered as the blackest hour in the history of Lloyd's. However, notwithstanding these grievous losses Lloyd's emerged from the ordeal with unimpaired credit and prestige.

The steady increase in the number and wealth of the subscribers of Lloyd's towards the turn of the century reflected the rapid expansion of seaborne commerce and of the capital available for its protection. The interval of peace between the American and the French Revolutionary Wars was on the whole a period of mounting prosperity; and this prosperity was carried over into the era of the long struggle against the French Republic and Empire. Lloyd's advanced rapidly in wealth and importance. High premiums had to be paid for the vastly increased volume of trade and shipping. Great fortunes were to be made by marine insurance. Merchants and financiers of high repute and ample resources were eager to share in these gains. The result was that very large insurances indeed could now be effected at Lloyd's.

A minor development at Lloyd's which is worth noticing is that the Coffee-Room had become so well patronized by shipmasters that it was already beginning to be referred to as 'The Captains' Room'.

The continued expansion of business called for additional accommodation. Shortly before the outbreak of the Revolutionary War there was a significant extension of the premises of Lloyd's. 'The new room just opened at this Coffee house,' announced the *Public Advertiser* in July 1791, 'for the use of the Underwriters, is in style of furnishing, and point of elegance, the first in the Kingdom; connected as it is with the other three, the *tout ensemble* forms the most perfect suite of any in Europe appropriated to commercial purposes. . . . In this room the daring hand of the Underwriter, with pen and paper, is to brave the united force of Neptune and Boreas.'

At the same time a process of weeding-out accompanied the expansion of maritime insurance business. Lloyd's in some degree represented the survival of the fittest. The weaklings went to the wall. How great the risks sometimes were may be gathered from the fact that one underwriter, Robert Sheddon, was obliged to pay out losses of £190,000.[2]

What is at first sight almost incredible is that anyone who had access to the room was free to write what he liked, without regard to his means or standing. The underwriters crowded round the tables comprised all sorts and conditions of men, from penniless, nameless clerks to some of the wealthiest and best-known merchants in Europe. What, however, in the main served as a cushion against bad debts—and did so very effectively—was the long credit which underwriters gave to brokers. In practice, therefore, the system worked remarkably well.[3] At any rate it is clear from the findings of the Parliamentary Commission of 1810 that failures were few and far between. The security of a Lloyd's policy during this period was very good. It attracted a large marine insurance business from all over the world.

Conditions in the Revolutionary and Napoleonic Wars were such as to demand a degree of caution, knowledge, and experience which no ordinary merchant could be expected to possess. As Joseph Marryat (Chairman of the Committee of Lloyd's and father of the novelist) declared in the House of Commons in 1810: 'He must be informed of the safety or danger of every port and road in every part of the world; of the nature of the navigation to and from every country; and of the proper season for undertaking different voyages; he should be acquainted, not only with the state, but the stations of the naval force of his own country, and of the enemy; he should watch the appearances of any change in the relations of all foreign powers, by which his foreign interests may be affected; and in short, constantly devote much time and attention to the pursuit in which he is engaged.'[4]

Though the State as yet made no provision for those who suffered by the war, Lloyd's initiated a series of subscriptions for their benefit, which culminated in the Patriotic Fund. This was launched in July 1803 after a general meeting of members of Lloyd's, more largely attended than any on record, in the course of which it was unanimously agreed to establish a fund 'for the Encouragement and Relief of those who may suffer in the Common Cause, and of those who may signalize themselves during the present most important contest'. The proposal excited immense enthusiasm throughout the country and brought in donations amounting to upwards of £20,000 within a few days. Subscriptions poured in from the highest and the lowest. The Bank of England and the East India Company each contributed £5,000, the City of London £2,500. The City companies, members of Lloyd's, and certain private individuals distinguished themselves by their extreme generosity. Some theatres donated the entire receipts of a night's performance. What was truly touching and impressive was the enormous number of small contributors, many of them anonymous, like the 'three Watermen of Shadwell Dock Stairs', 'A Journeyman Shoemaker', 'A Maidservant', 'A Labourer', etc. The Patriotic Fund became henceforth a national undertaking; though it remained, in effect, under the control of members of Lloyd's. It did much to alleviate the hard lot of the families of those killed in the war; and the work it did was greatly appreciated in the Services. Highly valued by the recipients, too, were the medals and swords which were awarded from time to time. It is not too much to say that it was essentially the Patriotic Fund which during this era made Lloyd's a familiar name throughout the length and breadth of the kingdom.

In the course of the eighteenth century, as has been said, Lloyd's had built up a unique and unrivalled system of shipping intelligence, which was further extended, during the Napoleonic War, by John Bennett the younger, who, in 1804, was appointed Secretary to the Committee. In 1811 the Committee established a system of agents throughout the world which provided the members with a continuous supply of news about the movements of ships. Intelligence of arrivals and departures, both at home and overseas, together with other news of naval and military importance, received from these agents, was sent on immediately to the Admiralty; and the Admiralty in turn forwarded convoy lists and other useful information to Lloyd's.

The Room at the height of the Napoleonic War presented a spectacle without parallel, surely, in any other capital on earth. In this extraordinary assemblage—part coffee-house, part market—several hundred men were ensconced at small tables, and perhaps as many more crowded in the gangways. The underwriters sat in their regular places. Around them surged a bustling, jostling crowd of brokers, clerks, and attorneys. The volume of business transacted in 'Eighteen-hundred and war-time' was enormous. (The risks covered at Lloyd's during the year 1809 totalled nearly £100 million.) It had become, and was to remain, the greatest centre of marine insurance in the world.

Most of the men who were responsible for this great achievement are today quite forgotten. Some of them are remembered for activities other than the work they did at Lloyd's. A few outstanding figures, nevertheless, may be mentioned.

A View of the Baltic Walk;
caricature of Richard Thornton
of Lloyd's by Richard Dighton,
1923.

Richard Thornton was renowned throughout the City for his daring speculations in foreign loans. He was no less eminent in the field of marine insurance. Once it happened that the house of Baring Bros. had occasion to ship gold to the value of £¼ million to Russia. With the intention of spreading this great risk over the market, they first approached 'Dicky' Thornton. 'The old man took the slip, very slowly put down the figures 25, and added nought after nought till he had completed the whole sum of £250,000. Looking up and seeing an expression of consternation on the broker's face he observed, "Young man, you can show this slip to Mr. Thomas Baring and if he thinks I have taken too much you can tell him that I will deposit Exchequer Bills to that amount till the risk is run off."' It is related that in his later years 'Dicky' Thornton used to stand with his back to the fire in the Subscribers' Room 'offering all newly married members to lay a hundred to one against the contingency of twins'.[5]

John Julius Angerstein, an immigrant from the Baltic, the friend of Dr. Johnson, Garrick, Sir Joshua Reynolds, and Sir Thomas Lawrence, now at the height of his fame and influence, has some claim to be regarded as 'the father of Lloyd's'. It was Angerstein who was chiefly responsible for arranging for the premises in the Royal Exchange to be let to Lloyd's. For the future the business of marine insurance was concentrated in the new premises instead of being scattered about London. He was a man of high abilities, integrity, and experience. The policies subscribed by Angerstein were honourably known as 'Julians'.

Sir Brook Watson had been a member of the original Committee of Lloyd's set up in 1771. Already Lord Mayor of London when he became Chairman of Lloyd's, he presided over the Committee during ten years of

John Julius Angerstein; oil painting by Thomas Lawrence,
1816.

soaring prosperity and unexampled expansion (1797–1806); to Watson, indeed, must be given much of the credit for the remarkable progress achieved by Lloyd's during those years.

The work of Angerstein and Sir Brook Watson was later carried on by Joseph Marryat, who was appointed Chairman in 1811. The latter had already shown his mettle during the Parliamentary Commission of 1810, when, as the principal representative of Lloyd's in the House of Commons, he had successfully borne the brunt of the battle in the inquiry. In the ensuing years Marryat's strong and autocratic personality, combined with his hard common sense and his ability in debate, well fitted him for the task of executing certain much needed reforms in the constitution of Lloyd's; of introducing more order and regularity into the proceedings of the Committee, and of establishing and developing the agency system.

The authority and prestige of Lloyd's were such that its recommendations in every branch of trade protection—especially with regard to the convoy system—received the most careful consideration from both Admiralty and government. The Convoy Acts of 1793, 1798, and 1803 had been largely due to the influence of Lloyd's: for the experience of successive generations of underwriters had proved that convoy afforded by far the most efficacious means of trade protection, as was soon shown by a significant reduction in the insurance rates of ships under convoy; and throughout the war Lloyd's co-operated with the Admiralty in enforcing these Acts.

Thus, following the disaster to the Newfoundland convoy in 1804, Lloyd's protested indignantly against the practice of entrusting convoys of from 50 to 70 merchantmen to the protection of only one small cruiser: with the result that soon after, escorts were substantially strengthened. In 1805 a request was made by the Committee of Lloyd's to the effect that copies of coastal signals should be distributed to merchant shipping so that they might receive timely warning of an enemy's approach from the signal stations which had lately been erected along the coasts of the United Kingdom; following which the Committee made urgent representations to merchantmen 'to keep near the English coast in proceeding up Channel, otherwise the Lieutenants at the Signal Posts cannot make known to Merchant Vessels the approach of any Enemy's cruizers'.[6] In the summer of 1809, in response to a pressing appeal from Lloyd's, the Admiralty hastened to provide stronger protection for the Archangel trade, which was then under attack from the Danes.[7] In the same year the Committee of Lloyd's drew up a strongly-worded complaint concerning the very severe losses sustained in the Channel during the previous six months. The Admiralty, however, responded with a detailed defence of its system of trade protection, observing that:

> many of these ships were taken in consequence of having quitted their convoys, in direct opposition to their orders, and frequently after every possible effort had been made by the commanders of convoys, to prevent them from parting convoy. Several of these captures were also made after the convoys, to which the vessels belonged, had been dispersed by stress of weather; and it has frequently happened during the last winter, that the cruizers in the Channel have been blown from their several positions, and that the enemy's privateers have thereby been afforded an opportunity of putting to sea, and committing depredations on that part of the coast which they could fetch, before it was possible for the cruizers to get back to their stations.[8]

Not only was the convoy system organized, during the French Revolutionary and Napoleonic Wars, far more elaborately and comprehensively than ever before, but individual convoys sometimes attained very large proportions. The strength of the escort force was proportionate to the size and value of the convoy and the degree of danger to be apprehended in the area through which the convoy was passing. Generally speaking, larger convoys and stronger escort forces were the rule than in earlier wars. Convoy, supplemented by cruiser patrols in the focal areas, proved, during the wars of 1793–1815, the most effectual means of protecting the vital long-distance trades upon which the prosperity of Great Britain in the last resort depended.

~~~~~~

CHAPTER 15

THE SOCIAL BACKGROUND

THE hierarchy of the Service reflected for the most part that of society ashore. In eighteenth-century England social distinctions were taken as a matter of course; the principle of subordination was regarded as part of the natural order of things: but relations between the classes were usually friendly. Even under the severe stress of the Revolutionary and Napoleonic Wars something of the old harmony, as well as the stability, of the social order still remained. In each class there existed various significant gradations; nor were the barriers between class and class absolutely rigid and impenetrable; the English aristocracy was never a close caste like the French *noblesse*. Generally speaking, everyone in the Service who was accounted a gentleman was placed at the outset of his career on the quarter-deck and could expect in due course to become a wardroom officer. For most of the others there was small prospect of their ever rising above the lower deck—though the best of them were not infrequently made warrant officers. From the great country houses came many an admiral; from the smaller manor-houses, the parsonages, and the like, a large proportion of the captains; from the farmsteads and the modest residences of merchants and ship-owners, the masters, pursers, gunners, and other warrant officers of the Service, a few of whom attained to commissioned rank.

The influence of the English class structure upon the Georgian Navy was in some ways a valuable source of strength: in others, a somewhat serious handicap. It was unquestionably advantageous to the Service that the landed aristocracy—perhaps the strongest and ablest ruling class which the world has ever known—should send its younger sons into the Navy, as in the same way it had fostered a close alliance with commerce and industry. Nor is it to be denied that Dr. Blane's superior social status was an important element in his successful endeavours to bring about much-needed reforms in the medical service of the Navy. On the other hand, it was deplorable that those favoured at birth were enabled all too often to rise to high rank, to the exclusion of better men. This was recognized and regretted, notably by Anson and St. Vincent. Moreover, the close association between leading flag officers and the great Whig oligarchs was to have disastrous consequences in the political crisis which arose early in George III's reign.

The struggle for mastery among the groups of Whig and Tory magnates, with the influence of the Crown (it was said) not only 'increased', but still 'increasing', finally resulted in a Cabinet headed by Lord North with Sandwich as First Lord. The new ministry had few adherents in the Service. Most of the principal flag-officers were strongly opposed to the Cabinet and to the First Lord. Following Keppel's court-martial and subsequent resignation a number of opposition flag-officers flatly refused to accept commands from the existing Board of Admiralty. Both Jervis and Duncan took Keppel's part in the quarrel—one of the fiercest which ever rent the Service. The tension continued so long as Sandwich held office. The First Lord, indeed, was not popular even with men promoted by his Board.

Despite the superior advantages enjoyed by the progeny of the upper class, however, it was still possible for a man born into the middle station to rise high in the Service. This happened often enough in real life to account for the aristocratic disdain with which Sir Walter Elliot, Bt., in Jane Austen's *Persuasion*, viewed such promotions. Sir Walter and his agent, John Shepherd, were discussing Admiral Croft, the prospective tenant of the baronet's country seat, Kellynch Hall; and Sir Walter expressed grave doubts about the Navy as a career for gentlemen.

> 'The profession has its utility, but I should be sorry to see any friend of mine belonging to it.'
>
> 'Indeed!' was the reply, and with a look of surprise.
>
> 'Yes; it is in two points offensive to me; I have two strong grounds of objection to it. First, as being the means of bringing persons of obscure birth into undue distinction, and raising men to honours which their fathers and grandfathers never dreamt of; and secondly, as it cuts up a man's youth and vigour most horribly; a sailor grows old sooner than any other man. I have observed it all my life. A man is in greater danger in the navy of being insulted by the rise of one whose father, his father might have disdained to speak to, and of becoming prematurely an object of disgust himself, than in any other line. One day last spring, in town, I was in company with two men, striking instances of what I am talking of: Lord St. Ives, whose father we all know to have been a country curate, without bread to eat: I was to give place to Lord

St. Ives, and a certain Admiral Baldwin, the most deplorable-looking personage you can imagine: his face the colour of mahogany, rough and rugged to the last degree; all lines and wrinkles, nine grey hairs of a side, and nothing but a dab of powder at top. "In the name of heaven, who is that old fellow?" said I, to a friend of mine who was standing near, (Sir Basil Morley.) "Old fellow!" cried Sir Basil, "it is Admiral Baldwin. What do you take his age to be?" "Sixty," said I, "or perhaps sixty-two." "Forty," replied Sir Basil, "forty, and no more." Picture to yourself my amazement: I shall not easily forget Admiral Baldwin. I never saw quite so wretched an example of what a sea-faring life can do; but to a degree, I know it is the same with them all: they are all knocked about, and exposed to every climate, and every weather, till they are not fit to be seen. It is a pity they are not knocked on the head at once, before they reach Admiral Baldwin's age.'

There was a fairly substantial intake of future officers of the Service from the sons of the clergy. Nelson, of course, is a sufficiently familiar example; but there were plenty of others. In the autumn of 1740 Captain Thomas Smith of the *Dursley* on his way up to town from Southampton stayed at Butleigh rectory. When appointed to command the *Romney* in the following year, he took two of the rector's sons to sea with him. Both of these boys—Samuel and Alexander Hood—attained to flag-rank and were raised to the peerage.[1] Captains Francis and Frederick Austen (brothers of Jane) were likewise sons of the parsonage. They occupied much the same position in society as Captain Wentworth in their sister's novel, *Persuasion*, which sheds a revealing light on the life of naval officers ashore.

The Scottish element in the Service came mostly from the lowlands. Apart from the landed gentry, there were many prosperous business families in that part of Scotland. In Midlothian there was a substantial seafaring community, better educated than Englishmen of the same calling. These were circumstances that held out strong possibilities of advancement. Ireland was represented by the sons of the dominant social and political class, the Ascendancy, who began to be an important element in the later eighteenth century. The future Sir Courtenay Boyle, Sir Henry Blackwood, Sir Robert Stopford, and Sir Thomas Pakenham were all of Ascendancy origin. A sprinkling of Irish officers came from professional families. Between the Irish peasantry and even the smaller squireens, however, there existed an unbridgeable gulf. The former, indeed, made first-class fighting seamen; but they had virtually no chance of reaching the quarter-deck.

The presence among Nelson's 'band of brothers' of Captains Miller and Hallowell, both of whom were born in New England, serves to remind us what a severe loss to our naval strength had been sustained through the revolt of the American colonies. Before the turn of the century the ports of New England were trading to the ends of the earth; and a large share of the world's carrying trade had passed into American keeping. The tough Yankee stock bred some of the finest seamen and shrewdest merchants of their day. Their ports and fishing villages possessed a substantial mercantile fleet and a proportionately abundant seafaring population. Navigation schools abounded in the northern colonies. Successive generations of masters and mates passed through their portals. Since the Declaration of Independence, all this had been lost to the mother country and the Navy.

A further deprivation, arising out of 'old, unhappy, far-off things' and deeply engrained prejudice, was actually self-inflicted. Throughout the whole of this era a small but by no means inconsiderable minority of the aristocracy and landed gentry were debarred, on account of their religion, from serving their country as sea-officers. These were the Catholics. The more rigorous of the penal laws against their community had long been relaxed, at any rate in the larger island. But the Test Act remained in force;[2] it was impossible, of course, for a Catholic to subscribe to it; and the supply of officers was in consequence restricted to the Protestant majority.

It is always to be remembered that the professional prospects of an officer in the era under review were very largely determined by the degree of interest he could command. It was here that background and family influence played such an important part. As Stephen Martin Leake observed in his *Life of Sir John Leake*: 'The sea officer is but occasionally employed, and at other times on half-pay only; which, if he has not a good interest at the Admiralty Board, may be always being forced to make fresh application to his friends every time his ship is paid off.' The situation as it was, nearly every officer who came to the top in the Service may be shown to have possessed some initial advantage in the way of Interest.

The late Professor Michael Lewis has produced a most interesting and illuminating analysis of 'Interest'.[3] As he points out, there was Service Interest, which could be exercised by captains, admirals, and the Board of Admiralty; and there was also Non-Service Interest, comprising that of peers, M.P.s, and other influential personages. Interest of one sort or another, indeed, was not only highly important to an officer, it was virtually indispensable, if he were to 'get on'. Without the favour of the captain, an aspirant to a naval career could not even reach the quarter-deck. Without Interest (particularly in peace-time), however promising an officer might be, his prospects of promotion were slender. Hawke owed much of his success in early life to one of his uncles, Colonel Martin Bladen—a good example of Non-Service Interest. The Hoods were brought on by Captain (later Admiral) Smith, a natural son of Sir Thomas Lyttleton, a member of the Board of Admiralty. The Lyttletons formed part of the powerful Grenville cousinhood. Troubridge, who commanded little Interest himself, was fortunate enough in his youth to find a patron in Sir John Jervis. In the same way the backing of Captain Palliser and Admiral Colville did much for Cook. A great nobleman, a county magnate, or some high official could be a very useful patron. Political Interest was so potent a factor in the procurement of promotion that it is not to be wondered at that so many of the most successful officers were also M.P.s. Nelson, be it noted, commanded much more than average Interest. His maternal uncle, Captain Maurice Suckling, rose to be Comptroller of the Navy; and later he enjoyed the favour of Admiral Peter Parker. An entry in one of Nelson's Mediterranean notebooks puts the whole thing in a nutshell. In this notebook is a significant memorandum to the effect that an officer then under his command, Lieutenant Peter Parker, was 'to get both steps as fast as possible—his grandfather made me what I am'. In other words, young Parker was to be made commander and then post-captain at the first opportunity. Favours of this kind, both given and returned, were taken entirely for granted. Some Service families, like the Parkers and the Cochranes, were adepts at the game. It was largely because he lacked Interest that promotion came but slowly to one of the best and ablest officers of this era, Richard Kempenfelt, with the result that he did not reach post-rank until he was nearly forty.

On the whole the system, blatantly unfair as it appears, worked better than at first sight would seem possible. There were occasions, of course, when it was carried to indefensible extremes. For example, Rodney's son was made a lieutenant when he was not sixteen; five weeks later his fond parent made him first commander and then a post-captain. Captain the Hon. John Rodney was not a success in the Service and was in fact court-martialled. It is not without significance that St. Vincent roundly denounced the abuses of Interest whereby 'the influential secured the plums of the Service for the inefficient and lazy'. But his was a voice crying in the wilderness. Interest long out-lived 'old Jarvie's' protests.

From Jane Austen's *Persuasion* it is possible to form a good idea of the kind of homes from which a fair proportion of the sea-officers came. They apparently belonged to families possessed of no great wealth—but families, notwithstanding, that enjoyed sufficient standing for the sons to be accounted gentlemen. Of such, in real life, were two of our greatest commanders, St. Vincent and Nelson. Of such, in fiction, were Admiral

Croft and his brother-in-law, Captain Wentworth, the devoted suitor of Anne Elliot. We see them and their brother officers settled in agreeable country houses and in modest but comfortable lodgings in Bath and Lyme. These men had begun life with certain advantages: for the future they must look to the lottery of war for prize-money and promotion alike (not for nothing was the wardroom toast so often heard, 'A bloody war and a sickly season').

In another of her novels, *Mansfield Park*, Jane Austen shows no less perspicuity in her portrayal of a very different circle to that of Admiral Croft and Captain Wentworth. The milieu of Fanny Price's father—a down-at-heels lieutenant in the marines—might be aptly described as shabby without being genteel. The setting is that of the back streets of Portsmouth with their aura of dingy paintwork, perpetually hanging strings of washing, crying children, prowling cats and dogs, raucous street cries, and slovenly domestics. Not a few among the lower strata of officers mentioned in Gardner's *Recollections* must have had this sort of background.

In one of the later chapters of the novel it is related that the young midshipman, William Price, and his sister Fanny had driven down from Mansfield Park to visit their family. They broke their journey, we are told, at Oxford.

> The next morning saw them off again at an early hour; and with no events, and no delays, they regularly advanced, and were in the environs of Portsmouth while there was yet daylight for Fanny to look around her, and wonder at the new buildings. They passed the Drawbridge, and entered the town; and the light was only beginning to fail, as, guided by William's powerful voice, they were rattled into a narrow street, leading from the high street, and drawn up before the door of a small house now inhabited by Mr. Price.
>
> Fanny was all agitation and flutter—all hope and apprehension. The moment they stopped, a trollopy-looking maid-servant, seemingly in waiting for them at the door, stepped forward, and more intent on telling them the news, than giving them any help, immediately began with, 'the Thrush is gone out of harbour, please sir, and one of the officers has been here to'— She was interrupted by a fine tall boy of eleven years old, who, rushing out of the house, pushed the maid aside, and while William was opening the chaise-door himself, called out, 'you are just in time. We have been looking for you this half hour. The Thrush went out of harbour this morning. I saw her. It was a beautiful sight. And they think she will have her orders in a day or two. And Mr. Campbell was here at four o'clock, to ask for you; he has got one of the Thrush's boats, and is going off to her at six, and hoped you would be here in time to go with him.'

A stare or two at Fanny, as William helped her out of the carriage, was all the voluntary notice which this brother bestowed;—but made no objection to her kissing him, though still entirely engaged in detailing further particulars of the Thrush's going out of harbour, in which he had a strong right of interest, being to commence his career of seamanship in her at this very time. . . .

Further discussion was prevented by various bustles; first, the driver came to be paid—then there was a squabble between Sam and Rebecca about the manner of carrying up his sister's trunk, which he would manage all his own way; and lastly in walked Mr. Price himself, his own loud voice preceding him, as with something of the oath kind he kicked away his son's portmanteau and his daughter's band-box in the passage, and called out for a candle; no candle was brought, however, and he walked into the room.

Fanny, with doubting feelings, had risen to meet him, but sank down again on finding herself undistinguished in the dusk, and unthought of. With a friendly shake of his son's hand, and an eager voice, he instantly began, 'Ha! welcome back, my boy. Glad to see you. Have you heard the news? the Thrush went out of harbour this morning. Sharp is the word, you see! By G——, you are just in time! The doctor has been here inquiring for you; he has got one of the boats, and is to be off Spithead by six, so you had better go with him. I have been to Turner's about your mess; it is all in a way to be done. I should not wonder if you had your orders to-morrow: but you cannot sail with this wind, if you are to cruize to the westward, with the Elephant. By G——, I wish you may. But old Scholey was saying, just now, that he thought you would be sent first to the Texel. Well, well, we are ready, whatever happens. But by G——, you lost a fine sight by not being here in the morning to see the Thrush go out of harbour. I would not have been out of the way for a thousand pounds. Old Scholey ran in at breakfast time, to say she had slipped her moorings and was coming out. I jumped up, and made but two steps to the platform. If ever there was a perfect beauty afloat, she is one; and there she lays at Spithead, and anybody in England would take her for an eight-and-twenty. I was upon the platform two hours this afternoon looking at her. She lays close to the Endymion, between her and the Cleopatra, just to the eastward of the sheer hulk.'

'Ha!' cried William, 'that's just where I should have put her myself. It's the best birth at Spithead. But here is my sister, Sir; here is Fanny;' turning and leading her forward;—'it is so dark you do not see her.'

With an acknowledgment that he had quite forgot her, Mr. Price now received his daughter; and having given her a cordial hug, and observed that she was grown into a woman, and he supposed would be wanting a husband soon, seemed very much inclined to forget her again.

Fanny Price's estimate of her father, Lieutenant Price, in the quality of both husband and parent was more faithful than flattering, and would have probably applied with equal justice to a not inconsiderable element among the lower ranks of officers. It is certainly borne out by various significant comments on a number of his shipmates by Commander Gardner in his *Recollections*.

> On her father, her confidence had not been sanguine, but he was more negligent of his family, his habits were worse, and his manners coarser, than she had been prepared for. He did not want abilities; but he had no curiosity, and no information beyond his profession; he read only the newspaper and the navy-list; he talked only of the dockyard, harbour, Spithead, and the Motherbank; he swore and drank, he was dirty and gross. . . .

Generally speaking, the families of masters and gunners hailed from the lower strata of the middle class, often long resident in some sea-port or fishing village. William Richardson was born at South Shields in 1768, the son of a shipmaster, with whom he sailed for three voyages before being apprenticed to the master of a Newcastle collier. In 1792 he was pressed into the Navy, and after two years received a gunner's warrant; in which capacity he remained during the rest of his service. George Patey was born in Plymouth in 1729 and entered the Navy as a coxswain in 1753. He was promoted to gunner four years later. Patey was gunner of the *Warrior* at The Saints in 1782. He had no less than ten sons, all of whom joined the Navy. The Pateys got on; a grandson of the first George Patey eventually reached flag rank.

It is not without significance that a number of good officers came from some of the smaller ports, such as Ilfracombe, in North Devon. If ever a place lived for and by the sea it was Ilfracombe. Surrounded by rugged hills, flanked by the precipitous, rocky coast of Exmoor, the terraced houses and steep cobbled lanes of the little town looked down on a commodious, well-sheltered tidal harbour which was usually crowded with shipping. Out of a total population of nearly 2,000, about the year 1800, it has been estimated that over one-tenth were seamen, and many more employed in ancillary occupations like shipbuilding and rope-making. During the Napoleonic War there were at least fifty Ilfracombe men serving in the Navy. In such close-knit communities enterprise and initiative flourished. Here were abundant opportunities for inherited aptitude and skill to be brought on by practical experience and training. Here was a likely breeding-ground of future sea-officers.

Ilfracombe; watercolour by Nicholas Pocock, 1797.

The five Bowen brothers were the sons of a merchant skipper of Ilfracombe. The eldest of them, James, learned his navigation in the merchant service and entered the Navy in that branch, as a master. He presently showed remarkable skill in running down smugglers in the revenue cutter *Wasp*. He served in the capacity of master for twelve years; then, under the patronage of Lord Howe, was made lieutenant after the Glorious First, was promoted to commander in 1795, to captain in 1797, and was appointed Commissioner of the Transport Board in 1803. For his services in the embarkation of the army at Corunna, in 1809, Bowen received the thanks of both Houses of Parliament. He retired, in 1825, with the rank of rear-admiral. It was apparently through his eldest brother's connection with the Transport Board that the second son, John, first gained a footing in the Service, receiving an appointment in the same branch. Richard, the third son, first went to sea with his father, entered the Navy under the auspices of his brother James, and later found an influential patron in Sir John Jervis, who first made him lieutenant and afterwards helped to get him promoted to commander and captain. Great things were predicted of Richard. But a brilliant career was cut short when Captain Bowen of the *Terpsichore* ('than whom', Nelson declared, 'a more enterprising, able, and

Rear-Admiral James Bowen; engraving after Joseph Slater.

gallant officer does not grace his majesty's naval service') was killed in the abortive attempt on Santa Cruz in 1797. The fourth son, George, who had followed him into the Service, ultimately rose to post-rank. The youngest of the five brothers, Thomas, who was also in the Navy, died as a midshipman in 1799.

Besides the elder Bowens and their progeny (James Bowen's two sons were both post-captains by 1810) another Ilfracombe man must be mentioned. Samuel Walters, the son of a carpenter of that town, first served his apprenticeship as a shipwright and then entered the Navy under the patronage of the Bowens. He became carpenter's mate in the transport *Ocean* and was later made lieutenant.

Of similar social standing and environment were such men as Brierly, who played an important part in the British attack at Copenhagen, and old Yawkins, master of the hired cutter *King George*, whom Nelson described as a 'knowing one', and in whom the Admiral put his trust during the operations off the Flanders coast in the summer of 1801.

The son of a coasting or fishing skipper would usually learn his trade under the watchful eye of his father; or else, perhaps, of an uncle, elder brother, or other older relation. The skill and experience of generations of mariners before him would thereby be passed on to him during the formative years of early youth—a firm grasp of the essentials of seamanship and navigation, a remarkable skill in forecasting the weather, and, above all, a close and intimate knowledge of the tides.

Between such stocks of middle-class origin and those of the common seamen there was a great gulf fixed. In the case of the latter the struggle for bare existence occupied most of their energies. They were perforce put to some trade or craft as soon as they were old enough to earn a few pence to eke out the family income; they were for the most part unable to read or write; usually they had no relative or friend to help them along the stony path to advancement. It followed that few among them were able to improve their condition to any notable extent. The ordinary run of fisher-boys could scarcely hope to own their own vessels. Most of the men who served in the merchantmen and in the Navy were unlikely ever to rise to a higher station than that of an able seaman.

According to the evidence of the muster-books, the majority of a ship's company, as might be expected, were of seafaring stock—a markedly hereditary calling. The homes from which they came were situated in London's 'sailor town', Wapping, and its environs; in the three great naval bases of Plymouth, Portsmouth, and Chatham; in the major sea-ports, Liverpool, Bristol, Glasgow, Dublin, and Cork; in the crowded coal ports of the north-east coast, and in innumerable small ports and fishing villages all over the kingdom. The inland regions of the country were mainly repre-sented by the Quota-men; otherwise they furnished only a low percentage of the total intake.

A former ploughman from Warnborough in Hampshire, who had somehow found his way on board the *Royal Sovereign* and was present at the battle of Trafalgar, formed part of the contingent of agricultural labourers in the Service which cannot at any time have been large. A few may have entered from time to time under a particular captain who came from their own part of the country.

The case of Captain Cook is probably unique. He was born on 27 October 1728, 'Ye son of a day labourer', in Cleveland, Yorkshire; and in his early years he followed the same calling. His is the only case on record of a farm labourer who succeeded in attaining, not merely to the quarter-deck, but to post rank. The circumstances, however, were exceptional. His father was a man of unusual ability who in his middle age managed a farm for his employer. Again, before he was nineteen, in 1746, the son was apprenticed to John Walker of Whitby, who with his brother owned a fleet of colliers. Whitby was then a flourishing port with a long tradition of shipbuilding. Young Cook now found himself in much the same kind of environment as that which had given the Bowens and Samuel Walters their opportunities for advancement. During the next few years he was engaged in the coal trade between Newcastle and London, with occasional voyages to the Baltic. In the winter, he applied himself to his studies in his master's house. From his early youth James Cook had given promise of outstanding qualities. In 1752 he became mate in the *Friendship*, and three years later the Walkers offered him the command of the same vessel. Instead of accepting this offer, however, Cook shortly after entered the Navy, at Wapping, as an able seaman. Within a few weeks he was appointed master's mate. From this time on he advanced steadily in the Service until, as he truly claimed, he had 'gone through all the Stations belonging to a Seaman, from a prentice boy in the Coal Trade to a Commander in the Navy'. In the course of his exploration of the South Pacific, Cook displayed qualities that came near akin to genius. The circumstances of the case, as has already been said, were exceptional. Nevertheless, when all possible allowance had been made for these extraordinary qualities of his, it is safe to say that Cook would never have attained to such an astonishing skill in seamanship and navigation had it not been for the thorough training he received in his early manhood in the North Sea.

CHAPTER 16

'SWEETHEARTS AND WIVES'

THE traditional Saturday night toast in the Navy was 'Sweethearts and wives'. That this remembrance of home and loved ones was no empty form may be seen in the eagerness with which the recipients would collect their letters and then take them below to digest—line by line, and paragraph by paragraph—at leisure; and in the lengthy epistles they would frequently write in reply. Something of this emotion is preserved for us in the evocative words and melody of the old song, telling how, after wine, in an agreeably sentimental mood, the wardroom would rise and drink to 'The wind that blows, The ship that goes, And the lass that loved a sailor'.

In most cases the sailor had to do his wooing during his infrequent spells ashore. Cases of courtship at sea, as one would expect, are extremely rare. The best known example, perhaps, is that of Captain Fremantle and Betsey Wynne, which is worth examining.

In the spring of 1796 Bonaparte overran the north of Italy, afterwards advancing southward down the peninsula. When the enemy forces closed in on Leghorn, the British colony in that town was hurriedly evacuated. Among the refugees was the Wynne family who, with their servitors, were taken off in Fremantle's frigate, the *Inconstant*, and afterwards transferred to the *Britannia* off Toulon. The eldest of the Wynne daughters, Betsey, seems to have fallen in love with the *Inconstant*'s commander almost as soon as she set eyes on him.

> All packing up and getting on board the ships. We hardly had time to get a little breakfast, they hurried us so terribly to quit the place and Captain Fremantle took us on board his Frigate the *Inconstant*. The sight of the sea gave me great joy I had not seen it so long. I found the Inconstant so fine so clean so

comfortable so many civil persons that I was quite delighted and regretted no more that the ffrench had obliged us to run away. How kind and amiable Captain Fremantle is. He pleases me more than any man I have yet seen. Not handsome, but there is something pleasing in his countenance and his fiery black eyes are quite captivating. He is good natured, kind, and amiable, gay and lively in short he seems to possess all the good and amiable qualities that are required to win everybodies heart the first moment one sees him.[1]

The situation was attended by every romantic circumstance of time and place—Jervis's squadron cruising before Toulon, moonlight nights at sea, the danger and exhilaration of war, parties and balls staged almost under the guns of the enemy, parental opposition to the match, alternating misery and bliss, separation and then reunion. In the middle-aged Captain Foley of the *Goliath* Fremantle had a formidable rival; who, apparently with Mr. and Mrs. Wynne's approval, had begun to press his unwelcome attentions on Betsey. 'Mamma', she wrote in her journal, 'says that I am not in the least engaged to Fremantle and that the matter is far from settled.' However, an unexpected ally appeared in the person of 'old Jarvie', Admiral Sir John Jervis, Commander-in-Chief on the Mediterranean station.

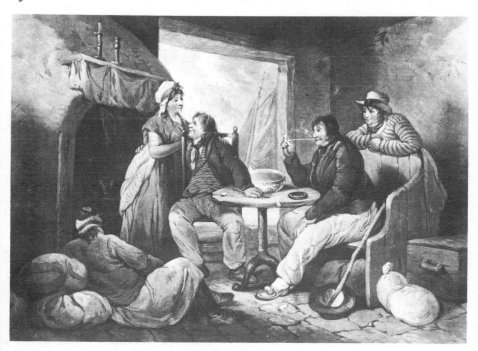

The Sailor's Return; engraving after G. Morland.

The Admiral was on Deck to receive us with the greatest civility and kindness nothing stiff or formal about him and we were not at all embarassed as I feared we should be. He desired we should pay the tribute that was due to him at our entering his Cabin, this was to kiss him which the Ladies did very willingly. . . . The good Admiral has a very high opinion of me. He told me that I should make the best wife in England. And indeed he made me so many such fine compliments that I was quite at a loss how to answer them. All the gentlemen that had been to see us in the morning dined with us. It was a large party and we were very gay, laughed much and made a monstrous noise at table. . . . We were obliged to sing a duet after dinner. We did not stay late for as Admiral Jervis gets up at two o'clock in the morning he goes to bed at half past eight. . . . We had a dance in the evening on board the Britannia all the gentlemen that dined with us and Captain Hallow[ell] and Captain Sotheby who commands the Bombay Castle came.[2]

Fremantle was presently sent away on a cruise by the Admiral, which held out a good prospect of prize-money. Early in 1797 Betsey and he were married in the British Embassy at Naples. His young wife was with him a few months later during the ill-fated attack on Santa Cruz, which cost Nelson his right arm and in which Fremantle also was wounded. Betsey subsequently retired to the village of Swanbourne in Buckinghamshire, whence she exchanged letters with Fremantle throughout the rest of the war.

During the Revolutionary and Napoleonic Wars a number of the officers' wives sought lodgings in various sea-ports and elsewhere on the coast in the hope of seeing something of their husbands whenever the Channel squadron returned to harbour. Brixham, Paignton, Tor Quay, and Flushing (near Falmouth) were the places chiefly favoured. Flushing offered more gaiety and congenial society than any of the others. Besides the frigates working out of Falmouth there were the famous Falmouth Packets which carried the mails. There was a constant coming and going of boats between the little quay and the shipping lying in the roads. In this pleasant village lived many of the wives of the commanders. Dinners, balls, and evening parties were of almost nightly occurrence.

In the early years of the war there was no attempt at the close blockade of Brest, and our captains were able to spend a good deal of their time ashore. But the appointment, in the spring of 1800, of St. Vincent to the command of the Channel fleet put a stop to the easy-going regimen exercised by Howe and Bridport. Henceforward captains were strictly forbidden to sleep out of their ships or proceed any distance from the shore.

'I am at my wits' end,' the new Commander-in-Chief declared, 'to meet every evasion and neglect of duty. Seven-eighths of the Captains who compose this fleet . . . are practising every subterfuge to get into harbour for the winter, and encouraging their carpenters to an exposition of defects, &c. &c.' St. Vincent had much the same sort of trouble with the 'captains of frigates whose dilatory conduct in port annoys me beyond expression. All the married ones have their wives there, which plays the devil with them.' 'When an officer marries,' he said on another occasion, 'he is d——d for the service.'

It is scarcely to be wondered at that St. Vincent's stern measures excited the resentment, not only of his officers, but also of their families living ashore; and the story is told that at a dinner party one good lady gave as a bumper toast, 'May his next glass of wine choke the wretch!'

In his second term in command of the Channel squadron St. Vincent encountered the same difficulties and reacted in the same way. 'Torbay is become a bugbear,' he told his secretary, 'and Falmouth Harbour preferred because of its repose and difficulty of getting out of it; our wives have found their way to Flushing, and ply on board the ships of their husbands the moment they appear, and inhabit the cabins, and even contrive to get into quarantine, to go a cruise.'

During St. Vincent's blockade of Brest in 1800–1 some of the captains' wives found temporary quarters on the wild and lovely shores of Torbay, where they might hope sometimes to see their husbands without infringing the Admiral's rules. Mrs. Collingwood and her small daughter, Sall, were settled at Paignton. Pellew's wife, Susan, was at Brixham. 'Summer is pleasant enough,' she declared; 'in June I have hopes we may all be . . . at Torbay, our cub is there.' A few others were lodging at Tor Quay, which was then no more than a fishing hamlet.

Captain Markham of the *Centaur* rented Livermead Cottage, hard by the shore near Torre Abbey, from a neighbouring squire, for his wife Anne. The cottage, sheltered from the north by steep rocky cliffs, looked out across Torbay towards Brixham and Berry Head. The roof was of thatch, the rooms were small but comfortable, and on one side were some outhouses, and on the other a wattle-and-daub wall with a door in it opening on to a small garden. In this modest retreat Mrs. Markham lived with Bob, their dog, cultivated flowers and vegetables for her husband and his officers, went on Sundays to worship at Tor church, and climbed the neighbouring hills to catch a glimpse of the distant topsails of the Channel fleet. It was a lonely life for a young woman, but there were compensations.

'I saw young Lady E—— at Becca yesterday,' wrote Mrs. Markham, 'and I could not help thinking how much happier am I than her. So beautiful, so pleasing as she is, to be thrown away upon a man who seems to be little worthy of her—there is no species of dissipation he is not engaged in, I understand; while I am married to an honest tar, who, though absent in the service of his country, is good and true.'

Anne's chief employments were writing long letters to her husband, working in the little garden of Livermead Cottage, and sketching. Occasionally she would stroll over to Tor Quay and sit with Mrs. Stopford, the wife of the captain of the *Phaeton*, one reading aloud while the other worked. So she passed the time while her husband was at sea.

In the month of July 1800, when the *Centaur* was docked for necessary repairs, and also the following Christmas, when the fleet lay windbound in Torbay, Captain Markham was able to pass his leisure hours ashore in the day-time. Mrs. Markham now had the opportunity of going on board the *Centaur*, arranging her husband's cabin, and meeting his officers. It was decided that mustard and cress should be sown in the captain's stern walk, and one quarter-gallery should be turned into a greenhouse. With much pride and satisfaction Mrs. Markham sent on board the *Centaur* the produce of her labours in the cottage garden.

'Strange as it may seem,' her husband informed her, the *Centaur* being once again at sea, 'the sight of the plants in the little greenhouse always makes me melancholy; I suppose from the idea of their having been your companions and favourites. I have to complain of you for sending the asparagus. My dear girl, you would strip yourself of every comfort for me, and never think of yourself. . . . It is strange that the only thing I can ever find fault with you for, should be your too great kindness and consideration for me. It is only a week since you sowed the seed.'[3]

To see their husbands the women often had to undertake long and wearisome journeys. The cost of travel, too, was a heavy drain on their resources. The expense of post-horses and inns may be gauged from the fact that these two items alone cost Mrs. Markham no less than 15 per cent of her income. There were occasions when husband and wife met only to be parted again in a matter of hours. When Collingwood was at Plymouth in January 1801 he went to dine with Nelson, and while the two were at dinner the arrival of his wife and child was announced to Collingwood. 'I flew to the inn where I had desired my wife to come, and I found her and little Sarah as well after their journey as if it had lasted only for the day. No greater happiness is human nature capable of than was mine that evening; but at dawn we parted, and I went to sea.' In a letter to a friend he added, 'How surprised you would have been to have popped in to the Fountain Inn and seen Lord Nelson, my wife, and myself sitting by the fireside cosing, and little Sarah teaching Phillis, her dog, to dance.'[4]

Jane Austen in *Persuasion*, which sheds a revealing light on the domestic side of a sailor's life, has well described such scenes of parting and reunion.

> 'Ah!' cried Captain Harville, in a tone of strong feeling, 'if I could but make you comprehend what a man suffers when he takes a last look at his wife and children, and watches the boat that he has sent them off in, as long as it is in sight, and then turns away and says, "God knows whether we ever meet again!" And then, if I could convey to you the glow of his soul when he does see them again; when, coming back after a twelvemonth's absence perhaps, and obliged to put into another port, he calculates how soon it would be possible to get them there, pretending to deceive himself, and saying, "They cannot be here till such a day," but all the while hoping for them twelve hours sooner, and seeing them arrive at last, as if Heaven had given them wings, by many hours sooner still!'

Captains would sometimes take their wives and daughters to sea with them and also give a passage to brother officers' families 'to oblige'. As to the desirability or otherwise of this practice in the Service opinions varied. Thus in *Persuasion* Captain Wentworth declared himself strongly opposed to the idea of having ladies on board a man-of-war; but his brother-in-law, Admiral Croft, it would seem, had often taken his wife to sea with him.

His sister informed Captain Wentworth:

> 'If you had been a week later at Lisbon, last spring, Frederick, you would have been asked to give a passage to Lady Mary Grierson and her daughters.'
>
> 'Should I? I am glad I was not a week later then.'
>
> The admiral abused him for his want of gallantry. He defended himself: though professing that he would never willingly admit any ladies on board a ship of his, excepting for a ball, or a visit, which a few hours might comprehend.
>
> 'But, if I know myself,' said he, 'this is from no want of gallantry towards them. It is rather from feeling how impossible it is, with all one's efforts, and all one's sacrifices, to make the accommodations on board, such as women ought to have. There can be no want of gallantry, admiral, in rating the claims of women to every personal comfort *high*—and this is what I do. I hate to hear of women on board, or to see them on board; and no ship, under my command, shall ever convey a family of ladies any where, if I can help it.'
>
> This brought his sister upon him. . . .
>
> 'But you, yourself, brought Mrs. Harville, her sister, her cousin, and the three children, round from Portsmouth to Plymouth. Where was this superfine, extraordinary sort of gallantry of yours, then?'

'All merged in my friendship, Sophia. I would assist any brother officer's wife that I could, and I would bring any thing of Harville's from the world's end, if he wanted it. But do not imagine that I did not feel it an evil in itself.'

'Depend upon it they were all perfectly comfortable.'

'I might not like them the better for that, perhaps. Such a number of women and children have no *right* to be comfortable on board.'

. . . He got up and moved away.

'What a great traveller you must have been, ma'am!' said Mrs. Musgrove to Mrs. Croft.

'Pretty well, ma'am, in the fifteen years of my marriage; though many women have done more. I have crossed the Atlantic four times, and have been once to the East Indies, and back again, and only once; besides being in different places about home—Cork, and Lisbon, and Gibraltar. But I never went beyond the Streights, and never was in the West Indies. We do not call Bermuda or Bahama, you know, the West Indies.'

Mrs. Musgrove had not a word to say in dissent; she could not accuse herself of having ever called them anything in the whole course of her life.

'And I do assure you, ma'am,' pursued Mrs. Croft, 'that nothing can exceed the accommodations of a man of war; I speak, you know, of the higher rates. When you come to a frigate, of course, you are more confined—though any reasonable woman may be perfectly happy in one of them; and I can safely say, that the happiest part of my life has been spent on board a ship.'

In harbour the seamen's wives were generally allowed to come on board freely. 'Where and when they were married was never inquired,' recorded a naval surgeon, 'the simple declaration was considered as sufficient to constitute a nautical and temporary union and which was authorized by long established custom as practised from time immemorial in His Majesty's Navy.[5] It is to be understood that there were wives and 'wives'—the latter, it appears, in considerable numbers. 'Jack Nasty-Face' has described in detail the customary procedure:

After having moored our ship, swarms of boats came round us: some were what are generally termed bomb-boats [bumboats], but are really nothing but floating chandler's shops; and a great many of them were freighted with cargoes of ladies, a sight that was truly gratifying, and a great treat; for our crew, consisting of six hundred and upwards, nearly all young men, had seen but one woman on board eighteen months; and that was the daughter of one of the Spanish chiefs, who made no stay on board, but went ashore again immediately. So soon as these boats were allowed to come alongside, the seamen flocked down pretty quick, one after the other, and brought their choice up, so that, in the course of the afternoon, we had about four hundred and fifty on board. Of all the human race, these poor young creatures are the most pitiable: the ill-usage and degradation they are driven to submit to are indescribable; but from habit they become callous, indifferent as to delicacy of speech and behaviour, and so totally lost to all sense of shame that they seem to retain no quality which properly belongs to woman but the shape and name. . . . On the arrival of any man-of-war in port, these girls flock down to the shore, where boats are always ready; and here may be witnessed a scene somewhat similar to the trafficking for slaves in the West Indies. As they approach the boat, old Charon, with painter in hand, before they step on board, surveys them from stem to stern with the eyes of a bargaining Jew; and carefully calls out the best looking, and the most dashingly dressed; and, in making up his complement for a load, it often happens that he refuses to take some of them, observing (very politely), and usually with some vulgar oath, to one that she is 'too old'; to another that she is 'too ugly'; and that he shall not be able 'to sell them'; and he'll be d——d if he has any notion of having his trouble for nothing. The only apology that can be made for the savage conduct of these unfeeling brutes is, that they run a chance of not being permitted to carry a cargo alongside, unless it makes a good show-off, for it has been often known that, on approaching a ship, the officer in command has so far forgot himself as to order the waterman to push off—that he should not bring such a cargo of d——d ugly devils on board, and that he would not allow any of his men to have them. . . . Here the waterman is a loser, for he takes them conditionally: that is, if they are made choice of, or what he calls 'sold', he receives three shillings each; and if not, then no pay: he has his labour for his pains: at least, these were the terms at Portsmouth and Plymouth in war-time. . . . A boat usually carries about ten of these poor creatures at a time, and will often bring off three cargoes of these ladies in a day; so that, if he is fortunate in his 'sales', as he calls them, he will make nearly five pounds by his three trips. . . . It may seem strange to many persons that seamen before the mast should be allowed to have these ladies on board, while the officers must not, on pain of being tried by a court-martial for disobedience of orders, the Admiralty having made a regulation to that effect. The reason of this is, that the seamen are not allowed to go ashore, but the officers are.[6]

Down to the peace of 1815 considerable numbers of women accompanied the crews to sea and used to assist the boys at quarters. When in 1806 the Princess of Wales was being shown over the *Caesar*, Sir Richard Strachan's flagship, all the women then on board, numbering several hundreds, received strict instructions to keep out of sight on the orlop deck until the Princess had left the ship. Earlier it is recorded that Jervis seized every opportunity to get rid of what he regarded as an intolerable abuse, complaining that 'the women, who still infest His Majesty's ships in great numbers, will have water to wash, that they and their reputed husbands may get drunk with the earnings, and where these vermin abound, the crews are so much addicted to drinking at sea as in port, and the hold is continually damp and a vapour rising from it highly pernicious to health'. Collingwood, too, was strongly opposed to the custom of permitting women to accompany the crews to sea. 'I have heard there was a woman in the *Pickle*,' he observed in August 1808. 'I never knew a woman brought to sea in a ship that some mischief did not befall the vessel.' 'Captain Carden had given permission for a number of women to come in this ship' [the *Ville de Paris*], he complained the following year. 'I have reproved him for this irregularity and considering the mischief they never fail to create wherever they are, I have ordered them all on board the *Ocean* to be conveyed to England again.'[7]

Captain James Gambier, a notorious 'Blue Light', when in command of the *Defence* at the beginning of the Revolutionary War took the extreme measure of ordering all women on board to show their marriage lines: a measure which (it is said) 'created a very unpleasant feeling among the tars'. Half a century later, soon after the accession of Queen Victoria, an even more zealous commander refused to allow women on board at all. As this was in direct breach of an old-established custom of the Service, it is not to be wondered at that there was serious trouble; in fact, mutiny broke out. When the mutiny, and the *causa causans*, were reported to the port admiral—a hard-bitten veteran of the Nile—it is related that the old commander's language was lurid and unrestrained. He immediately ordered the signal to be made, 'Send 200 women from the —— to the ——' ... and with that the mutiny ended.[8]

CHAPTER 17

JACK ASHORE

FROM published anecdotes, ballads, woodcuts, cartoons, and other contemporary sources it is possible to form a vivid impression of the British tar as he appeared to a spectator in the streets of our naval ports and coastal towns. With his distinctive attire, mahogany-hued complexion, rolling gait, and strange, outlandish speech, the seaman stood out in sharp contrast to the landsman. There was no mistaking him for anything but a sailor.

It was when he was 'on the spree' that he generally attracted attention. Of his quieter moments, passed in the lowly cottage home which saw him so seldom, much less is known. Jane Austen has with admirable skill depicted the officer ashore among his family and friends. We have no comparable impressions of the humble tar. Little, indeed, beyond prints portraying his faithful Nan's sorrowing at her tar's departure and rejoicing on his return.

In his reminiscences Robert Hay, a pressed man, has given a lively description of Jack ashore at the time of the Napoleonic War. Hay relates how from the windows of one of the houses on the water-front at Plymouth overlooking the harbour hundreds of vessels of all sizes and rigs could be seen anchored in Hamoaze.

> Pinnaces, cutters, gigs, etc., were every moment landing. Porters were trudging along under their ponderous burdens. Women of pleasure flitting about in all directions watching for their prey, jews stalking about with hypocritical gravity hunting for dupes, and lastly the jolly tar himself was seen with his white demity trowsers fringed at the bottom, his fine scarlet waistcoat bound with black ribbon, his dark blue broadcloth jacket studded with pearl buttons, his black silk neckcloth thrown carelessly about his sunburnt neck. An elegant hat of straw, indication of a recent return from a foreign station,

Sailors carousing, or a Peep in the Long Room; caricature by George Cruikshank, 1825.

cocked on one side; a head of hair reaching to his waistband; a smart switch made from the backbone of a shark under one arm, his doxy under the other, a huge chaw of tobacco in his cheek, and a good throat season of double stingo recently deposited within his belt by way of fending off care. Thus fitted out, in good sailing trim, as he himself styles it, he strides along with all the importance of an Indian Nabob.[1]

When Jack was ashore it was generally a case of *Tout aux tavernes et aux filles.* His capacity for liquor, indeed, would seem to have been practically inexhaustible. His shore leave was apt all too frequently to take the form of one long debauch. At sea, he suffered punishment for drunkenness oftener than for any other misdemeanour. In port, he was adept in smuggling spirits on board by one stratagem or another. When sent ashore on duty, the officers were hard put to it to keep the men sober. One of the most onerous duties of midshipmen placed in charge of boats ordered away to Portsmouth was to flush their crews out of the Blue Anchor and other favoured boozing-kens on the Point.

The tar's other pressing need was for a congenial doxy. It would appear that the latter was only too willing to meet him more than half-way. 'In some quarters,' Dr. Pinckard remarks severely, 'Portsmouth is not only filthy, and crowded, but crowded with a class of low and abandoned beings, who seem to have declared open war against every habit of common decency and decorum.' Even during the few short weeks that the good doctor spent in the town he had seen enough of these 'Portsmouth Polls', as they were called, to denounce, in no uncertain terms, their conduct, 'which', he writes, 'puts the great orb of noon to the blush.'

> Callous to every sense of shame, these daring objects reel about the streets, lie in wait at the corners, or, like the devouring Kite, hover over every landing place, eager to pounce upon their prey; and each unhappy tar, who has the misfortune to fall under their talons, has no hope of escape till plucked of every feather. The instant he sets foot on dry land he is embraced by the neck, hugged round the waist, or hooked in the arm by one or more of these tender Dulcineas; and thus poor Jack, with pockets full of prize money, or rich with the wages of a long and dangerous cruise, is, instantly, dragged (though, it must be confessed, not always against his consent) to a bagnio, or some filthy pot-house, where he is kept drinking, smoking, singing, dancing, swearing, and rioting, amidst one continual scene of debauchery, all day and all night, and all night and all day, until his every farthing is gone. He is then left to sleep till he is sober, and awakes to return, penniless, to his ship, with much cause to think himself fortunate if an empty purse be the worst consequence of his long wished for ramble ashore.[2]

When Jack came ashore he not infrequently combined the pleasure of female society with that of carriage exercise. There was a custom in the naval ports of hiring out single-horse chaises to carry seamen and their girls in and around the town. 'It was not uncommon to see, at all times of the day, several of these carriages filled with a jolly tar and three girls, besides the driver, who must always be taken as an agreeable companion on these excursions; and, when it rains, perhaps, Jack has a boat cloak, with which he covers himself and the whole group. . . .'[3]

These delights were liable at all times to be abruptly terminated by the activities of the Impress Service. This, according to Hay (who had plenty of experience of the press in person), greatly damped the enjoyment which sailors experienced ashore. Merchant seamen, he said, scarcely dared show their faces in the street. After nightfall, however, fortified by a few drams of good Jamaica, they would sometimes become foolhardy and sally out for a ramble. 'Many, very many,' declared Hay, 'instead of finding themselves in the morning in the arms of Polly would find themselves in the press room of a receiving ship in the more rough and unceremonious hands of a corporal of marines.'[4]

There was a commonly accepted, and by no means unfounded, belief that Jack's one aim and object, on setting foot on shore, was to get through his hard-earned wages as quickly as possible. This he usually succeeded in doing within the bounds of his home port. But on occasions he would go further afield.

After the action of The Saints, in 1782, there was a general distribution of prize money amounting to upwards of £80 per man. One of the fortunate recipients of this windfall promptly went off and hired the London stage coach for himself and his wife. As the coach was about to drive off an officer came up and asked the coachman to open the coach door.

'The coach is full, sir,' said the coachman, as he touched his hat and smiled.

'How can that be?' said the officer. 'You have only *two* passengers.'

'True, your honour,' replied the coachman. 'It is one of the crew of the *Magnificent* and he has engaged the entire coach for himself and his party.'

'Oh, if that's the case,' said the lieutenant, 'only let me see him, and I'll soon settle the business.' Whereon the lieutenant made no more ado but opened the coach door, and would have entered, but Jack, who had got his grog aboard, hailed him:

'What ship, hey? Where the devil are you steering to? Don't you know that I'm the captain of this here craft?'

'I know it, Jack,' said the lieutenant, 'and you must give me a berth aboard to London.'

'I'll be d———d if I do, though,' says Jack. 'This is *my ship*, and nobody shall come aboard without I says the word.'

The coachman here spoke to Jack, and said, 'It is Lieutenant G——— wants to take a berth in your cabin.'

'I'll be d———d if he shall, though,' replied Jack. 'He never axed me into the cabin aboard the *Magnificent*. Howsomever, tell him he may go upon deck if he likes; and I hope he'll look after you, and see that you are steady at the helm, and don't sarve us the same as one of you land-lubbers did about three years ago, when he ran foul of one of the landmarks, and pitched us all overboard.'

The lieutenant heard Jack's reply, and, taking it all in good part, mounted the coach and rolled away to London.[5]

Such local jollifications as Free Mart Fair at Portsmouth attracted the seamen in considerable numbers. It might even be said that the success or failure of the Fair generally depended upon the number of ships assembled in the anchorage at Spithead. In 1800 the Fair was a really good one; but in the following year there were fewer booths and the attendance was smaller than for many years past, and in 1804 the Fair was ruined by a deluge of rain. It is recorded that the stands for the sale of useful articles became fewer and fewer each year, 'while their place was taken by peep-shows, menageries, circuses, theatres, and many more or less questionable entertainments'. The following is a contemporary description, in doggerel, of the delights of Free Mart Fair as it was about the year 1800.

Ye lovers of fun, to Portsmouth repair,
And see the delights that abound at our Fair;
Here baboons and monkeys display all their tricks,
To show that with coxcombs they ever should mix;
And tigers and lions and leopards are seen,
And gentle as lambs—to their keepers I mean,
For they, like the world, can flatter and fawn,
But they want a meal's victuals at evening or dawn;
But if any on whom they depend not for bread
Too near them approach, they would bite off his head.
Merry Andrews, with salt-boxes, gather a crowd,
With gestures, grimaces too freely allowed;
A giant behold, with a voice fierce and grum;
Says Morgan, the fairy, 'I'll dance on my thumb,
And the lions of Pedcock I'd strangle with ease,
And throw bombs at a town like a handful of peas.'

Here's a negro from Guinea will greatly delight,
She proves to the world that a black may be white;
Some feet to the left—just on the parade,
Are battles—engagements on pasteboard display'd;
But those who love fighting, at Hatch's may see
Ships sunk and blown up, from firing free;
And there's plenty of smoke and bursting of flames
Without thunder to frighten young ladies and dames,
Though L'Orient exploding terrific appears,
No danger is near to excite any fears.

But now to return to our famed Grand Parade,
Where the ponies of Saunders great fortune have made,
And equestrians and tumblers your notice invite,
While your wonder they raise and your senses delight.

Adjoining to this, Pizarro is seen,
For murder prepared both in action and mien,
Thus on slaughter determined for fame or for pelf,
He thinks it all fair to murder himself;
Not far from this booth, for theatres removed,

Is, for boobies and babies, a merry-go-round,
Where Paddy may travel and not stir a foot,
Without baiting a horse or soiling a boot,
And here you may journey aloft in the air
In a chaise without wheels or horses, I swear,
And ne'er be afraid of turnpikes to pay,
Or of robbers who plunder by night or by day.

Near this is erected a camera box,
Where the tell-tale mirror the populace mocks;
Here horses and booths on parchment advancing
Seems as if the world on a drum-head was dancing.

But to notice what may in this great Mart be seen,
Would require such a pen as never has been. . . .[6]

Wherever he went, whenever he got shore leave, Jack usually managed to entertain himself—and others. The following passage gives some idea of the kind of ploy calculated to appeal to the lower deck of that era: rough, reckless, uproarious, and entirely characteristic. It refers to a visit which the crew of the frigate *Unité* paid to Malta in 1808.

Had glorious fun there; liberty on shore except those who got themselves in the black list. They used by way of joke to wear yellow ribands round their hats and yellow tyers in their shoes to denote that they were in quarantine and could not go on shore until they received practique. Those that did go on shore, kicked up what sailors call 'Bob's a-dying'. They hired every horse, jackass and coach, that they could find. They formed themselves into fleets (opponents) and performed several nautical manoeuvres on horseback, which of course must be very diverting. The one that personated the English Admiral was one David Robinson, who rode the ass he was on to such a degree that he broke the poor animal's neck and very near breaking his own. After paying for the loss of the poor beast, he mounted another, which he termed shifting his flag, his last vessel having foundered. Captain Campbell who had seen the accident and fearing that he could hurt himself, if he got another beast, ordered him not to hire another, so when he saw the Admiral again mounted, he said to him, 'Why, Robinson, I thought I told you to ride no more.' 'Oh! sir, I intend to ride his tail off.' 'I'll pay you for that, sir.' 'I paid the man already'; and away he scampered, tail up on end, leaving the captain and several officers ready to die with laughing.[7]

The prospect of action was doubly welcome to the British seaman. There was, first and foremost, his congenial love of a scrap—so that he looked

forward to a close engagement with 'Monsoo' with the keenest relish and
anticipation. Further, action as a rule meant a fair chance of prize money;
and prize money meant a glorious spree at Portsmouth Point, Wapping
Town, or some other congenial quarter ashore. The joys he had in mind are
hymned in a favourite ballad of the period, 'The *Arrow* sloop of war'.

> The action being over, and the pris'ners safe on board,
> We'll keep safe on board, my boys, and toss a can of grog.
> And when we come to Portsmouth, with a girl on each knee,
> We'll spend our money cheerfully, and then again to sea.[8]

The tars crowded every hostelry and tavern on the water-front; they
exchanged greetings, jests, and witticisms up and down the public ways;
they joyfully took their choice of the local Polls; they hired coaches and
fiddlers for the common entertainment; they packed the theatre galleries of
every naval port in England; and, as long as the ships were in harbour and
the men were granted shore leave, they kept those ports in one continuous
roar of revelry and jubilation.

CHAPTER 18

THE LETTERS OF SAILORS

BOSCAWEN'S correspondence with his wife, Fanny (a great-grand-niece of John Evelyn the diarist) may be accounted among the best of the letters written by sailors. Boscawen would write freely and amusingly about his family and his home and his ship alike. It was almost impossible for him or for his wife to be dull when they wrote to each other. Fanny was a well-known figure in London society, acclaimed across the Channel as 'La Sévigné d'Angleterre', the friend of Dr. Johnson, David Garrick, and Sir Joshua Reynolds; together with her friend, Mrs. Montagu, she inaugurated the famous 'Blue Stocking Assemblies', where conversation took the place of cards: but it was in her well-loved country home, Hatchlands, with her children, that she was most truly herself. The two were married when Boscawen was a young captain, and Fanny a girl of eighteen. The marriage was fated to be one of continual separations; but letters passed between them constantly.

Early in the Seven Years War—on 2 August 1756—Boscawen wrote to his wife from the Bay of Biscay:

> Yesterday evening I was joined by the *Seaford* and received my love's long letter of the 16th July. Your elegant description of your haymaking, your relation of summer delices, are things we sailors are quite strangers to, and can only know in the books of the poets, to which we give some poetical licence. You well know I believe you, and that you take your full swing of the fine things you talk of. I don't envy you, though heartily wish to partake of them for the sake of your company. . . . I am very sorry your housekeeper thinks of leaving you. Your decayed gentlewomen seldom are good for anything, they want a place where there is nothing to be done. When I come home you will not much want a housekeeper, the fellow I have got is so handy and clever. But

for what I know, some fly may sting him and he may leave me.

Apropos of your health, you give me a charming account of our boys and girls, as well as of your own health, and I assure you mine is as good as you could wish. I have two cows, but I cannot use their milk raw. I drink it in my tea, make puddings with it, etc., but my stomach won't let me drink it otherwise. I have attempted it but it won't do. It makes me sick. I eat very little meat and therefore it is impossible the sea scurvy should ever take hold of me. Besides, we have Dr. Hales's ventilator on board and find the good effects of it.

This letter will go to-morrow, I believe, by Captain Roddam, who has written me a complaining letter of his ship.

My blessing to the dear children. I am your faithful and affectionate husband.

ED. BOSCAWEN

The Admiral must have smiled at Fanny's account of their little boy's recovery from inoculation against small-pox, which was then quite a recent innovation. It seemed that during the child's convalescence discipline had been relaxed so long 'it is unknown how perverse and saucy we are, and how much we deal in the words won't, can't, shan't, etc.' Billy apparently would not take milk one morning, 'but the rod and I went to breakfast with him, and though we did not come into action, nor anything like it, yet the bottom of the porringer was very fairly revealed and a declaration made by him; indeed he could not but say it was very good milk.'

On 18 August Boscawen wrote:

Sixteen weeks at sea but, my dear love, in very good spirits and health. Yesterday I sent you a long letter, and also received one as long from you, the latest date of it 26th of last month, and with it came the table cloths from you, and at the same time clean linen, etc., from Plymouth, with peas, beans, and cauliflowers from my friends on board the *Invincible*.

I am afraid, as my dearest love expected me the 8th of this month, that you will cease writing. But when I wrote you that, I did not expect the *Royal George*. And now I must truly tell you I don't know when I shall return. I will only promise to you that it is a thing I much wish for.

. . . I am very sensible of the condescencion in letting me have the direction of our building, and much more so for your owning you do not understand it. Most wives meddle with all concerns, understanding or not. In return, you shall have the principal hand in furnishing, that is in directing all that is to be new, not but that I own I have a plan for the disposal of the furniture we have and for putting up the china, taffeta, and paper, as well as the chintz. The latter I propose for our bedchamber and dressing room. I don't forget the inlaid ebony doors for a cabinet for the best dressing room, which is to be on the ground floor, and serve for a drawing room, or a fine dressing room on grand occasions. We have ebony in the tower to complete it, if not stolen.

I promise you it shall be a good house to live in, bar the colour of the bricks and smoky chimneys, which I can't prevent. But about the latter we will consult the most learned.

The large room, one pair of stairs, and that under it, will be entirely at your discretion as to furniture, though I own I have thought of Cornish marble for the table below stairs, and a fine but plain white chimney piece. The chimney pieces of the two best bedchambers and dressing [rooms] I shall like to have elegant.

My dear love, I have written you a long letter for one sitting, but I can't finish without telling you I have written a sharp letter to the Admiralty today in answer to one of Cleveland's, who had written me a letter which I conclude is designed to be shown in case of any public noise about our ships. It is written by Mr Clevland himself and very likely never shown to the Board, which has made me very particular in my answer to him. I have written two lines of explanation to Lord Anson, and my answer, I think, will bear showing. I will keep both letter and answer for you to see.

I conclude your house is full now, though before you can receive this, Lady Smythe will have left you. I wish I made one amongst you.

My love to the dear children and compliments to all friends.

From your faithful and affectionate

ED. BOSCAWEN

Hawke's splendid dispatch of 24 November 1759 announcing the victory of Quiberon Bay is sufficiently familiar. Not so well known is the short but revealing letter which the Admiral sent to a member of his household, Miss Sally Birt, who had been in charge of his children since their mother's death some years earlier. Some of the credit for many of Hawke's official letters must go to his secretary, John Hay; but the letter reproduced below is Hawke's work, and Hawke's alone, and is entirely characteristic of the man and his simple, direct style in writing private letters.

Dear Sall,

My Express being just agoing away for England, I have only time to tell you, that wee got up with the French fleet off this place, and have beat them, and dispers'd their fleet. We have burnt two of their ships of seventy four and eighty four guns; wee sunk two, one of seventy four and another of seventy guns, and have taken the *Formidable*, a ship of eighty four guns. In the Evening near dark, and blowing fresh and bad Weather, some of them run away, clear out; seven of them with two Frigates, anchor'd so near the shore that wee cou'd not get at them, and the second day, they flung every thing over board (for fear the Wea.ʳ shou'd moderate, and that we should get at them) and got into a little harbour near the place they were lying at. There they must remain this

Winter at least without anything in, and can be of no service to the french till we please to permit them.

Thank God. I am very well, tho' almost starved with Cold; I hope to be allow'd to go home soon, for I have a long and tiresome service of it.

Write to My Children, the instant you receive this, and give My Love and blessing to them, and make My Compliments to all My Neighbours, and believe me that I am truly,

Dear Sall,

Your sincere Friend,
E. HAWKE.

P.S. Two of our ships had the Ill luck to run ashore and was lost; but these accidents can't be help'd on these occasions, for it was next akin to a Miracle that half our ships was not ashore in the pursuit of the Enemy, upon their own coast, which wee were unacquainted with; besides its blowing strongly and squally, and having no pilots. I am so cold I can scarce write.

Pray write to Mr. Brown, and make My Compliments to him and his sons.[1]

An endearing trait in Rodney's character was his devotion to his wife and daughters, to whom he wrote long, informative letters. He appears to have inspired deep devotion in his dog Loup, judging from the fact that when he went to sea in 1779 Loup remained for three whole days in the Admiral's room watching his coat and refusing to take any food. Rodney wrote to his wife from Spithead on 17 December 1779:

> George [his son] came on board this day, and brought me your letter, and one from Jenny. To hear that you and the girls are well is always the greatest pleasure I can receive. May you ever continue so is my most sincere wish!
>
> . . . Jenny's account of Loup's knowing my purse when she dropped it, shows what a sensible dog he is, and must, as she says, endear him more to me, but she must pardon me if I say, *non credo*.
>
> Everything here is noise and hurry. The wind continuing westerly gives more time to the fleet to get ready. I wish I was once at sea. You know that an admiral has not a tenth part of the trouble and fatigue as when in port. Ministers and merchants are eager to have me gone, but I cannot command the seasons. Adieu.[2]

When Rodney was in the West Indies he received all the news from home in a long letter from his daughter Jane. 'My sisters are quite well, and poor Loup is in perfect health, and as fat as when you left him. He knows your name very well; and even now, when he hears a carriage, he runs to the door, and listens very attentively.' He later told Lady Rodney that 'Jenny', in one of her letters, had informed him that Loup appeared highly offended at his having forgotten to mention him in writing. He wrote again, towards the end of 1780, to his wife in reference to Lady Rodney's visit to Brighton.

> I have received my dear Jenny's letter from Brighton, for which I think myself highly obliged by the description she has given of her own bathing, and the affection of my dog Loup, when the women took hold of you. She seems more pleased with the nice souse, as she calls it, than with the affection that caused it. I am sorry, however, he was so displeased with his bathing as not to suffer anybody to speak to him.
>
> Notwithstanding I am so pleased with her letter, I am not quite so with her writing: I fear her master is a bad performer, and does not teach her a woman's hand. Nothing is so shocking in a lady than a masculine hand. Pray tell her so. . . . Pray don't let any of my girls go to a boarding-school. I cannot bear it. They will learn nothing there but mischief.[3]

Of particular interest are the letters which sailors wrote, not to wives or daughters, but to one another. Gardner, after sundry experiences as prizemaster on board a captured French privateer, which included an ordeal in the Portland Race ('this infernal race was worse than all, and I expected every moment we should founder'), eventually arrived safely at Plymouth, where he received this letter from the captain of his ship, the *Hind*.

> Gardner, my good friend, I am truly happy to find you are in the land of the living, and that it was through necessity you put into Plymouth. We are ordered to Sheerness to dock, where I shall be devilish glad to see you; so get on board some vessel bound to the Downs with your party, and be sure to call on my father, who will be very glad to see you and will send some craft to take you to the Nore. We are all well.—Believe me to remain, with best wishes,
>
> Yours most faithfully,
JOHN BAZELY, JUNR.[4]

One of the most prolific and entertaining correspondents in the Service during this era was the future Sir William Hoste, son of the rector of Godwick in Norfolk, who had gone to sea with Nelson in the *Agamemnon* in 1793 and who in the spring of 1798 was a lieutenant in the *Theseus*. Writing to his sister of a visit which the *Theseus* had just made to Gibraltar, Hoste observed:

> General O'Hara gave a ball to the officers of the army and navy whilst we were there. I was not of the party, though invited; you know I never cut a *figure* in dancing when in England, and I assure you that I have not improved much since, for God knows we have something else to do besides dancing. We have

often a reel on board, and I am a capital hand at it; but a country dance is quite out of my latitude. I am sure you would laugh heartily were you to see our ball-room and music. Figure to yourself a poor unfortunate fiddler, stuck up in one corner of the ward-room, striking up some merry tune, whilst we, from the rolling of the ship, or the creaking of her sides, can hardly hear him at the other: however, it is what we are used to, and it gives us as much pleasure for the moment as the best band at St. James's.[5]

It is worth noticing that many of the letters which sailors would send home were concerned with the ordinary, everyday details of life at sea which they knew would interest their womenfolk. In this vein Sir James Saumarez, in command of the inshore squadron moored off the Black Rocks, in the Iroise, wrote to his wife on 21 October 1800:

I am now *solus*. Captain Brenton, who I mentioned had been staying with me, is gone to the *Ville de Paris*. I know no one I should prefer as captain under my flag. He is a steady, sensible, good officer, and of great experience, having served several years with admirals as a lieutenant. Captain Cook dined with me today on a *Black Rock* dinner, viz. a fine piece of salmon and a nice little cochon-de-lait, with entremêts, removes, &c. The salmon was sent me with a basket of vegetables from Plymouth, I suspect from Captain Markham; the roaster was a present from Captain Hood, who, being under sail, could not dine with me. I mention these trifles because I know they please you. The boats occasionally go to the small islands and procure bullocks, &c.; and, as fast as the stock is purchased, they contrive to replenish it from the mainland,—a proof they are well satisfied with the price we pay for it, which is fixed by themselves.[6]

It might be said that for all practical purposes Midshipman Bernard Coleridge was a contemporary of the much better known Marjory Fleming. Both belonged to the Regency era and to much the same social class; though one was English and the other was Scots. Neither of them lived to grow up. Bernard was thirteen when he fell from aloft in the *Phoenix*. Marjory died of mastoid, following measles, before she was nine. The boy is known to us through his letters, and the girl through her journal. Both were 'characters' and possessed of intense vitality. Across the gulf of time Bernard and Marjory are living, breathing youngsters; personalities as vivid as Harry and Laura Graham in *The Holiday House*—a once famous children's classic treating of the same era.

Bernard Coleridge, midshipman;
contemporary silhouette.

My dear Father,—I received your packet with great joy on Wednesday about 1 o'clock from Mr. Baker, and ran down into the cockpit to examine the contents, and I was a great deal more delighted with the letters than with the sweetmeats, but those were very acceptable indeed also. I tore open Frank's [his brother's] letter first and I was much delighted with the contents of it, but I could not read any more before dinner, I being invited to-day to the Wardroom to dine upon green peas and mutton and other good things. . . . After dinner I had strawberries and wine, but wine is no luxury to me, for I have two glasses at dinner every day and two at supper, which is my half allowance, I not liking grog. I go into the Captain's cabbin every day for two hours and read and write whatever we choose, and I assure you that these two hours are the happiest in the day to me; but altogether I am very happy indeed, seeing Brest and Ushant every day, and the other day we were so near that with Mr. Baker's glass which he lent me I could see everything, even to perceive two boys riding across a gate on a plank, and so did two or three others with me. . . . I thought you would sooner have something than nothing, for the boat is waiting.

So I remain your dutiful son,
B. F. COLERIDGE[7]

In his subsequent letters Bernard gives his parents some account of life at sea in the midshipmen's berth.

We have twelve-shilling tea for breakfast, and biscuit, which is very good indeed, but rather maggoty. We play at marbles on the poop, and yesterday I lost ninety to Hood while we were in the boat alongside the *Trenon*. We have very good dinners and teas and suppers, tea and sugar is allowed by the purser, but we have our own; we have also ham, coffee, and cocoa, and we have a nice berth with candles all day.[8]

During the long weeks of the blockade, when provisions ran short, the boy's thoughts turned hungrily to the abundant fare and well-stocked garden of his Devonshire home.

I wish James would change grub with me for a week. I believe I should be twice as strong as I am. We have had nothing now for the last month but salt beef, biscuit, stinking water, and brandy. . . . I assure you when you write about sallads, green peas, and strawberries my mouth waters and I wish could only be in our garden for twenty-four hours! . . . I often think what I would give for two or three quarendons off the tree on the lawn with their rosy cheeks![9]

In September 1805 Bernard wrote briefly of a brush with the enemy off Brest. He was still only twelve years old; but nothing could be more concise, effective, and revealing than the report in question. He had evidently profited by his studies in the captain's cabin.

Seven of the enemy's fleet weighed and stood towards us under an easy sail, so the headmost French ship, with a Rear-Admiral's flag, poured a broadside into the *Indefatigable*, and then stood in for Brest, to which she returned. At quarter past ten we were stripped and stood in close order for the enemy's fleet. At half-past ten the batteries opened a tremendous fire of shot and shell, one of which struck the *Ville de Paris*, and a splinter of it striking the Admiral, he said, 'Damme, but I will have some of you out for this!'[10]

In October, Bernard was granted a week's leave. He planted a pine-tree on the terrace of his home at Ottery St. Mary and carved his name on an oak-tree in the garden (the letters were still faintly visible more than a century later). He was then gazetted to the *Phoenix* and killed shortly afterwards.

The last and greatest of all general actions fought under sail produced a rich harvest of correspondence, both before and after Trafalgar.

It was shortly after daybreak on 19 October 1805 that the signal had been made by the *Sirius*—that one of Blackwood's five frigates which lay closest inshore: 'Enemy have their topsail yards hoisted.' An hour later the enemy's ships began to leave port. The news flashed from ship to ship to Nelson's squadron far out in the Atlantic. That day Captain Codrington of the *Orion* sat down and wrote a long letter to his wife.

How would your heart beat for me, dearest Jane, did you but know that we are
now under every stitch of sail we can set, steering for the enemy, whom we
suppose to be come out of Cadiz! Lord Nelson had just hoisted his *dinner flag* to
several captains at 9 o'clock this morning, when to my great astonishment he
wore ship and made the signal for a general chase to windward. It was nearly
calm, and has continued so ever since, till towards evening: but we have now a
nice air, which fills our flying kites and drives us along four knots an hour. . . .
We are now fully prepared in every respect, and I have every confidence in the
result being such as will at last keep up and justify the esteem you have for your
husband. As to my coming out of the battle alive or dead, that is the affair of
chance and the little cherub: but that I shall come out without dishonour is my
affair; and yet I have but little apprehension about the matter, so great is my
confidence in my ship, and in our excellent Admiral. . . . However, it will be
all over before you get this, and it is, therefore, needless to dwell longer on the
subject. I feel a little tired; and, as I have now nothing to do but keep the ship's
head the right way, and take care that the sails are well trimmed, in readiness
for the morning, I shall even make that over to the officer of the watch and go
to my cot; nor do I think I shall sleep the worse for my cabin being only
divided from the quarter-deck by a boat's sail. And so, dear, I shall wish thee
once more a good night, and that thy husband's conduct in the hour of battle
may prove worthy of thee and thy children . . .[11]

Francis William Austen, one of Jane's two sailor brothers, was directed to
report on the possibilities of a French descent on the Kentish coast during the
invasion scare of 1803, and during this time he became engaged to a Miss
Mary Gibson at Ramsgate. In the spring of 1805 he sailed with Nelson to the
West Indies in pursuit of Villeneuve and was one of the captains who
welcomed the Admiral on his return to the Mediterranean fleet at the end of
September. The *Canopus* was one of the ships detached under Rear-Admiral
Louis to revictual at Gibraltar and to act as escort vessels to a convoy. It was
while engaged in these duties that he learned, to his chagrin, that he had
missed the battle of Trafalgar.

My dearest Mary,—Having now got over the hurry and bustle which
unavoidably attends every ship while in the act of compleating provisions,
water and stores, I think it high time to devote some part of my attention to
your amusement, and to be in a state of preparation for any opportunities
which may offer of dispatching letters to England.

. . . Our stay at Gibraltar was not productive of much gaiety to us; we dined
only twice on shore, and both times with General Fox, the Governor. We had
engagements for several succeeding days on our hands; but this change of wind
making it necessary to move off, our friends were left to lament our absence,

and eat the fatted calf without us. . . . The last evening of our stay at Gibraltar we went, after dining with the General, to see *Othello* performed by some of the officers of the garrison. The theatre is small, but very neatly fitted up; the dresses and scenery appeared good, and I might say the same of the acting could I have seen or heard anything of it; but, although I was honoured with a seat in the Governor's box at the commencement of the programme, yet I did not long profit by it, for one of his aide-de-camps, happening to be married, and his lady happening also to come in during the first scene, I was obliged to resign my situation, happy to have it in my power to accommodate a fair one.

The play was *Othello*, and by what I have been able to collect from the opinions of those who were more advantageously situated for seeing and hearing them myself, I did not experience a very severe loss from my complaisance. I believe the Admiral was not much better amused than I was, for, at the expiration of the first act, he proposed departing, which I readily agreed to, as I had for some time found the house insufferably hot and close.

October 21.—We have just bid adieu to the convoy, without attending them quite so far as was originally intended, having this day received intelligence, by a vessel dispatched in pursuit of us, that on Saturday, 19th, the enemy's fleet was actually seen under way, and coming out of Cadiz.

Our situation is peculiarly unpleasant and distressing, for if they escape Lord Nelson's vigilance and get into the Mediterranean, which is not very likely, we shall be obliged, with our small force, to keep out of their way; and on the other hand, should an action take place, it must be decided long before we could possibly get down even were the wind fair, which at present it is not. As I have no doubt but the event would be highly honourable to our arms, and be at the same time productive of some good prizes, I shall have to lament our absence on such an occasion on a double account, the loss of pecuniary advantage as well as of professional credit.

October 27, off Tetuan.—Alas! my dearest Mary, all my fears are but too fully justified. The fleets have met, and, after a very severe contest, a most decisive victory has been gained by the English twenty-seven over the enemy's thirty-three. Seventeen of the ships are taken and one is burnt; but I am truly sorry to add that this splendid affair has cost us many lives, and amongst them the most invaluable one to the nation, that of our gallant, and ever-to-be-regretted Commander in Chief, Lord Nelson, who was mortally wounded by a musket shot, and only lived long enough to know his fleet successful. . . . As a national benefit I cannot but rejoice that our arms have been once again successful, but at the same time I cannot help feeling how very unfortunate we have been to be away at such a moment, and, by a fatal combination of unfortunate though unavoidable events, to lose all share in the glory of a day which surpasses all which ever went before, is what I cannot think of with any degree of patience; but, as I cannot write upon that subject without complaining, I will drop it for the present, till time and reflection reconcile me a little more to what I know is now inevitable.[12]

Unlike so many of his brethren, Captain Thomas Fremantle was able to write freely and lucidly in his letters home about the daily happenings at sea in the weeks before Trafalgar. His letters supply a wealth of interesting detail which is by no means forthcoming in the correspondence of, say, Captain Thomas Hardy. The fact that his 'Tussy', as a young girl, had spent a good deal of time on shipboard and was very well acquainted with several other captains in the fleet may partly account for this.

Shortly before the action Fremantle received the offer of his old place in the line of battle, which was Nelson's second. On 19 October, Fremantle had all the captains in the fleet to dinner on board the *Neptune*. Tussy's anxiety for her husband when the news reached Swanbourne of a great battle fought at Cadiz, and several captains having been killed and twenty ships taken, was intense. 'I really felt indescribable misery until the arrival of the Post, but was relieved from such a wretched state of anxious suspence by a Letter from Lord Garlies, who congratulated me on Fremantle's safety & the conspicuous share he had in the Victory gained on the 21st off Cadiz.' Fremantle's preoccupation with the main chance is both amusing and characteristic. The truth is, the captain of the *Neptune* was a good deal less concerned with Nelson's vision of Glory than with the tangible benefits which might be expected to accrue from a great victory over the Combined Fleet.

My ever Dearest and best of Women,—

If I know your heart, or your sentiments I think I may depend that you will be truly happy to hear that I am well after the very severe action we have had,—This last Week has been a scene of Anxiety and fatigue beyond any, I ever experienced but I trust in God that I have gained considerable credit, and that it will ultimately tend to the benefit of you and my dear little Children for when—alone I am now here,—I am at present towing the *Victory* and the Admiral has just made the signal for me to go with her to Gibraltar, which is a satisfactory proof to my mind that he is perfectly satisfied with old *Neptune*, who behaves as well as I could wish, The loss of Nelson is a death blow to my future prospects here, he knew well how to appreciate Abilities and Zeal, and I am aware that I shall never cease to lament his loss whilst I live. We have ten Men killed and 37 Wounded, which is very trifling when compared to some other Ships, however we alone have certainly the whole credit of taking the

Santissima Trinidada, who struck to *us alone*. Adml. Villeneuve was with me on board the *Neptune* over two days, I found him a very pleasant and Gentlemanlike man, the poor man was very low. Yesterday I put him on board the *Euryalus* with Admiral Collingwood, but I still have the pleasure of feeding and accommodating his Captain and his 2 Aid du Camps and his Adjutant General, who are true Frenchmen, but with whom I am much amused, I have also 450 poor Spaniards from the *Santissima Trinidada*, with a true Italian priest born at Malta,—I have found also an excellent French cook and a true Spanish pug dog. . . . I am afraid this brilliant Action will not put much money in my pocket, but I think much may arise out of it ultimately, I shall with this send you a copy of the Minutes kept by my old Lieut. Mr. Green, I hope with the Line of battle and the drawing you will be enabled to make it out, you may give the Ringers I think a Guinea on the occasion to save your credit to my brother William I send one also that you may show your plan over Buckinghamshire as much as you please,—My Cabin that was so elegant and neat is as dirty as a pig Stye and many parts of the bulk heads are thrown overboard, however I shall find amusement and indeed employment in having them fitted in some new way. . . . The French Captain drinks your health regularly every day at dinner, The poor man is married and laments his lot, one of the younger ones is desperately in love with a lady at Cadiz and Frenchmanlike carries her picture in his pocket—

Ever your most affectionate husband

T. F. F.[13]

The following letter from 'Sam' (surname unknown), one of the crew of the *Royal Sovereign*, is one of a large number of such communications which issued from the fleet in the aftermath of Trafalgar. Like so many of the others, it is compounded of jubilation over the brilliant victory and sorrow for Lord Nelson's death. A point of some interest is how a country lad like 'Sam' came to be on board the *Royal Sovereign* at all. Usually the press-gang would not operate so far inland. In any case a ploughboy should—in theory—have been exempt from impressment. Did 'Sam' pay a visit to the coast and was apprehended there? Or had he perhaps run away to sea for the sake of adventure? This particular letter is all the more welcome in that it is the work of a common seaman and the voice of the lower deck is so seldom heard in this era.

Honoured Father,

This comes to tell you I am alive and hearty except three fingers; but that's not much, it might have been my head. I told brother Tom I should like to see a greadly battle, and I have seen one, and we have peppered the Combined rarely; and for matter of that, they fought us pretty tightish for French and Spaniards. Three of our mess are killed, and four more of us winged. But to tell you the truth of it, when the game began, I wished myself at Warnborough with my plough again; but when they had given us one duster, and I found myself snug and tight, I bid Fear kiss my bottom, and set to in good earnest, and thought no more about being killed than if I were at Murrel Green Fair; and I was presently as busy and as black as a collier. How my fingers got knocked overboard I don't know; but off they are, and I never missed them till I wanted them. You see, by my writing, it was my left hand, so I can write to you, and fight for my King yet. We have taken a rare parcel of ships, but the wind is so rough we cannot bring them home, else I should roll in money, so we are busy smashing 'em, and blowing 'em up wholesale.

Our dear Admiral Nelson is killed! So we have paid pretty sharply for licking 'em. I never set eyes on him, for which I am both sorry and glad; for, to be sure, I should like to have seen him—but then, all the men in our ship who have seen him are such soft toads, they have done nothing but blast their eyes, and cry, ever since he was killed.—God bless you! chaps that fought like the Devil, sit down and cry like a wench. I am still in the *Royal Sovereign*, but the Admiral has left her, for she is like a horse without a bridle, so he is in a frigate that he may be here and there and everywhere, for he's as *cute* as here and there one, and as bold as a lion, for all he can cry!—I saw his tears with my own eyes, when the boat hailed and said my lord was dead. So no more at present from your dutiful son,

SAM.[14]

'The Admiral', observed Hoste of Collingwood shortly after Trafalgar, 'is a very different man from Lord Nelson, but as brave an old boy as ever stood.' The future Admiral Sir George Elliot, then a young captain, received a much less favourable impression of the Commander-in-Chief. 'I was many years in company with him and always considered him a selfish old bear. That he was brave, stubborn, persevering, and determined an officer as was known everyone acknowledged; but he had few if any friends, and no admirers. In body and mind he was iron, and very cold iron—in heart I believe the same, except one small soft corner, accessible only to his family.'

Elliot's estimate of Collingwood's character is to some extent borne out by the Admiral's correspondence. There is none of the warmth and quick sympathy in his letters which one finds in those of Boscawen half a century before; or, for that matter, in his friend Nelson's. Even when writing to his beloved young daughters, Collingwood was apt to be lamentably prolix, prosy, and dull. He appears to have devoted considerable thought to the subject of education, especially the education of young ladies; and he endeavours to impart these ideas to the two girls, aged fifteen and fourteen respectively.

> Never forget for one moment that you are gentlewomen; and all your words and actions should make you gentle. . . . So much for mind and manners; next for accomplishments. No sportsman ever hits a partridge without aiming at it; and skill is acquired by repeated attempts. It is the same thing in every art: unless you aim at perfection, you will never attain it; but frequent attempts will make it easy. Never, though, do anything with indifference. Whether it be to mend a rent in your garment, or finish the most delicate piece of art, endeavour to do it as perfectly as possible.
>
> When you write a letter, give it your greatest care, that it may be as perfect in all its parts as you can make it. Let the subject be sense, expressed in the most plain, intelligible, and elegant manner that you are capable of. If in a familiar epistle you should be playful and jocular, guard carefully that your wit be not sharp, so as to give pain to any person; and before you write a sentence, examine it, even the words of which it is composed, that there be nothing vulgar or inelegant in them.
>
> . . . Remember that gentle manners are the first grace which a lady can possess. Whether she differ in her opinion from others, or be of the same sentiment, her expressions should be equally mild. A positive contradiction is vulgar and ill-bred; but I shall never suspect you of being uncivil to any person.
>
> . . . Your application must be to useful knowledge. Such, I hope, applies to geometry, and Mary makes good progress in arithmetic. Independently of their use in every situation in life, they are sciences so curious in their nature, and so many things that cannot be comprehended without them are made easy, that were it only to gratify a curiosity which all women have, and to be let into secrets that cannot be learned without that knowledge, it would be a sufficient inducement to acquire them. Then do, my sweet girls, study to be wise.[15]

The general dullness of Collingwood's private letters is at times relieved by his vivid evocation of the familiar sight and sounds of his well-loved Morpeth. Nowhere in the correspondence of sailors, indeed, is there to be found a more moving and more revealing expression of the exile's pent-up longing for wife and children and home than in these letters of Collingwood's.

'God knows when we shall meet again,' he had written despondently to Nelson in 1792, when some of the most promising officers in the Service were vainly seeking employment, 'unless some chance should draw us again to the Sea-shore.' Nevertheless, before the Peace of Amiens was concluded he was longing to be on shore again. 'Then I will plant my cabbages again,' he wrote hopefully, 'and prune my gooseberry trees, cultivate roses, and twist the woodbine through the hawthorn hedge with as much satisfaction in my improvement as ever Diocletian had.' 'This is the third summer that I have hardly seen the leaf of the trees.' he lamented, 'except through a glass at the distance of some leagues.' And again: 'How I long to have a peep into my own home, and walk in my own garden!' In the summer of 1806 he wrote to his wife: 'This day, my love, is the anniversary of our marriage and I wish you many happy returns of it. If ever we have peace I hope to spend my latter days among my family. Should we decide to change the place of our dwelling our route would of course be to the southward of Morpeth; but then I would be for ever regretting those beautiful views which are nowhere to be exceeded; and even the rattling of that old waggon that used to pass our door at six o'clock of a winter's morning had its charms. . . . Tell me, how do the trees that I planted thrive? Is there shade under the three oaks for a considerable summer seat? Do the poplars grow at the walk and does the wall of the terrace stand firm?'[16]

Another appealing trait in Collingwood's character was his devotion, which was apparently fully reciprocated, to his dog Bounce. Collingwood and Bounce were known to every member of the crew on board the *Culloden*. 'Accompanied by Bounce,' says Hay, 'he would stand on the weather gangway breathing the midnight air, levelling his night glass all round the horizon, or fixed on the light carried by Cornwallis in the *Ville de Paris*, the van ship of the weather line.'[17] No doubt Bounce was regarded as something of a friend at court and he became the object of general solicitude. The future Admiral Hercules Robinson, then a midshipman, attributed his advance under Collingwood to his practice of making a favourite of Bounce.

It is not surprising that there is a good deal about Bounce in the Admiral's correspondence. 'He sleeps by the side of my cot', he confided to his wife, '. . . until the time of tacking and then marches off to be out of hearing of the guns.' History does not record what happened to Bounce at Trafalgar. He probably followed his usual practice of retiring below while the guns were going off. Even so, the shock to his nervous system must have been considerable. Bounce seems to have been fully aware of his elevated position as Dog to Admiral Lord Collingwood. 'The consequential airs he gives himself since he became a right honourable dog are insufferable. He considers it beneath his dignity to play with commoners' dogs, and truly thinks that he does them grace when he condescends to lift up his leg against them. This', observed the Admiral, 'I think is carrying the insolence of rank too far.'[18]

Admiral Lord Collingwood; contemporary portrait.

Bounce even had a poem composed in his honour. For the two girls their father wrote these lines:

> Sigh no more, Bouncey, sigh no more,
>   Dogs were deceivers never:
> Tho' ne'er you put one foot on shore,
>   True to your master ever.
> Then sigh not so, but let us go,
>   Where dinner's daily ready,
> Converting all the sounds of woe
>   To heigh phiddy diddy.[19]

During all these years of his sea service, indeed, Bounce must almost have forgotten the sights and scents of the shore. 'Poor Bounce is growing very old,' his master declared. 'I once thought of having his picture taken, but he had the good fortune to escape that.' Finally, off Toulon on 13 August 1808, Collingwood in the *Ville de Paris* wrote sorrowfully to his sister: 'You will be sorry to hear my poor dog Bounce is dead. I am afraid he fell overboard in the night. He is a great loss to me. I have few comforts, but he was one, for he loved me. Everybody sorrows for him'.[20]

CHAPTER 19

STORY AND SONG

CONSIDERING how very important a part was played in the Georgian era by British seamen, it is surprising how little is said about them in the literature of the period. Only a handful of writers, of whom Daniel Defoe, Jane Austen, and Frederick Marryat are the most eminent, can be cited. Probably the reason for this is that sailors, as in the days of Chaucer and Shakespeare, were still regarded very much as a body separate and apart from the general population.

In his novels and other works Defoe occasionally wrote of the sea and seamen; but only, as it were, incidentally. Defoe must have listened to many a yarn in inns and coffee-houses, and with his reporter's acumen he made good use of what he learned; but his knowledge, after all, was only second-hand, and he cannot be regarded in any way as one of the greatest writers of the sea.

It was not Defoe, but Smollett, who revealed to the reading public the British seaman; who sketched his appearance and his character; who familiarized us with his peculiar lingo. With his penetrating powers of observation and description Smollett went to the root of the matter. His characters, eccentric and exaggerated as they are, are true seamen. Through his service in the Navy, he knew them at first hand.

Best of all Smollett's naval figures is Lieutenant Tom Bowling, uncle of the hero in *Roderick Random*. The lieutenant's speech breathes the very tang of the sea, in his character is the frank and breezy disposition of the sailor, his courage, his manliness, his simplicity, his hard common sense, his kindness and generosity, his ignorance of men and affairs ashore. The humorous study of Commodore Trunnion in *Peregrine Pickle*, exaggerated as it certainly is, is also very good.

The world of Jane Austen was far removed from that of Smollett. Her link with the Service was through her two brothers, Francis and Frederick Austen. There were still rough customers among naval officers in Jane's time: but nothing like to the same extent as in Smollett's. Jane felt herself entirely at home when she wrote about the domestic side of a sea-officer's life and when she portrayed such characters as Admiral Croft, Captain Wentworth, and Midshipman Price. She must have learned much from her brothers' letters and more from their conversation. She knew very well how the sea-officer comported himself when he was ashore: how he spoke and acted, and, one might even add, how he felt and thought.

In *Persuasion* Jane Austen admirably depicts the mood of the peace following the great war of 1793–1815 and of officers being reunited with their families after long years of separation. While such scenes were fresh in her memory, she relates how some of these officers on a visit to Bath would form 'a little knot of the Navy' whenever they happened to meet in the streets. The account of Anne Elliot's meeting with her father's tenant, Admiral Croft, is one of the most effective pieces of characterization she ever did.

> He was standing by himself, at a printshop window, with his hands behind him, in earnest contemplation of some print, and she not only might have passed him unseen, but was obliged to touch as well as address him before she could catch his notice. When he did perceive and acknowledge her, however, it was done with all his usual frankness and good humour. 'Ha! is it you? Thank you, thank you. This is treating me like a friend. Here I am, you see, staring at a picture. I can never get by this shop without stopping. But what a thing here is, by way of a boat. Do look at it. Did you ever see the like? What queer fellows your fine painters must be, to think that any body would venture their lives in such a shapeless old cockleshell as that? And yet, here are two gentlemen stuck up in it mightily at their ease, and looking about them at the rocks and mountains, as if they were not to be upset the next moment, which they certainly must be. I wonder where that boat was built!' (laughing heartily); 'I would not venture over a horsepond in it. Well' (turning away) 'now, where are you bound? Can I go anywhere for you, or with you? Can I be of any use?'
>
> 'None, I thank you, unless you will give me the pleasure of your company the little way our road lies together. I am going home.'
>
> 'That I will, with all my heart, and farther too. Yes, yes, we will have a snug walk together; and I have something to tell you as we go along. There, take my arm; that's right; I do not feel comfortable if I have not a woman there. Lord! what a boat it is!' taking a last look at the picture, as they began to be in motion.
>
> 'Did you say that you had something to tell me, sir?'

'Yes, I have. Presently. But here comes a friend, Captain Brigden; I shall only say "How d'ye do," as we pass, however. I shall not stop. "How d'ye do." Brigden stares to see anybody with me but my wife. She, poor soul, is tied by the leg. She has a blister on one of her heels, as large as a three shilling piece. If you look across the street, you will see Admiral Brand coming down and his brother. Shabby fellows, both of them! I am glad they are not on this side of the way. Sophy cannot bear them. They played me a pitiful trick once—got away some of my best men. I will tell you the whole story another time. There comes old Sir Archibald Drew and his grandson. Look, he sees us; he kisses his hand to you; he takes you for my wife. Ah! the peace has come too soon for that younker. Poor old Sir Archibald! How do you like Bath, Miss Elliot? It suits us very well. We are always meeting with some old friend or other; the streets full of them every morning; sure to have plenty of chat; and then we get away from them all, and shut ourselves into our lodgings, and draw in our chairs, and are as snug as if we were at Kellynch, ay, or as we used to be even at North Yarmouth and Deal. We do not like our lodgings here the worse, I can tell you, for putting us in mind of those we first had at North Yarmouth. The wind blows through one of the cupboards just in the same way.'

In the same novel Jane Austen paints an excellent portrait of the keen young frigate captain, Frederick Wentworth, and in *Mansfield Park* there is a warm and sympathetic study of a young midshipman, William Price, the brother of the heroine.

Frederick Marryat entered the Navy in 1806 at the age of fourteen and served for three years under Cochrane in the *Impérieuse*, a crack frigate with a fine crew, several of whom long afterwards figured in his naval novels. Those three years of active and adventurous life made an ineffaceable impression upon the young officer. His subsequent service took him to the West Indies, North America, and St. Helena. He had, therefore, rich stores of experience to draw on when he began to write. In 1830 he retired from the Navy, having already published the first of his novels, *Frank Mildmay*, in 1829. With the serialization of *Peter Simple* in 1832–3 Marryat's fame was secure. It was the jolliest, gayest, and most enthralling of all his works. The scenes of comedy and adventure, and the rich array of characters, were drawn from his own recollections. How Marryat must have enjoyed writing this book! It is impossible not to believe that he must have known how good it was. The earlier experiences of the hero in the midshipmen's berth, Portsdown Fair, the club-hauling of the *Diomede*, the escape of Peter Simple and his friend, Terence O'Brien, from a French prison, old Swinburne's yarns, the Dignity Ball, passing for lieutenant, the hurricane in Martinique, and the brush with the Danish gun-boats in the Sound, are among the best things that ever came from his pen. As to the characters in *Peter Simple*, 'Gentleman Chucks' is, perhaps, Marryat's masterpiece. But almost all the characters in the book, major and minor alike, are excellent in their way.

Marryat possessed a good, clear narrative style which was admirably adapted to his subject. In *Peter Simple* this style was seen at its best. He

Captain Frederick Marryat; oil painting by J. Simpson, c. *1835.*

thoroughly understood what he was writing about and had no difficulty in expressing himself well and intelligibly over a wide range of topics. He compelled his reader's interest from the first page and held it to the last. *Peter Simple* has given delight to successive generations of grown men, as well as youngsters. A good example of Marryat's lucid, workmanlike style may be seen in his account of the press-gang at work on the eve of the *Diomede's* departure from Portsmouth Harbour.

About dusk we rowed on shore, and landed on the Gosport side: the men were all armed with cutlasses, and wore pea jackets, which are very short great-coats made of what they call Flushing. We did not stop to look at any of the grog-shops in the town, as it was too early, but walked out about three miles in the suburbs, and went to a house, the door of which was locked, but we forced it open in a minute, and hastened to enter the passage, where we found the landlady standing to defend the entrance.

The passage was narrow, and her body so large that she almost filled it up. She stood there holding in her hands a long spit with which she threatened the invaders. By this means she held them off until all the seamen who had been drinking inside had safely made their escape, after which she made a rush at them with the spit, and they fled before her—'so there we were, three officers and fifteen armed men, fairly beat off by a fat old woman'.

We then called at other houses, where we picked up one or two men, but most of them escaped us, by getting out at the windows or the back doors, as we entered the front. Now there was a grog-shop which was a very favourite rendezvous of the seamen belonging to the merchant vessels, and to which they were accustomed to retreat when they heard that the pressgangs were out. Our officers were aware of this, and were therefore indifferent as to the escape of the men, as they knew that they would all go to that place, and confide in their numbers for beating us off: As it was then one o'clock, they thought it time to go there; we proceeded without any noise, but they had people on the look-out, and as soon as we turned the corner of the lane the alarm was given. I was afraid that they would all run away, and we should lose them; but, on the contrary, they mustered very strong on that night, and they had resolved to 'give fight'. The men remained in the house, but an advanced guard of about thirty of their wives saluted us with a shower of stones and mud. Some of our sailors were hurt, but they did not appear to mind what the women did. They rushed on, and then they were attacked by the women with their fists and nails. Notwithstanding this, the sailors only laughed, pushing the women on one side, and saying, 'Be quiet, Poll';—'Don't be foolish, Molly';—'Out of the way, Sukey; we an't come to take away your fancy man'; with expressions of that sort, although the blood trickled down many of their faces, from the way in which they had been clawed. . . . The seamen of the merchant ships had armed themselves with bludgeons and other weapons, and had taken a position on the tables. They were more than two to one against us, and there was a dreadful fight, as their resistance was very desperate. Our sailors were obliged to use their cutlasses, and for a few minutes I was quite bewildered with the shouting and swearing, pushing and scuffling, collaring and fighting, together with the dust raised up, which not only blinded, but nearly choked me. By the time that my breath was nearly squeezed out of my body, our sailors got the best of it, which the landlady and women of the house perceiving, they put out all the lights, so that I could not tell where I was; but our sailors had every one seized his man, and contrived to haul him out of the street door, where they were collected together, and secured.

Another passage from *Peter Simple* which ought to be quoted occurs a little later in the story when the *Diomede*, cruising in the Bay of Biscay, was caught by a gale on a dead lee shore. While they were endeavouring to claw off the coast the wind headed them suddenly, and the captain was obliged to club-haul his ship. That saved them for the moment, and the ship went away on the other tack: but about thirteen miles beyond there was a rocky point which they would have to weather. Such hazardous situations are succinctly mentioned or implied in many a ship's log; but here, in good seamanlike narrative, the whole stormy scene is vividly conjured up.

Before twelve o'clock, the rocky point which we so much dreaded was in sight, broad on the lee-bow; and if the low sandy coast appeared terrible, how much more did this, even at a distance: the black masses of rock, covered with foam, which each minute dashed up in the air, higher than our lower mast-heads. The captain eyed it for some minutes in silence, as if in calculation.

'Mr. Falcon,' said he at last, 'we must put the main-sail on her.'

'She can never bear it, sir.'

'She *must* bear it,' was the reply. 'Send the men aft to the mainsheet. See that careful men attend the buntlines.'

The mainsail was set, and the effect of it upon the ship was tremendous. She careened over so that her lee channels were under water, and when pressed by a sea, the lee-side of the quarter-deck and gangway were afloat. She now reminded me of a goaded and fiery horse, mad with the stimulus applied; not rising as before, but forcing herself through whole seas, and dividing the waves, which poured in one continual torrent from the forecastle down upon the decks below. Four men were secured to the wheel—the sailors were obliged to cling, to prevent being washed away—the ropes were thrown in confusion to leeward, the shot rolled out of the lockers, and every eye was fixed aloft, watching the masts, which were expected every moment to go over the side. A heavy sea struck us on the broadside, and it was some moments before the ship appeared to recover herself; she reeled, trembled, and stopped her way, as if it had stupified her. The first lieutenant looked at the captain, as if to say, 'This will not do'. 'It is our only chance,' answered the captain to the appeal. That the ship went faster through the water, and held a better wind, was certain; but just before we arrived at the point the gale increased in force . . .

The captain and the first lieutenant went aft, and took the forespokes of the wheel, and O'Brien, at a sign made by the captain, laid hold of the spokes behind him. An old quarter-master kept his station at the fourth. The roaring of the seas on the rocks, with the howling of the wind, were dreadful; but the sight was more dreadful than the noise. For a few moments I shut my eyes, but anxiety forced me to open them again, As near as I could judge, we were not twenty yards from the rocks, at the time that the ship passed abreast of them. We were in the midst of the foam, which boiled around us; and as the ship was driven nearer to them, and careened with the wave, I thought that our main-yard-arm would have touched the rock; and at this moment a gust of wind came on, which laid the ship on her beam-ends, and checked her progress through the water, while the accumulated noise was deafening. A few moments more the ship dragged on, another wave dashed over and spent itself upon the rocks, while the spray was dashed back from them, and returned upon the decks. The main rock was within ten yards of her counter, when another gust of wind laid us on our beam-ends, the foresail and mainsail split, and were blown clean out of the bolt-ropes—the ship righted, trembling fore and aft. I looked astern: the rocks were to windward on our quarter, and we were safe. . . .

If the maritime element in English literature must be admitted to be disappointingly meagre, of 'ballads, songs, and snatches' of the sea there is enough and to spare. Though the majority of these are lost, or at any rate forgotten, a considerable number still live on; and very good they are.

Finest of all these airs, a song which was old in Nelson's boyhood and which seems to hold in its melody all the heave and surge of the sea, is 'Spanish Ladies'. Words and music are in perfect accord in this classic lay of a ship, homeward bound, entering soundings and standing up Channel with a fair wind.

> Farewell and adieu to you, Spanish ladies,
> Farewell and adieu to you, ladies of Spain;
> For to-day we've received orders to sail for Old England,
> But we hope very soon to be with you again.
>> Now we'll rant and we'll roar like true British sailormen,
>> We'll rant and we'll roar across the salt seas,
>> Until we strike soundings in the Channel of Old England;
>> From Ushant to Scilly is thirty-five leagues.
>
> We hove the ship to with the wind at sou'-west, my boys,
> We hove the ship to for to strike soundings clear:
> Then we squared the main topsail and bore right away, my boys,
> And straight up the Channel of Old England did steer.
>> Now we'll rant and we'll roar, &c.
>
> The first land we made 'twas a point called the Dodman,
> Next Rame Head off Plymouth, Start, Portland, and Wight;
> We passed up by Beachy, and Farley, and Dungeness,
> And hove our ship to off the South Foreland light.
>> Now we'll rant and we'll roar, &c.

To this era belong some of the most celebrated patriotic songs in the language. 'Rule, Britannia', composed by Thomas Arne in 1740, was destined to become virtually our second national anthem. At the news of a great victory at sea 'Rule, Britannia' would be played by the orchestra at Covent Garden and Drury Lane—sometimes the performance would be abruptly broken off for the purpose, and the chorus enthusiastically sung by both players and audience. During the long blockade of the enemy's ports in the Napoleonic War 'Rule, Britannia' was one of the favourite choruses roared out on the mess decks of a Saturday night; and in certain ships the evening's entertainment would be regularly wound up by the singing of 'Rule, Britannia'.

To the Year of Victories, 'the Great Fifty-nine', belongs the stirring sea-song 'Heart of Oak', written by David Garrick and set to music by William Boyce. In the ensuing decades it became part of the warp and woof of naval tradition. To the fiercely exhilarating double-double-double beat of 'Heart of Oak', the drums beat to quarters when our ships went into action. It was played on the quarter-decks of the flagships at Algeciras and Trafalgar. It was sung by the great Incledon in wardroom and concert hall.

> Come cheer up, my lads, 'tis to glory we steer,
> To add something more to this wonderful year:
> To honour we call you, not press you like slaves,
> For who are so free as the sons of the waves?
>> Heart of oak are our ships, heart of oak are our men;
>> We always are ready, steady boys, steady,
>> We'll fight, and we'll conquer again and again.
>
> We ne'er see our foes, but we wish them to stay;
> They never see us, but they wish us away;
> If they run, why we follow, and run them ashore;
> For, if they won't fight us, we cannot do more.
>> Heart of oak, &c.
>
> They swear they'll invade us, these terrible foes;
> They frighten our women, our children, and beaus;
> But, should their flat-bottoms in darkness get o'er,
> Still Britons they'll find, to receive them on shore.
>> Heart of oak, &c.
>
> We'll still make 'em run, and we'll still make 'em sweat,
> In spite of the Devil, and Brussel's gazette;
> Then cheer up, my lads, with one heart let us sing,
> Our soldiers, our sailors, our statesmen and King.
>> Heart of oak, &c.[1]

An interesting variant of the patriotic *genre* was 'Rodney's Glory', by Eoghan Ruadh (*anglice* Owen O'Sullivan), celebrating the victory over De Grasse off The Saints in 1782. Eoghan had been gathered in by the all-embracing net of the press-gang, and was then serving as a common seaman. Though written in English, in the popular 'Come all ye' form, it was the work of one of the greatest Irish poets who ever lived, whose mother tongue was Gaelic and for whom English was a foreign language. Eoghan may well stand as an exemplar of his race, the 'wild Irish', as they were called—i.e. the native Irish, the Gaels, as contrasted with the Ascendancy or, again, the 'stage Irishman' so often encountered in the novels of Captain Marryat.

> Give ear, ye British hearts of gold,
> That e'er disdain to be controlled,
> Good news to you I will unfold,
>   'Tis of brave Rodney's glory . . .
>
> 'Twas in the year of Eighty Two,
> The Frenchmen know full well 'tis true,
> Brave Rodney did their fleet subdue,
>   Not far from old Fort Royal.
> Full early by the morning's light,
> The proud De Grasse appeared in sight,
> And thought brave Rodney to affright,
> With colours spread at each mast-head,
> Long pendants, too, both white and red,
>   A signal for engagement . . .
>
> From morning's dawn to fall of night,
> We did maintain this bloody fight,
> Being still regardless of their might,
>   We fought like Irish heroes.
> Though on the deck did bleeding lie
> Many of our men in agony,
> We resolved to conquer or die,
> To gain the glorious victory,
> And would rather suffer to sink or die
>   Than offer to surrender.
>
> So well our quarters we maintained,
> Five captured ships we have obtained,
> And thousands of their men were slain,
>   During this hot engagement;

Our British metal flew like hail,
Until at length the French turned tail,
Drew in their colours and made sail
In deep distress, as you made guess,
And when they got in readiness
    They sailed down to Fort Royal . . .

The song was brought to Rodney in the first flush of victory. He was plainly delighted, and summoned the author to his cabin. Escorted by a fellow-countryman, an officer named MacCarthy, Eoghan arrived in the great man's presence. The Admiral received him kindly and offered him promotion; but Eoghan's only desire was to be released from the Service. Before Rodney could reply, MacCarthy interrupted: 'Anything but that; we would not part with you for love or money.' Eoghan turned away sullenly, muttering that he would 'play some other trick' on the speaker—'Imireochaimíd beart éigin eile oraibh.' MacCarthy replied in English: 'I'll take good care, O'Sullivan, that you will not'.[2]

A ballad which long enjoyed a considerable vogue, though nowadays it is not so well known, was 'The Arethusa'.

Come, all ye jolly sailors bold,
Whose hearts are cast in honour's mould,
While British glory I unfold
    Huzza to the *Arethusa*!
She is a frigate tight and brave
As ever stemm'd the dashing wave:
    Her men are staunch
    To their favourite launch;
And when the foe shall meet our fire,
Sooner than strike we'll all expire
    On board of the *Arethusa*.

'Twas with the spring flood she went out,
The English Channel to cruize about,
When four French sail, in show so stout,
    Bore down on the *Arethusa*.
The fam'd *Belle Poule* straight ahead did lie:
The *Arethusa* seem'd to fly;
    Not a sheet nor a tack
    Or a brace did she slack,

Though the Frenchman laugh'd, and thought it stuff
But they knew not the handful of men how tough
    On board of the *Arethusa*.

On deck five hundred men did dance,
The stoutest they could find in France;
We with two hundred did advance,
    On board of the *Arethusa*.
Our captain hail'd the Frenchman, 'Ho!'
The Frenchman then cried out, 'Hullo!'
    'Bear down; d'ye see?
    To our admiral's lee.'
'No, no,' says the Frenchman, 'that can't be!'
'Then I must lug you along with me,'
    Says the saucy *Arethusa*.

The fight was off the Frenchman's land.
We forc'd them back upon the strand;
For we fought till not a stick would stand
    Of the gallant *Arethusa*.
And, now we have driven the foe ashore,
Never to fight with Britons more,
    Let each fill a glass
    To his favourite lass;
A health to the captain and officers true
And all that belongs to the jovial crew
    On board of the *Arethusa*.[3]

The year 1811 saw the production at the Lyceum of Braham's operetta, *The Americans*, containing the celebrated song 'The Death of Nelson'. This was sung by Braham himself and received terrific and reiterated applause. It was sung again at Covent Garden during the season of 1812. 'The Death of Nelson' may be accounted one of the most stirring and nostalgic 'period pieces' of the Napoleonic War; it later became a favourite Victorian ballad, carrying the Nelson legend down to the end of the century.

> 'Twas in Trafalgar's bay
> We saw the Frenchman lay
>   Each heart was bounding then;
> We scorn'd the foreign yoke,
> Our Ships were British oak,
>   And hearts of oak our men.

John Braham; engraving after Wageman.

Our Nelson mark'd them on the wave,
Three cheers our gallant Seamen gave,
  Nor thought of home or beauty,
Along the line this signal ran,
'England expects that every man
  This day will do his duty.'

And now the Cannons roar
Along th' affrighted shore;
  Our Nelson led the way.
His ship the *Victory* nam'd,
Long be that *Victory* fam'd,
  For victory crown'd the day.
But dearly was that conquest bought,
Too well the gallant Hero fought,
  For England, home, and beauty, &c.

The War of 1812 had begun badly for Great Britain with the three disastrous frigate duels which terminated in the surrender successively of the *Guerrière*, *Macdeonian*, and *Java*. Several American sloops-of-war had likewise proved too much for their British opponents. The national faith and trust in the Royal Navy had been rudely shaken. It could not be too deeply felt, Canning avowed in the House of Commons, that 'the sacred spell of the invincibility of the British Navy was broken by these unfortunate captures'. It was largely on account of the run of defeats in 1812 that the capture of the *Chesapeake* by the *Shannon*, Captain Philip Vere Broke, outside Boston on 1 June 1813 was received with such jubilation, which was reflected in the following famous ballad entitled 'The *Shannon* and the *Chesapeake*'.

> The *Chesapeake* so bold,
> Out of Boston, we've been told,
> Came to take the British frigate
>   Neat and handy, O!
> All the people of the port
> They came out to see the sport,
> And the bands were playing
>   'Yankee doodle dandy, O!'
>
> Now before the fight begun,
> The Yankees with much fun,
> Said they'd take the British frigate
>   Neat and handy, O!
> And after that they'd dine,
> Treat their sweethearts all with wine,
> And the band should play up
>   'Yankee doodle dandy, O!'
>
> We no sooner had begun,
> Than from their guns they run,
> Though before they thought they worked 'em
>   Neat and handy, O!
> Brave Broke he waved his sword,
> Crying, 'Now, my lads, we'll board,
> And we'll stop their playing
>   "Yankee doodle dandy, O!"'
>
> Here's a health to Captain Broke,
> And all the hearts of oak,
> That took the Yankee frigate
>   Neat and handy, O!

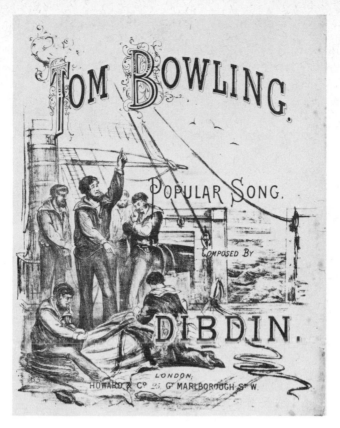

Music cover for 'Tom Bowling' by Dibdin; nineteenth century.

And may we always prove
That in fighting as in love,
The true British sailor
Is the dandy, O![4]

A favourite *motif* was the sentimental. The sailor songs of Charles Dibdin were an outstanding example of the sentimental ballad. His tender and evocative melodies are in a class by themselves. Music and words came together; and Dibdin's airs were admirably suited to his words. They served to establish the 'image' of the British seaman as he was in the days of Nelson. The most celebrated of all, 'Tom Bowling', is said to have been inspired by the death of Dibdin's brother in the merchant service. 'Tom Bowling' immortalized the British tar as he existed in the imagination of landsmen; and, to a large extent, in fact, as he truly was. It was closely followed in popular esteem by 'Poor Jack'. Dibdin's sailor songs came out just in time to satisfy the strong patriotic fervour which had been evoked by the Revolutionary and Napoleonic Wars. The vogue they enjoyed was enormous. They not only appealed to the general public but were immensely and deservedly popular with sailors. Dibdin could justly claim: 'My songs have been the solace of sailors in long voyages, in storms, in battle; and they have been quoted in mutiny to the restoration of order and discipline.'

The seaman of old revelled in the melancholy ballads of which the tune was as doleful as the words. Sung in a minor, dirge-like key, these airs centred on such subjects as drownings, mutiny, pestilence, and piracy on the high seas. The more dismal, the more horrific, the more generally ghastly they were, the better the seaman was pleased. Ballads concerning highwaymen, robberies, murders, and hangings enjoyed a similar vogue on land. To this category belong 'The Mermaid', 'Captain Kidd', 'Brave Benbow', 'Disconsolate Judy's Lament', 'Hosier's Ghost', and 'The Wreck of the *Ramillies*'.

Not a few of the songs popular with seamen were impromptu, including the ballad made by the Irishman, Fegan, when he was sent on board the *Conquistador*, 60, then lying as a guard-ship at the Nore, during the War of American Independence.

> At the beginning of the war they hobbled poor Fegan,
>   And sent him on board of the *Conquistador*;
> That floating old gin shop, who struck upon her beef bones,
>   While laying as a guard ship near the buoy of the Nore.
>
> When first they lugged him before Justice Fielding,
>   Fegan thus to him did say:
> 'You may be damned, you old blind b——,
>   I will be back again before Christmas day.'
>
> 'By my sowl, Mr. Fegan, you are a fine fellow,
>   It's you that have done the king much wrong;
> Call Kit Jourdan, the master at arms, sir,
>   And put Mr. Fegan in double irons strong.'
>
> 'Step here, boatswain's mate, and give him a starting';
>   Says the first lieutenant, 'it's always my way;
> And you shall have many before the day of parting—
>   I think, Mr. Fegan, you mentioned Christmas day.'[5]

Others were traditional.

I hate this damned watching and trudging the deck;
The most we can get, boys, at best is a check;
Sit still then, and let the lieutenants all rail,
We'll ride out the breeze—says Commodore Gale.[6]

Not all these songs were about the sea. There were popular airs of the day which also had their vogue on shipboard. There were songs belonging to particular localities. Almost any song which had a 'catchy' tune and a good chorus would probably be taken up in this way. From Gardner's *Recollections* it is possible to get some idea of the wide range of songs which were in demand in wardroom and midshipmen's berth in his time. In his *Recollections* there is an unforgettable description of the old gunner of the *Gorgon* comfortably ensconced on the forecastle, in the lee of a tarpaulin set up in the weather fore rigging, 'the ship rolling gunwale under', singing 'Bryan O'Lynn' for the amusement of the midshipmen assembled there.

Bryan O'Lynn and his wife, and wife's mother,
They all hid under a hedge together;
But the rain came so fast they got wet to the skin—
We'll shall catch a damned cold, says Bryan O'Lynn.

Bryan O'Lynn and his wife, and wife's mother,
They went in a boat to catch sprats together;
A butt end got stove and the water rushed in—
We're drowned, by the holy, says Bryan O'Lynn.

Bryan O'Lynn and his wife, and wife's mother,
They went with a priest to a wake together,
Where they all got drunk and thought it no sin—
It keeps out the cold, says Bryan O'Lynn.

Bryan O'Lynn and his wife, and wife's mother,
They went to the grave with the corpse together;
The earth being loose they all fell in—
Bear a hand and jump out, says Bryan O'Lynn.

Bryan O'Lynn and his wife, and wife's mother,
When the berring was over went home together;
In crossing a bog they got up to the chin—
I'm damned but we're smothered, says Bryan O'Lynn.

Bryan O'Lynn and his wife, and wife's mother,
By good luck got out of the bog together;

They went to confess to Father O'Flinn—
We're damnation sinners, says Bryan O'Lynn.

Bryan O'Lynn and his wife, and wife's mother,
Resolved to lead a new life together;
And from that day to this have committed no sin—
In the calendar stands SAINT BRYAN O'LYNN. [7]

Charles Incledon; drawing by G. Dance, 1798.

The era under review produced two remarkable singers of sea songs. Charles Incledon, who was one of the finest tenors of his day, was the son of a country surgeon, born at St. Keverne, in Cornwall. In his early youth Incledon ran away to sea, and in 1779 sailed to the West Indies; in the *Raisonnable* he was present at the battle of The Saints. Becoming a great favourite with both officers and men, he was presently released from all the duties of a common seaman. According to tradition, Incledon used to be summoned, first to the wardroom, and afterwards to the Admiral's cabin, to sing to them after dinner. When he left the Service he was furnished with letters of recommendation from Admiral Pigot and others. After a hard struggle he eventually achieved success, singing from 1786 to 1789 at

Vauxhall Gardens, and from 1790 to 1815 at Covent Garden, where Mrs. Billington and he were the principal singers. He played the part of Macheath in the revival of *The Beggars' Opera* and also sang in oratorio. Incledon is said to have sung best of all in ballads, 'rolling his voice upwards like a surge of the sea'; his rendering of 'Heart of Oak' at Vauxhall Gardens was long remembered, and has probably never been surpassed; sometimes at Covent Garden he sang sailor songs in costume between the acts, such as 'The Storm', 'Heaving the Lead', and 'Black-Eyed Susan', which were received with immense acclamation. He died in 1826.

John Braham (whose real name was Abraham) was another renowned tenor, born in London in 1774. He made his début at Covent Garden in 1787 and, reappearing at the theatre in 1801, created a constant furore. It was said by foreign visitors to this country that there was not a tenor in Italy to compare with him. Braham was at his best, perhaps, during the long-drawn-out struggle against Napoleon—especially during the great invasion scare of 1803–5, when the Grand Army was encamped just across the Channel, and popular pride and confidence in the Navy reached their peak. He is associated with such airs as 'Bay of Biscay', 'Heart of Oak', and 'Rule, Britannia'. During his last weeks in England, Nelson went to the house of the eminent banker, Abraham Goldsmid, to hear this great singer. Braham lived until 1856.

The national instinct and inclination for the sea is reflected in the names of a good many of the country dances of the period. Some of the earlier dances are listed in John Playford's collections, which date back to the seventeenth century. These include 'The Boatman', 'About Ship', 'Captain's Maggot', 'Dutch Skipper', and 'Gunfleet'. Others belong to the later Georgian era; and among these may be noted 'The Hardy Sailor', 'Admiral Keppel's Minuet', 'Admiral Nelson's Rout', 'Admiral MacBride's Fancy', 'Nymph of the Ocean', and 'Bonny Jack Tar'.

It may have been one of these dances which was in progress late that night during the ball given in Fanny Price's honour, in *Mansfield Park*, when her uncle, Sir Thomas Bertram, knowing that the girl wished to be up in good time on the morrow to breakfast with her sailor brother before his departure, advised her to go to bed immediately. '"Advise" was his word, but it was the advice of absolute power, and she had only to rise and . . . pass quietly away; stopping at the entrance door, like the Lady of Branxholm Hall, "one moment and no more", to view the happy scene, and take a last look at the five or six determined couples, who were still hard at work—and then, creeping slowly up the principal staircase, pursued by the ceaseless country-dance.'

CHAPTER 20

AFTERMATH

NAPOLEON'S downfall was the signal for an outburst of revelry and rejoicing throughout Great Britain such as this island had not experienced since the Year of Victories, 'the Great Fifty-nine'. From Land's End to John of Groats there were processions, bands, concerts, balls, bonfires, cricket matches, entertainments for the poor, feasting in taverns, bedecking of houses with flags and foliage, display of transparencies, ringing of church-bells, fireworks, maypoles, and dancing on the green. The celebrations were kept up throughout the spring and summer of 1814 and resumed after The Hundred Days and the final triumph of Waterloo.

Early in June, London was *en fête* for the visit of the Allied Sovereigns, the Tsar of Russia and the King of Prussia. For several nights the metropolis was illuminated with fairy lamps and transparencies. The singing and cheering went on far into the night. Later in the month the 'illustrious visitants' went down to Portsmouth to see a grand naval review, comprising more than fifty sail, which attracted vast crowds of spectators. Southsea Common and all the beaches from Fort Monckton to Blockhouse Point were thronged with holiday-makers. 'All seemed to exult with just satisfaction and patriotic joy at a view not more magnificent as a picture', *The Times* declared, 'than honour and glory to the great nation which alone could present it.' An interesting feature of the peace celebrations was the carefree mingling of the different social classes in mutual enjoyment and goodwill. At Southampton, at long tables set up in streets which were adorned with triumphal arches, the gentlemen of the town served and waited on the diners. At Brixham, between 2,000 and 3,000 persons sat down at a table more than 2,000 feet long in the public street. The usual fare at these entertainments was the time-honoured roast beef and plum pudding, with a plentiful supply of beer or cider; and the diners would take their seats to the joyful strains of 'The Roast Beef of Old England'. There was endless drinking of loyal toasts, dancing through town streets, chorusing of patriotic ballads, and banging and blazing of fireworks.

Nowhere were the celebrations carried out with greater enthusiasm or superior effect than in the ports and coastal towns of the West Country, which throughout the long struggle had furnished so many men for the Navy and the merchant service. At Bideford, a grand procession of trumpeters, cavalry, shipwrights, sawyers, blacksmiths, ropemakers, sailors, farmers, gardeners, woolcombers, potters, shoemakers, coopers, masons, etc., presented a striking spectacle as it crossed the ancient bridge over the Torridge. At the neighbouring town of Ilfracombe, then at the height of its prosperity as a sea-port, they also made a great day of it.

> The day began with the ringing of bells, parading the streets with flags, drums, &c. In the evening the battery fired, as a signal for lighting; in front of Nathaniel P. Lee, esq's, house, was the word *'Peace'* in most elegant variegated lamps, the letters of an immense size. At Reeve's Hotel, a number of very grand transparencies were shown; and the whole town was enlivened with the decorations of flowers, transparencies, &c. of the latter of which we counted above fifty set off in a most tasteful and handsome manner. At ten at night, the battery fired a Royal salute, and the ships in the harbour, with the *Alarm* cutter, off at sea, all the ships covered with flags, returned the fire.—Every countenance bespoke the pleasure it experienced, and the whole went off without the least accident.—On Wednesday there will be a very gay ball at Reeve's Hotel.[1]

At the little fishing port of Clovelly, where the houses cling to the cliff-side alongside what must surely be the most precipitous High Street in England, they celebrated the peace a few weeks later. 'At nine o'clock in the morning all the houses in the principal street were most beautifully and profusely decorated with branches of laurel, oak, &c. and the colours of the different nations were proudly displayed from the houses of merchants, masters of vessels and others. About eleven o'clock a procession moved from the quays in the following order. 'Preceded by drums and fifes, there came a long train of young girls dressed in white, then the clergymen, surgeon, principal merchants, etc., the shipwrights, sailors carrying a model full-rigged ship, 'followed by their brother tars two and two, bearing flags with appropriate mottoes, and a party with the fallen tyrant, closely guarded'. At two o'clock a cannon announced the dinner-hour, when nearly five hundred of the inhabitants, including all the poor of the parish, sat down, at a long range of tables in the street, 'to a plentiful dinner of good old English fare—beef, plum-pudding, and beer'. After dinner 'God Save the King' and 'Rule, Britannia' were sung in full chorus. In the evening there was a general illumination; 'which from the peculiar situation of the houses, had a very novel and picturesque appearance from the quay'. A fireworks display concluded the festivities.[2]

All these celebrations, however, did little to alleviate the hardships and misery endured by so many of the working-class throughout the war. The general suffering was actually aggravated, during the early years of the peace, by the multitude of men thrown suddenly on the labour market, which was quite unable to absorb them. The seamen suffered grievously. On the restoration of peace in 1814 about 50,000 of them were paid off almost immediately; in 1816 nearly 60,000 were discharged, and in 1817 another 14,000. Within a few years well over 500 men-of-war were laid up, broken up, or sold out of the Service.

A visitor to Portsmouth in those years has given us a vivid if somewhat fanciful impression of the transformation which had come over the town with the cessation of hostilities. All the liveliness and excitement which had formerly reigned among the inhabitants had given way to lassitude and desolation; the Point was scarcely recognizable, so quiet things had become. Two old men-of-war's men were lamenting the change.

> 'But, my toplights, Tom!' continued he, 'where's all the girls, and the fiddlers, and the Jews, and bumboat-women that used to crowd all sail to pick up a spare hand ashore? Not a shark have I seen in the harbour, and all the old grog-shops with their foul-weather battens up and colours half-mast.' 'All in mourning for Mr. Nap, shipmate,' says Tom; 'we've had no fun here since they cooped him up on board the *Bellerophon* and stowed him away at St. Helena. All the Jews have cut and run, and all the bumboat-women retired upon their fortunes; the poor landlords are most of them in the bilboes at Winchester: and as for a pretty girl—whew!—not such an article to be had at Point now, either for love or money: and all this comes of the peace—shiver my odd forelight! mate, if it lasts much longer, it will be the ruin of the navy.'[3]

Though many of the men discharged at the peace eventually found employment in the mercantile marine or in the fisheries, large numbers of them were reduced to destitution. For years to come bands of seamen, idle, ragged, and half-starved, roamed the streets of the larger towns.

The fate of John Nicol is worth recalling. This man had served for twenty-five years in the Navy; he had been present at two of the greatest actions of the war—St. Vincent and Aboukir Bay; during his service he had

A dinner held to celebrate the Peace of 1814.

sailed all over the world. In his old age, through no fault of his own, he fell upon hard times, and made the long journey from his home in Scotland to London in the hope of securing a pension. But on his arrival in the metropolis he found that his old captain was dead, and at the Admiralty he was refused the necessary certificate of service on the grounds that he had been too long in applying for it. In his last years too often his staple fare was a handful of potatoes and coffee 'made from the raspings of bread'. To warm his old body he would sometimes pick up a few coals in the streets. Nicol lived alone in a small room and also owned a cellar in which he was accustomed to do any little work he managed to obtain. 'Should I be forced to sell it, all I would obtain could not keep me, and pay for lodgings for one year; then I must go to the poor's house, which God in his mercy forbid.'[4]

It was peculiarly appropriate that the Navy which, to a greater degree than any other single factor, had been responsible for the final frustration of Napoleon's bid for world supremacy, should have been entrusted with the duty of conveying the illustrious prisoner to his place of exile and ensuring his safe custody. John Barrow, Second Secretary of the Admiralty, appears to have been chiefly responsible for the decision to send Napoleon to St.

Helena. 'At such a distance and in such a place,' he declared, 'all intrigue would be impossible, and being withdrawn so far from the European world, he would very soon be forgotten.' St. Helena lay far out in the lonely wastes of the South Atlantic, approximately half-way between Africa and South America. The look-out post upon the heights commanded the waters around for a distance of sixty miles. From such a place escape was virtually impossible. Thither the *Northumberland* sailed with Napoleon and his suite, arriving on 20 October 1815—just three months after the Emperor's surrender to Captain Maitland in the *Bellerophon*.

Four British warships were permanently stationed there (one of them continually cruising to the westward of the island). 'My cruisers', declared Cockburn, who during the first months of Napoleon's exile was both Governor of St. Helena and Commander-in-Chief of the station, 'are so well posted round the island that the devil himself could not get out of it.' In addition to this the island was strongly fortified. When Cockburn dispatched the *Peruvian* to claim Ascension Island, one of the two nearest islands (the other was Tristan da Cunha) for Great Britain, he informed the Admiralty that he had done so to prevent the United States or any other nation from establishing themselves there for the purpose of assisting Napoleon's escape.

> I conceived it to be essential to possess ourselves of the Island of Ascension because it is situated within the limit of the same Trade wind with St. Helena, is of course within the invariably moderate weather precincts, and being but a short distance and directly to leeward, a boat or small vessel might have run down to it from St. Helena in three or four days, but the Island of Tristan da Cunha being above twenty degrees of latitude south of St. Helena, of course out of the Trade wind, and situated in a generally stormy region, no small vessel or boat could (with adequate prospect of success) attempt to reach the former Island from the latter.[5]

Sir Hudson Lowe, however, was of a different opinion; and, in the early summer of 1816, Rear-Admiral Pulteney Malcolm, who succeeded Cockburn, sent a cruiser to take possession of Tristan da Cunha—formerly a refuge for privateers. A small garrison was installed; and provision and stores for their sustenance were hauled, not without difficulty, up the 100-foot cliff. A year later the garrison was withdrawn, the Admiralty being now convinced that the occupation of the island was in no way important for the security of St. Helena.[6]

This remote and lonely outpost, on which the greatest military genius that the world has ever known was to live out the brief remainder of his days,

Napoleon on board the Bellerophon *at* Plymouth; *oil painting by J. J. Chalon, 1816.*

exiled from France and civilization, with British cruisers maintaining their silent, unremitting watch off its rugged shores, might well have stood, like the Rock of Gibraltar, for a symbol of the victorious and unchallengeable maritime supremacy of Great Britain throughout the long peace. The imprisonment of Napoleon on St. Helena, indeed, set the seal on the triumph of the great Sea Power over the great Land Power.

Shortly before Trafalgar *The Times* had declared, 'We will retain the empire of the ocean'. This prediction had been fulfilled to the letter. Surely, if ever there was an empire of the ocean in the history of mankind, it was England's. At the close of the war the British Empire was enormous in area and its population more than trebled. The menace which had overhung her territories in the Orient and in the Americas was finally and effectively removed. There was much truth in the claim of the Prussian General von Gneisenau that it was to Napoleon and his overweening ambitions that the aggrandizement of the British Empire might properly be attributed. 'Great Britain has no greater obligations to any mortal on earth than to this ruffian,' he declared. 'For through the events which he has brought about, England's greatness, prosperity, and wealth have risen high. She is the mistress of the sea and neither in this dominion nor in world-trade has she now a single rival to fear.'

For years after the *Northumberland* had carried off Napoleon and his train to their place of exile, old salts were wont to foregather upon The Hard at Portsmouth. There, seated on a wooden bench beside some iron railings overlooking the beach, they would revive memories of the great days that had been—of Black Dick and the Glorious First of June; of the Mediterranean squadron cruising proudly before Toulon; of old Jarvie, and what a taut 'un he was; of the action of St. Valentine's Day, and of the boarding of the huge *Sans Josef* by way of the captured *San Nicolas* (an achievement gleefully acclaimed by the lower deck as '*Nelson's Patent Bridge for boarding First-Rates*'); of stormy days off Ushant and the Black Rocks; of the blowing-up of *L'Orient* at the battle of the Nile; of Saumarez's flagship hauling out of the mole at Gibraltar, before the action of Algeciras, to the strains of 'Heart of Oak'; of the tremendous winter gales of '03; of Trafalgar, and the death of Nelson; of the old 'Billy Ruffian' (*Bellerophon*) cruising off the Brittany coast after Waterloo, and of Napoleon's surrender to her captain.

There would be similar gatherings and much the same kind of reminiscences in almost every port in the kingdom, great and small. In the quieter, more rural places these stories would sometimes survive for generations. At Appledore in North Devon the tradition is still current, or was until very recently, that it was a forebear of the Cox family of   place who had hoisted Nelson's famous signal before Trafalgar. At Port Isaac in Cornwall old fishermen yarning on the Plat would sometimes recount how lookouts were posted on the cliffs to give warning to the men in the boats of the approach of a press-gang; and they would recall how 'Thomas Thomas' had always been regarded as an ill-omened name in the locality—a Port Isaac man of that name having fought and died at the battle of the Nile. For years to come these yarns would be handed down in remote little ports redolent of Stockholm tar, canvas, cordage, newly sawn timber, and seaweed, where the screech of straining blocks mingled with the busy clink of caulking mallets and the recurrent clunk of shipwrights' adzes, and where wooden coasters were still occasionally to be seen which had been afloat in the Napoleonic War and even before.

One of the greatest figures of this era, 'old Jarvie', long outlived his friend and pupil. He had been with his old school-fellow, General Wolfe, at Quebec, and he was still active in the reign of George IV. Early one morning in 1823 four old Greenwich pensioners, having learned that St. Vincent was to pass the previous night at the Hospital, with the Governor, Sir Richard Keats, presented themselves on the terrace in their best uniforms. They were all acquainted with St. Vincent's habit of early rising. One of the four had seen the great Admiral pace the quarter-deck as long ago as St. Valentine's

Day, 1797. Two of them had served in the *Victory*, the others in the *Ville de Paris*. Long before six o'clock St. Vincent was seen on the terrace, with the four old seamen walking stiffly to leeward of him. The Admiral and his former shipmates continued in close conversation for upwards of an hour, to their mutual satisfaction. 'We all in our day', St. Vincent remarked in parting, 'were smart fellows.'

Among the pensioners in Greenwich Hospital in his later years was the famous Tom Allen. Born and bred at Burnham Thorpe and a former retainer of the Nelson family, the 'Norfolk bor' had followed the parson's son to sea, in 1793, in the *Agamemnon*. Tom always declared that he had accompanied Nelson at the boarding of the *San Nicolas* at the battle of St. Vincent and had followed him 'in fourteen scrimmages and fifteen reg'lar engagements'. To the end of his life he claimed that he had prevented Nelson from putting on a brand-new uniform at the Nile, and would never have permitted him to appear on deck with all his decorations had he been present at Trafalgar. Clumsy, uncouth, and illiterate, the Admiral's *wally de cham* (as he liked to style himself) was whole-heartedly attached to his master and watched over him with devoted care. Tom had only lately been married and was down at Burnham Thorpe on his honeymoon when Nelson received his orders. Directed to join the Admiral immediately, Tom arrived at Portsmouth only to find that the *Victory* had sailed twenty-four hours earlier; whereupon he made his way back to Burnham Thorpe. In 1831 Hardy (who was then Governor) got him into Greenwich Hospital, where he passed the remainder of his life in comfort. Hardy caused a memorial to be erected in the Hospital Cemetery, bearing the inscription: 'To the memory of Tom Allen, the faithful servant of Lord Nelson, born at Burnham Thorpe, in the county of Norfolk, 1764, and died at the Royal Hospital, Greenwich, on 23rd November, 1838'.[7]

The fame of Nelson still shone with undiminished lustre. It was, as Codrington declared, 'as if it were determined by fate, that as he distanced those who preceded him, nobody should approach him in these after times; but that he should stand so conspicuously aloof from all the lesser constellations, as to make a greater impression on ages yet to come'. By this time many memoirs of Nelson had appeared, the best known being Robert Southey's which had come out within eight years of the battle of Trafalgar. Monuments to his memory had been erected all over the kingdom. Concert audiences continued to be visibly moved by 'The Death of Nelson'. But the number of men and women who had actually seen Nelson was growing smaller every year.

The Nelson Column in Trafalgar Square, begun in 1840, was completed three years later: but Landseer's famous lions, which were to take their place at the base of the Column, were long in arriving; so long, in fact, that the comic papers of the day were full of witticisms about the interminable delay in their delivery. Quite a number of wonderful things, it was said, were going to happen 'when the lions come to Trafalgar Square'. It was not until the year 1868 that the lions actually arrived.

Throughout the nineteenth century the awe in which the Royal Navy was held by the rest of the world was an abiding source of security and strength. It ruled supreme on every sea and ocean on the face of the globe. There never was a time when this country was so absolutely and completely free from risk of hostile attack. There never was a population—with the exception of the kindred people of the United States—so essentially civilian in its outlook and mentality. In the ensuing decades the aura of invincibility which hung over the victors of St. Vincent, the Nile, and Trafalgar served to tide us safely over many a spell of transient weakness and unpreparedness. It lent force and substance to Palmerston's ringing policy of 'Civis Romanus sum'. It was a main contributory factor in Beaconsfield's bloodless triumph of 1878. It enabled us for many years to exercise world power at an astonishingly low cost. That was the matchless legacy bequeathed to us by the Old Navy, and one of the most truly impressive of all the manifestations of the influence of sea power upon history.

REFERENCES AND NOTES

CHAPTER 1   THE WOODEN WALLS

[1] A. J. Holland, *British Ships of Oak* (1965), pp. 134–5, 141.
[2] Charnock, *History of Marine Architecture* (1801), III, p. 172.
[3] ibid., p. 138.
[4] ibid., p. 203.
[5] ibid., 204.
[6] *Sandwich Papers*, IV, ed. Barnes and Owen (N.R.S., 1938), p. 285.
[7] *Barham Papers*, I, ed. J. K. Laughton (N.R.S., 1907), p. 55.
[8] *Sandwich Papers*, III, ed. Barnes and Owen (N.R.S., 1938), p. 207.
[9] Bogart, *The Economic History of the American People* (1942), p. 22.
[10] Roger Fisher, *Heart of Oak, The British Bulwark* (1763), *passim*.
[11] R. G. Albion, *Forests and Sea Power* (1926), p. 295.
[12] See *Select Naval Documents*, ed. Hughes and Hodges (1936), pp. 151–2.
[13] Holland, op. cit., p. 32.
[14] Albion, op. cit., pp. 295 sqq.
[15] ibid., p. 347. See also Bamford, *Forests and French Sea Power, 1660–1789* (1956), pp. 207–8.
[16] Quoted by E. Berckman, *Nelson's Dear Lord* (1962), p. 73.
[17] *Barham Papers*, III, ed. J. K. Laughton (1911), p. 69.
[18] ibid., pp. 44–5; Barrow, *An Auto-Biographical Memoir* (1847), p. 264.

CHAPTER 2   STRATEGY AND TACTICS

[1] *Vernon Papers*, ed. B. McL. Ranft (N.R.S., 1958), p. 451.
[2] Stetson Conn, *Gibraltar in British Diplomacy in the Eighteenth Century* (1942), p. 265.
[3] See G. J. Marcus, *Quiberon Bay* (1960), pp. 89–96.
[4] ibid., pp. 143–4.
[5] See G. J. Marcus, *A Naval History of England, II. The Age of Nelson*, pp. 49–50.
[6] *Vernon Papers*, p. 287.
[7] 'The latest Additional Fighting Instructions will reveal to us how ripe and sound a system of tactics had been reached. The idea of crushing part of the enemy by concentration had replaced the primitive intention of crowding him into a confusion; a swift and vigorous attack had replaced the watchful defensive, and above all the true method of concentration had been established; for although a concentration on the van was still permissible in

exceptional circumstances, the chief of the new articles are devoted to concentration on the rear. Thus our tacticians had worked out the fundamental principles on which Nelson's system rested, even to breaking up the line into two divisions. "Containing" alone was not yet clearly enunciated, but by Hood's signals for breaking the line, the best method of effecting it was made possible. Everything indeed lay ready for the hands of Howe and Nelson to strike into life.' See J. S. Corbett, *Fighting Instructions, 1530–1816* (N.R.S., 1905), pp. 213–14. But see also John Creswell, *British Admirals of the Eighteenth Century* (1972).

[8] Add. Mss. 37,953.

[9] The later edition of the Signal Book was used on the Glorious First, and also in the actions of St. Vincent and the Nile.

[10] The carronade, first cast in the Carron foundry in Stirlingshire, was described by W. Laird Clowes as 'a quick-firer of large calibre but very short range'. On 4 September 1782, the French frigate *Hébé* was attacked by the British frigate *Rainbow* off the Île de Batz: such was the force of the *Rainbow*'s carronade that the captain of the *Hébé*, believing his opponent to be a ship of the line, immediately hauled down his colours.

CHAPTER 3   SEAMANSHIP AND NAVIGATION

[1] *Above and Under Hatches*, ed. C. C. Lloyd (1957), pp. 159–60.

[2] *Recollections of my Sea Life, 1808–1830* by J. H. Boteler (N.R.S., 1942), p. 14. Cf. Adm. 51/2293, 27 February 1811. One of the earliest accounts of this interesting evolution (which was only attempted in a desperate emergency) was by William Hutchinson, a shipmaster in the Newcastle coal trade and author of a widely-read manual on seamanship. 'There is a saying amongst seamen, if a ship will not stay, you must ware her; and if she will not ware, you must box haul; and if you cannot box haul her, you must club haul her; that is, let go the anchor, to get her about on the other tack.' Club-hauling a ship, he goes on to explain, 'is to get a ship from one tack to the other, by letting go an anchor, when by an eddy tide, or by a ruff sea, or being out of trim, or from any other cause, she refuses to stay or ware, in time to avoid danger. When this happens in shoal water, found by the lead, that if the ship has not water over her anchor, she should have sternway given her, and not headway when the anchor is let go, and the weather anchor is likelier to go clear of the ship than the lee one, therefore both bower anchors should be ready on these occasions.' (William Hutchinson, *A Treatise on Practical Seamanship*, pp. 52, 54.)

[3] *Naval Chronicle*, Vol. 29, pp. 19–21. Cf. Adm. 51/2546, 16–18 December 1812.

[4] Adm. 1/503, 11 May 1813.

[5] Adm. 1/508, 17 January 1815; 51/2543, 13–15 January 1815.

[6] Pellew possessed to a very remarkable extent that delicate art of seamanship which consists in so handling a ship as to make her do just what you want, and to put her just where she should be' (Mahan, *Types of Naval Officers*), p. 446.

[7] Quoted by Mahan, *Types of Naval Officers* (1901), pp. 444–5.

[8] *Five Naval Journals*, ed. H. G. Thursfield (N.R.S., 1951), p. 255.

[9] John Nicol, *Adventures of John Nicol, Mariner* (1822), pp. 1–2.

[10] Quoted by E. G. R. Taylor, *The Haven-Finding Art* (1956), p. 256.

[11] How extremely baffling this problem appeared in the eyes of the contemporary world may be gauged from a significant observation of young Marlow's in Goldsmith's comedy, *She Stoops to Conquer*—'Zounds, man! we could as soon find out the longitude'.

[12] Until Graeme Spence carried out his admirable survey of the Goodwin Sands and the

Downs in 1794–5, these dangerous sands had never been systematically and accurately surveyed.

[13] As used in 1825, this term of course refers to an enclosed dock in which ships lay afloat at all states of the tide—not to the modern 'floating dock' in which, by pumping out compartments, a ship is raised out of the water.

[14] Quoted by Sir Archibald Day, *The Admiralty Hydrographic Service* (1967), p. 15.

[15] ibid., pp. 27, 29.

[16] The work of Rennell was continued and amplified by Lieutenant M. F. Maury of the United States Navy, who published in the middle of the nineteenth century his celebrated *Wind and Current Charts*.

CHAPTER 4   MARITIME RIGHTS

[1] Quoted by Pares, *Colonial Blockade and Neutral Rights* (1936), p. 181.

[2] ibid., p. 180.

[3] Quoted by Hotblack, *Chatham's Colonial Policy* (1917), pp. 142–3.

[4] Quoted by Kulrud, *Maritime Neutrality to 1780* (1936), p. 323.

[5] Quoted by H. W. Briggs, *The Doctrine of Continuous Voyage* (1926), p. 16.

[6] Quoted by E. S. Roscoe, *Lord Stowell* (1916), pp. 60–1.

[7] James Stephen, *War in Disguise, or the Frauds of the Neutral Flags* (1805), pp. 94–5.

[8] *War Speeches of William Pitt*, ed. R. Coupland (1940), p. 300.

[9] ibid., p. 299.

[10] Stephen, op. cit., pp. 43–4.

[11] Quoted by Bradford Perkins, *Prologue to the War between England and the United States, 1805–1812* (1961), p. 75.

CHAPTER 5   THE OFFICERS OF THE SERVICE

[1] *Above and Under Hatches*, ed. C. C. Lloyd (1957), pp. 50–1.

[2] E. Thompson, *A Sailor's Letters* (1767).

[3] Quoted by L. B. Namier, *Structure of Politics at the Accession of George III* (1960), I, pp. 43–4.

[4] Nor, judging from the following excerpt from a letter written by Admiral Thomas Pye to Lord Sandwich, would it appear that all gentlemen were men of education. 'Give me leave my Lord to make one observation more and I have Don—and that is When You peruse Admiral Pyes Letters you will please not to Scrutinize too close either to the speling or the Grammatical Part as I allow my Self to be no proficient in either. I had the Mortification to be neglected in my education, went to sea at 14 without any, and a Man of War was my University' (*Sandwich Papers*, I, ed. J. S. Corbett, p. 35).

[5] Quoted by H. W. Richmond, *The War of 1739–48* (1920), I, p. xii.

[6] E. H. Locker, *Memoirs of Celebrated Commanders* (1830).

[7] See *infra*, pp. 85–6.

[8] Quoted by Dundonald, *Autobiography of a Seaman* (1861), p. 32.

[9] *Above and Under Hatches*, pp. 162–4.

[10] ibid., pp. 75, 78–9.

[11] ibid., pp. 111–12.

[12] Misappropriation of Government stores.

[13] ibid., pp. 125–6.

[14] E. Fraser, *Famous Fighters of the Fleet* (1904), p. 78.

[15] John Creswell, *Naval Warfare* (ed. 1942), p. 6.

[16] *Spencer Papers*, ed. J. S. Corbett (N.R.S., 1913), I, pp. 379–81.

CHAPTER 6   THE YOUNG GENTLEMEN

[1] *Letters of Sir Thomas Byam Martin*, ed. R. V. Hamilton (N.R.S., 1902), I, pp. 4–5.

[2] *Above and Under Hatches*, ed. C. C. Lloyd (1957), pp. 12–13.

[3] Sir George Elliot, *Memoirs* (1863), p. 424.

[4] W. S. Lovell, *Personal Narrative of Events from 1799 to 1815* (1879), p. 4.

[5] *Above and Under Hatches*, pp. 62, 104–6.

[6] ibid., pp. 124–5.

[7] J. H. Boteler, *Reflections of my Sea Life, 1808–1830*, p. 14.

[8] W. S . Lovell, *Personal Recollections of Events from 1799 to 1815* (1879), p. 5. Such lively pastimes as 'able wackets' and 'goose' had their counterparts, of course, in many a modern gunroom: for instance, 'the priest of the parish and his man John' and 'dogs of war'—the first of which was fairly rowdy, while the second was definitely *rough*!

[9] ibid, p. 6.

[10] *Above and Under Hatches*, p. 43.

[11] 'At the inn where I dined I saw a great number of young midshipmen; some of them were tender boys who seemed more fit subjects for maternal care than for war and bloodshed; it is from such beginnings, however, that *Blakes* and *Nelsons* are formed, and I could easily imagine that I saw among them the future Admirals of England'. See Silliman, *Journal of Travels in England, Holland, and Scotland* (1812), I, p. 117.

[12] *Recollections of my Sea Life*, p. 49.

[13] Lovell, op. cit., pp. 41–2.

[14] George Elliot, *Memoirs* (1863), p. 25.

CHAPTER 7   THE MANNING OF THE FLEET

[1] R. Edington, *A Treatise on the Coal Trade* (1813), p. 227.

[2] And not always then. It is said that on one occasion John Wesley was impressed. See J. R. Hutchinson, *The Press-Gang Afloat and Ashore* (1913).

[3] Silliman, *Journal of Travels in England, Holland, and Scotland* (1812), I, p. 50.

[4] Quoted by David Mathew, *The Naval Heritage* (1944), p. 98.

[5] *Above and Under Hatches*, ed. C. C. Lloyd (1957), p. 74.

[6] Quoted by Mathew, op. cit., pp. 98–9.

[7] *Naval Miscellany*, I, ed. J. K. Laughton (N.R.S., 1930), pp. 320–1.

[8] *Landsman Hay*, ed. M. D. Hay (1953), pp. 218–20.

[9] 'Jack Nasty-Face', *Nautical Economy* (1836), pp. 2–3.

[10] Quoted by C. N. Robinson, *The British Fleet* (1894). p. 438.

[11] *Five Naval Journals*, ed. H. G. Thursfield (N.R.S., 1951), p. 19.

[12] *The Naval Sketch Book*. By an Officer of Rank (1826).

[13] 'Jack Nasty-Face', op. cit., pp. 5–12.

CHAPTER 8   DISCIPLINE AND MORALE

[1] *Select Naval Documents*, ed. Hodges and Hughes (ed. 1936), pp. 174–8.

[2] *Barham Papers*, I, ed. J. S. Corbett (N.R.S., 1906), p. 305.

[3] John Owen, *The War at Sea under Queen Anne* (1938), p. 25.

[4] 'Jack Nasty-Face', *Nautical Economy* (1836), p. 110. The evidence of 'Jack Nasty-Face' is not always to be relied on: but in this case it is fully confirmed by other sources.

[5] ibid., pp. 110–13. Admiral William Smyth, who first went to sea during the Napoleonic War, in his *A Sailor's Word-Book* bluntly describes the punishment of flogging through the fleet as 'diabolical'.

[6] *Adventures of John Wetherell*, ed. C. S. Forester (1954), p. 61.

[7] J. H. Boteler, *Recollections of my Sea Life, 1808–1830* (N.R.S., 1942), p. 48.

[8] *Landsman Hay*, ed. M. D. Hay (1953), p. 77.

[9] C. R. Pemberton, *Autobiography of Pel Verjuice*.

[10] John Nicol, *Adventures of John Nicol, Mariner* (1822), p. 186; *Above and Under Hatches*, ed. C. C. Lloyd (1957), pp. 96–7.

[11] Nicol, op. cit., p. 186.

[12] Joseph Allen, *Memoir of Sir William Hargood* (1841), pp. 278–81; Edward Fraser, *The Sailors Whom Nelson led* (1913), pp. 215–16.

[13] *Above and Under Hatches*, p. 10.

[14] Beatson, *Naval and Military Memoirs of Great Britain* (1790), II, p. 588.

[15] P. K. Kemp, *Prize Money* (1946), p. 23.

[16] James Stephen, *War in Disguise, or the Frauds of the Neutral Flags* (1805), pp. 125–7.

CHAPTER 9   HYGIENE AND SUPPLY

[1] L. H. Roddis, *James Lind* (1950).

[2] *Naval Yarns*, ed. W. H. Long (1899), p. 65.

[3] Gilbert Blane, *The Health of Seamen* (1780), pp. 19–20.

[4] Quoted in *The Health of Seamen*, ed. C. C. Lloyd (N.R.S., 1965), p. 118.

[5] His great contribution to the subject was his realization that what was needed was fresh food in general, and clean water, and, as a counter to depression, variety of food; and, as another contribution, cleanliness of person, clothes and quarters; and, as an aid to that, a dry and disinfected ship' (J. C. Beaglehole in *The Geographical Journal*, CXXII, p. 425).

[6] *The Health of Seamen*, ed. C. C. Lloyd (N.R.S., 1965), p. 30.

[7] Blane, *Observations on the Diseases Incident to Seamen* (1785), p. 184.

[8] *The Health of Seamen*, ed. C. C. Lloyd (N.R.S., 1965), p. 30.

[9] *Observations on the Diseases Incident to Seamen*, pp. 332–3.

[10] William Thompson, *The Royal-Navy Man's Advocate* (1757).

[11] William Thompson, *An Appeal to the Public* (1761).

[12] Adm. 1/92, 21 June, 22, 24 July, 28 August 1759.

[13] Adm. 2/83, 2 August 1759.

[14] *The Health of Seamen*, ed. C. C. Lloyd (N.R.S., 1965), p. 121.

[15] *Barham Papers*, ed. J. K. Laughton (N.R.S., 1907), I, 74–5.

[16] Quoted in *Medicine and the Navy, 1714–1815*, p. 324.

[1] 'Turn out,' bawled the master of the *Brunswick*, banging on Gardner's door as the 'buzz' went round that the war was ending (this was in 1802), 'and hurrah for the back of the Point and Capstan Square! paid off by the hokey, in a few days.' See *Above and Under Hatches*, ed. C. C. Lloyd (1957), p. 235.

[2] W. G. Gates, *Free Mart Fair* (1897), p. 40.

[3] In 1805, both the number and speed of the coaches were considerably augmented. At this time the coaches for London were the 'Royal Mail' and the 'Regulator', which both started from the George; the 'Hero', from the Fountain, the 'Nelson' from the Blue Posts, and the 'Rocket' from the Quebec.

[4] *Above and Under Hatches*, ed. C. C. Lloyd (1957), p. 178. It is good to know that Methusalah Wills, a very decent old fellow, died, then the senior master on the list, at the ripe age of eighty-three.

[5] Henry Slight, *The Royal Port . . . of Portsmouth* (1843), pp. 101–2.

[6] George Pinckard, *Notes on the West Indies* (1813), pp. 18–19.

[7] Pinckard, op. cit., p. 32.

[8] William James, *Naval History of Great Britain, 1793–1820* (1837), II, p. 63.

[9] Landmann, *Adventures and Recollections* (1852), II, pp. 259–63.

[1] It will be remembered how in Marryat's naval novel, *Peter Simple*, the hero's friend, Terence O'Brien, having lately been promoted to post-rank, hurried down to Portsmouth to read himself in before his commission could be cancelled as the result of an intrigue—'I looked up at the sky as soon as I left the Admiralty portico, and was glad to see that the weather was so thick and the telegraph not at work, or I might have been too late'.

[2] C. C. Lloyd, *Mr. Barrow of the Admiralty* (1970), pp. 74–8.

[3] The allusion was to Jemmy Twitcher in *The Beggars' Opera*, who had peached upon Captain Macheath. It was Sandwich's betrayal of his former boon-companion, John Wilkes, that had gained for him this unsavoury nickname.

[4] Sir John Barrow, *An Auto-biographical Memoir* (1847), pp. 255–6.

[1] *Memoir of Sir Edward Codrington*, ed. Lady Bourchier (1873), I, p. 73.

[2] *Above and Under Hatches*, ed. C. C. Lloyd (1957), pp. 116–17.

[3] See G. J. Marcus, 'The Loss of the *Ramillies*', *Royal United Service Institution Journal*, Vol. 105, pp. 510–14.

[4] Quoted by Bourchier, op. cit., I, pp. 16–17. cf. Howe's *Journal*, Adm. 1/391, 11 December 1793.

[5] See the admirable account of the disaster by A. N. Ryan in *Mariner's Mirror*, Vol. 50, pp. 123–34.

CHAPTER 13   LONDON RIVER

[1] William Hutchinson, *A Treatise on Practical Seamanship* (1777), p. 75.

[2] ibid., pp. 76, 120–1.

[3] ibid., p. 121.

[4] ibid., pp. 123–4.

[5] ibid., p. 124.

[6] Edington, *A Treatise on the Coral Trade* (1813), p. 234.

[7] G. G. Harris, *The Trinity House of Deptford* (1969), pp. 81, 89, 125, 162.

[8] ibid., pp. 92–3, 173–4.

[9] Hutchinson, op. cit., p. 135.

[10] Graeme Spence, *Nautical Descriptions of the Banks and Channels of the Thames Estuary* (1804), *passim*; G. S. Ritchie, *The Admiralty Chart* (1965), pp. 92–3, 343.

[11] Joseph Cotton, *A Memoir on the Origin and Incorporation of the Trinity House of Deptford Strond* (1818), pp. 152–3.

[12] Daniel Defoe, *Tour through Great Britain* (ed. 1928), I, p. 202.

[13] Quoted in *Johnson's England*, ed. A. S. Turbeville (1933), I, p. 171.

[14] J. R. McCulloch, *Dictionary of Commerce* (1832), p. 450.

[15] Quoted by James Elmes, *Survey of the Harbour and Port of London* (1838), p. 33. See also *The Select Committee on the Improvement of the Port of London, 1796* (Parliamentary Papers, XIV, 1836), and P. Colquhoun, *A Treatise on the Commerce and Police of the River Thames* (1800).

CHAPTER 14   LLOYD'S

[1] D. E. W. Gibb, *Lloyd's of London* (1957), p. 38.

[2] Wright and Fayle, *A History of Lloyd's* (1928), p. 192.

[3] Gibb, op. cit., pp. 56–7; Wright and Fayle, op. cit., p. 193.

[4] Quoted by F. Martin, *The History of Lloyd's* (1876), pp. 239–40.

[5] Wright and Fayle, op. cit., p. 197.

[6] Adm. 1/3993, 7 November 1805.

[7] Adm. 1/3993, 6 September 1809.

[8] Adm. 1/3993, 8 March 1809.

CHAPTER 15   THE SOCIAL BACKGROUND

[1] David Mathew, *A Naval Heritage* (1944), pp. 82–3.

[2] The Test Act required 'all persons holding any office of profit or trust, civil or military, under the crown, to take oaths of allegiance and supremacy, receive the sacrament of the Lord's Supper according to the rites of the Church of England, and subscribe the declaration against transubstantiation'.

[3] M. A. Lewis, *The Social History of the Royal Navy, 1793–1815* (1960), p. 38 *et passim*.

CHAPTER 16   'SWEETHEARTS AND WIVES'

[1] *The Wynne Diaries*, ed. A. Fremantle (1940), II, pp. 97–8.

[2] ibid., p. 118.

[3] J. Markham, *A Naval Career during the Old War* (1883), pp. 154–5, 169–74.

[4] *Public and Private Correspondence of Vice-Admiral Lord Collingwood*, ed. G. L. Newnham Collingwood (1829), pp. 84–5.

[5] *Naval Yarns*, ed. W. H. Long (1899), p. 63.

[6] 'Jack Nasty-Face', *Nautical Economy* (1836), pp. 58–9.

[7] *Private Correspondence of Admiral Lord Collingwood*, ed. E. A. Hughes (1957), p. 251.

[8] David Hannay, 'Odds and Ends of the Old Navy', *Mariner's Mirror*, Vol. 4, p. 181.

CHAPTER 17   JACK ASHORE

[1] *Landsman Hay*, ed. M. D. Hay (1953), p. 190.

[2] Geo. Pinckard, *Notes on the West Indies* (1813), p. 14.

[3] Quoted by W. G. Gates, *History of Portsmouth* (1900), p. 534.

[4] Hay, *op. cit.*, pp. 190–1.

[5] *Naval Yarns*, ed. W. H. Long (1899), pp. 150–1.

[6] Quoted by W. G. Gates, *Free Mart Fair* (1897), pp. 9–11.

[7] *Five Naval Journals*, ed. Thursfield (N.R.S.), p. 240.

[8] *Naval Songs and Ballads*, ed. C. H. Firth (N.R.S., 1907), p. 289.

CHAPTER 18   THE LETTERS OF SAILORS

[1] Quoted by Mackay, *Admiral Lord Hawke* (1965), pp. 255–6.

[2] Quoted by G. B. Mundy, *Life of Admiral Lord Rodney* (1830), I, pp. 208–9.

[3] ibid., p. 458.

[4] *Above and Under Hatches*, ed. C. C. Lloyd (1957), p. 144.

[5] Hoste, *Memoirs and Letters of Captain Sir William Hoste* (1833), p. 85.

[6] Sir John Ross, *Memoirs and Correspondence of Admiral Lord de Saumarez* (1838), I, p. 312.

[7] Coleridge, *The Story of a Devonshire House* (1905), pp. 92–3.

[8] ibid., p. 94.

[9] ibid., pp. 92–4, 100.

[10] ibid., p. 113.

[11] *Memoir of Admiral Sir Edward Codrington*, ed. Lady Bourchier (1872), I, p. 57.

[12] Quoted by J. H. and H. C. Hubback, *Jane Austen's Sailor Brothers* (1906), pp. 151–2, 154–6.

[13] *The Wynne Diaries*, ed. A. Fremantle (1940), III, pp. 216, 221–2.

[14] *Naval Yarns*, ed. W. H. Long (1899), pp. 233–4.

[15] *Public and Private Correspondence of Vice Admiral Lord Collingwood*, ed. G. L. Newnham Collingwood (1829), pp. 327–8, 492–4.

[16] *Private Correspondence of Admiral Lord Collingwood*, ed. E. A. Hughes (1957), pp. 109, 129; Newnham Collingwood, op. cit., pp. 227, 233–5.

[17] *Landsman Hay*, ed. M. D. Hay (1953), p. 76.

[18] Newnham Collingwood, op. cit., pp. 112, 167–8.

[19] ibid., p. 262.

[20] Hughes, op. cit., p. 291.

CHAPTER 19   STORY AND SONG

[1] David Garrick, *Harlequin's Invasion, or a Christmas Gambol* (1759).

[2] Daniel Corkery, *The Hidden Ireland* (1925), pp. 207–11; Tunstall, *Flights of Naval Genius* (1930), p. 119.

[3] *Naval Songs and Ballads*, ed. C. H. Firth (N.R.S., 1907), pp. 248–9.

[4] Firth, op. cit., pp. 311–12.

[5] *Above and Under Hatches*, ed C. C. Lloyd (1957), p. 163.

[6] ibid., p. 49.

[7] ibid., pp. 127–8.

CHAPTER 20   AFTERMATH

[1] *Western Luminary*, 16 June 1814.

[2] ibid., 28 June 1814.

[3] B. Blackmantle, *The English Spy* (1826), II, p. 184.

[4] John Nicol, *Adventures of John Nicol, Mariner* (1822), p. 211.

[5] Quoted by J. Brander, *Tristan da Cunha, 1506–1902* (1940), p. 86.

[6] ibid., pp. 84–6.

[7] G. S. Parsons, *Nelsonian Reminiscences* (1905), pp. 267–79.

BIBLIOGRAPHY

CHAPTER 1   THE WOODEN WALLS

The main authority for the essential raw material of naval construction in this era is R. G. Albion's *Forests and Sea Power* (1926), a work which is as interesting and stimulating as it is informative and important. See also G. S. Laird Clowes's *Sailing Ships, their History and Development* (1936) and G. Blake's *British Ships and Shipbuilders* (1946). Design and rigging are covered by Sir Alan Moore's *Rig in the North* (1956). For the grave timber crisis of 1803–5, see *Nelson's Dear Lord* by E. Berckman (1962).

Important primary sources are Fisher's *Heart of Oak, The British Bulwark* (1763), Charnock's *History of Marine Architecture* (1801), *Letters and Papers of Charles, Lord Barham*, III, ed. J. K. Laughton (N.R.S., 1911), *Letters of Admiral the Earl of St. Vincent*, ed. D. Bonner-Smith (N.R.S., 1927), and *The Private Papers of John, Earl of Sandwich*, IV, ed. G. R. Barnes and J. H. Owen (N.R.S., 1938).

CHAPTER 2   STRATEGY AND TACTICS

An indispensable authority on naval strategy in general is *Some Principles of Maritime Strategy* by J. S. Corbett (1911), which has recently been reprinted. Other important works which should be consulted are *Naval Warfare* (2nd ed. 1942) and *Statesmen and Sea Power* by H. W. Richmond (1946).

For the role played by the Western Squadron and the investment of Brest in our naval strategy, see A. T. Mahan's *The Influence of Sea Power upon History* (1890) and *The Influence of Sea Power upon the French Revolution and Empire* (1892), J. S. Corbett's *The Seven Years War* (1907) and *The Campaign of Trafalgar* (1910), H. W. Richmond's *The War of 1739–1748* (1920), A. T. Patterson's *The Other Armada* (1961), G. J. Marcus's *A Naval History of England, I. The Formative Centuries* (1961) and *II. The Age of Nelson* (1971), and Piers Mackesy's *The War for America* (1964).

Reference should also be made to such important primary sources as *Papers relating to the Blockade of Brest*, ed. J. Leyland (N.R.S., 1901), *Letters and Papers of Charles, Lord Barham*, ed. J. K. Laughton (N.R.S., 1910), *The Private Papers of John, Earl of Sandwich*, I and II, ed. J. S. Corbett (1913) and III and IV, ed. H. W. Richmond (1924), and *The Keith Papers*, III, ed. C. C. Lloyd (1955).

On the French side see Jurien de la Gravière's *Guerres maritimes de la France sous la république et l'empire* (1883), E. Desbrière's *La Campagne de 1805* (1907), Eng. trans.

The Trafalgar Campaign by C. Eastwick (1933), R. V. Castex's *Théories stratégiques* (1935), and L. Nicolas's *La puissance navale dans l'histoire* (1958).

For the Baltic, see *Memoirs and Correspondence of Admiral Lord de Saumarez* by Sir John Ross (1838) and *The Saumarez Papers*, ed. A. N. Ryan (N.R.S., 1968); for the Mediterranean, *The Mastery of the Mediterranean* by Sir Thomas Maitland (1897), *Gibraltar in British Diplomacy in the Eighteenth Century* by Stetson Conn (1942), and *The War in the Mediterranean, 1803–1810* by Piers Mackesy (1957); for the Indian Ocean, *War in the Eastern Seas* by C. N. Parkinson (1954) and *Great Britain in the Indian Ocean* by G. S. Graham (1969).

For the use, and misuse, of intelligence in naval warfare, see J. S. Corbett's *The Seven Years War* and *The Campaign of Trafalgar*, John Creswell's *Naval Warfare*, E. H. Stuart Jones's *An Invasion that Failed* (1950), G. J. Marcus's *Quiberon Bay* and *A Naval History of England, I. The Formative Centuries* and *II. The Age of Nelson*.

For an admirable account of the development of naval tactics, see M. A. Lewis's *The Navy of Britain* (1948) and John Creswell's *British Admirals of the Eighteenth Century* (1972). See also *Fighting Instructions, 1530–1816* (1905) and *Signals and Instructions* (1908), both by J. S. Corbett, and *A History of Naval Tactics from 1530 to 1930* by S. and M. Robinson (1942). An important contemporary work on tactics is Clerk of Eldin's *An Essay on Naval Tactics* (1797).

For gunnery, see H. Douglas's *A Treatise on Naval Gunnery* (1820), F. L. Robertson's *Evolution of Naval Armament* (1921), Dudley Pope's *Guns* (1965), and Peter Padfield's *Broke of the 'Shannon'* (1966).

CHAPTER 3   SEAMANSHIP AND NAVIGATION

Seamanship as a factor in naval warfare has been grievously neglected by the majority of historians. Nevertheless, it is of necessity very closely linked with other vital factors such as strategy, tactics, and maritime rights; and in the hands of a professional seaman like Mahan it receives the attention it deserves. See A. T. Mahan's *The Influence of Sea Power upon History* (1890), *The Influence of Sea Power upon the French Revolution and Empire* (1892), and *Sea Power in its Relations to the War of 1812* (1905).

Two contemporary works which are of considerable interest are W. Hutchinson's *A Treatise on Practical Seamanship* (1777) and R. Edington's *A Treatise on the Coal Trade* (1813).

There is no really authoritative work treating of navigation in the era under survey comparable, for instance, with D. W. Waters's *The Art of Navigation in Elizabethan and Early Stuart Times* (1958). The best of the general studies is E. G. R. Taylor's *The Haven-Finding Art* (1956).

On particular aspects of the subject see *Harbour and Port Works* by L. V. Harcourt (1868), *The Marine Chronometer: Its History and Development* by R. T. Gould (1923),

From Lodestone to Gyro-Compass by H. L. Hitchins and W. E. May (1953), *The World's Lighthouses before 1820* by D. A. Stevenson (1959), *The Life and Voyages of Captain George Vancouver* by B. Anderson (1960), *The Admiralty Chart* by G. S. Ritchie (1967), *The Journals of Captain Cook on His Voyages of Discovery*, ed. J. C. Beaglehole (1967), and *The Admiralty Hydrographic Service* by Sir A. Day (1967).

CHAPTER 4   MARITIME RIGHTS

The crucial issue of maritime rights is treated by the following authorities: *War in Disguise, or the Frauds of the Neutral Flags* by James Stephen (1805), *Lord Stowell* by Roscoe (1916), *The Documentary History of the Armed Neutralities* by Piggott and Omond (1919), *The Doctrine of Continuous Voyage* by H. W. Briggs (1926), *Neutrality I, The Origins* by Jessup and Deak (1935) and *II, The Napoleonic Period* by W. A. Phillips and A. H. Reade (1936), *Maritime Neutrality to 1780* by Kulrud (1936), and *Colonial Blockade and Neutral Rights* by R. Pares (1936).

CHAPTER 5   THE OFFICERS OF THE SERVICE

The leading authority on this subject is the late Professor M. A. Lewis with his *England's Sea Officers* (1939) and *The Social History of the Royal Navy* (1960).

Other works, contemporary and historical, which may be consulted are *Memoirs of Celebrated Commanders* by E. H. Locker (1830), *Life and Correspondence of the Earl of St. Vincent* by E. P. Brenton (1838), *Memoirs of the Earl of St. Vincent* by J. S. Tucker (1844), *Memoirs* by the Hon. Sir George Elliot (1863), *Nelson and his Captains* by W. H. Fitchett (1902), *Types of Naval Officers* by A. T. Mahan (1902), *The Wynne Diaries*, ed. A. Fremantle (1940), *Recollections of my Sea Life, 1808–1830* by J. H. Boteler (N.R.S., 1942), *Years of Endurance* (1943) and *Years of Victory* (1944), both by Sir Arthur Bryant, *Nelson's Band of Brothers* by L. Kennedy (1951), *Above and Under Hatches (Recollections of James Anthony Gardner)*, ed. C. C. Lloyd (1957), and *The Dress of Naval Officers* by W. E. May (1966).

CHAPTER 6   THE YOUNG GENTLEMEN

C. F. Walker's *Young Gentlemen* (1938) is of considerable interest and appeal; but it devotes comparatively little space to the era under survey. The most dependable authority is the late Professor Lewis with his *England's Sea Officers* (1939) and *The Social History of the Navy* (1960).

Among the numerous primary sources the following works may be mentioned as of particular interest: *Memoirs and Letters of Captain Sir William Hoste* by Lady Harriet Hoste (1833), *Memoirs* by the Hon. Sir George Elliot (1863), *The Life of Sir William Parker* by A. Phillimore (1876), *Personal Narrative of Events from 1799 to 1815* by W. S. Lovell (1879), *Letters and Papers of Thomas Byam Martin*, I, ed. J. K.

Laughton (1901), *The Story of a Devonshire House* by Lord Coleridge (1905), *Recollections of my Sea Life, 1808–1830*, by J. H. Boteler (N.R.S., 1942), and *Above and Under Hatches (Recollections of James Anthony Gardner)*, ed. C. C. Lloyd (1957).

CHAPTER 7   THE MANNING OF THE FLEET

The manning of the Fleet is treated from various viewpoints in the following works: C. N. Robinson's *The British Fleet* (1894), John Masefield's *Sea Life in Nelson's Time* (1905), J. R. Hutchinson's *The Press-Gang Afloat and Ashore* (1913), G. M. Trevelyan's *English Social History* (1944), and M. A. Lewis's *The Social History of the Royal Navy, 1793–1815* (1960).

Interesting and informative primary sources are *A Treatise on Practical Seamanship* by W. Hutchinson (1777), *A Treatise on the Coal Trade* by R. Edington (1813), *Nautical Economy* by 'Jack Nasty-Face' (1836), *Landsman Hay*, ed. M. D. Hay (1953), *Adventures of John Wetherell*, ed. C. S. Forester (1954), and H. Baynham, *From the Lower Deck* (1969).

CHAPTER 8   DISCIPLINE AND MORALE

This aspect of life at sea is at present rather inadequately covered. John Masefield's well-known work, *Sea Life in Nelson's Time* (1905) is in some respects prejudiced and misleading. Other authorities to be consulted are Edward Brenton's *The Naval History of Great Britain* (1823) and his *Life and Correspondence of the Earl of St. Vincent* (1838), J. S. Tucker's *Memoirs of the Earl of St. Vincent* (1844), C. N. Robinson's *The British Fleet* (1894), David Hannay's *A Short History of the British Navy* (1909), O. A. Sherrard's *A Life of Lord St. Vincent* (1933), P. K. Kemp's *Prize Money* (1946), L. Kennedy's *Nelson's Band of Brothers* (1951), D. Pope's *The Black Ship* (1963), and J. Dugan's *The Great Mutiny* (1965). Among the primary sources the following are particularly interesting and revealing: *Adventures of John Nicol, Mariner*, by John Nicol (1822), *A Farewell to my old Shipmates and Messmates* by Béchervause (1847), *Autobiography of Pel. Verjuice* by C. R. Pemberton (ed. 1929), *Landsman Hay* (1953), ed. M. D. Hay, and *Adventures of John Wetherell*, ed. C. S. Forester (1954).

CHAPTER 9   HYGIENE AND SUPPLY

The outstanding authority on hygiene and supply is Lloyd and Coulter's *Medicine and the Navy, 1714–1815*, II (1961). Other works which may be consulted are W. Tait's *The History of Haslar Hospital* (1906), J. S. Corbett's *England in the Seven Years War* (1907), H. W. Richmond's *The Navy in the War of 1739–1748* (1920), O. A. Sherrard's *A Life of Lord St. Vincent* (1933), R. S. Allison's *Sea Diseases* (1943), L. H. Roddis's *James Lind* (1950), O. Warner's *Portrait of Lord Nelson* (1958), G. J. Marcus's *Quiberon Bay* (1960), A. T. Patterson's *The Other Armada* (1961), and R. Mackay's *Admiral Lord Hawke* (1965).

Important primary sources on this subject are *The Adventures of Roderick Random* by Tobias Smollett (1748), *A Treatise of the Scurvy* (1753) and *An Essay on . . . the Health of Seamen* (1757), both by James Lind, *Observations on the Diseases Incident to Seamen* by Gilbert Blane (1785), and *Observations on the Scurvy* by Thomas Trotter (1786).

CHAPTER 10   'FAIR PORTSMOUTH TOWN'

For the history of Portsmouth in the Georgian era, see *The Royal Port . . . of Portsmouth* by Henry Slight (1843), *Free Mart Fair and Other Sketches* by W. G. Gates (1897), and *The History of Portsmouth* (1900) by the same author. The great naval mutinies are covered by the following works: Conrad Gill's *The Naval Mutinies of 1797* (1913), Manwaring and Dobrée's *The Floating Republic* (1935), and J. Dugan's *The Great Mutiny* (1965).

Interesting contemporary accounts of the great naval port are to be found in Silliman's *Journal of Travels in England, Holland, and Scotland* (1812), Dr. George Pinckard's *Notes on the West Indies* (1813), and Landmann's *Adventures and Recollections* (1852).

CHAPTER 11   ADMIRALTY

A most interesting and important work on the Admiralty in the era under survey is C. C. Lloyd's *Mr. Barrow of the Admiralty* (1970). Reference should also be made to Sir John Barrow's *An Auto-Biographical Memoir* (1847).

For the various First Lords and their Boards, see J. S. Corbett's *England in the Seven Years War* (1907) and *The Campaign of Trafalgar* (1910), H. W. Richmond's *The Navy in the War of 1739–1748* (1920), J. H. Plumb's *Sir Robert Walpole* (1956), G. Martelli's *Jemmy Twitcher* (1962), Piers Mackesy's *The War for America* (1964), D. A. Baugh's *British Naval Administration in the Age of Walpole* (1965), and R. Mackay's *Admiral Lord Hawke*.

CHAPTER 12   'THE DANGERS OF THE SEA'

For detailed tables of losses sustained by the Navy during this era, see W. Laird Clowes, *The Royal Navy*, III and IV. The heavy toll of ships and lives exacted by 'the dangers of the sea' is lucidly and comprehensively analysed by M. A. Lewis in his *The Social History of the Royal Navy* (1960). See also Gardner, Leyland, Boteler, as above.

CHAPTER 13   LONDON RIVER

An important contemporary authority on the coasting trade in general and the navigation of the Thames estuary in particular is William Hutchinson, whose *A Treatise on Practical Seamanship* (1777), based on considerable experience in the Newcastle coal trade, attained to several editions. This work may be usefully supplemented by Robert Edington's *Treatise on the Coal Trade* (1813).

For the beaconage and buoyage of the Thames estuary, see Graeme Spence's *Nautical Description of the Banks and Channels of the Thames Estuary* (1804), Joseph Cotton's *Memoir on the Origin and Incorporation of the Trinity House of Deptford Strond* (1818), H. P. Mead's *The Trinity House: Its Unique Record from the Days of Henry VIII* (1947), and G. G. Harris's *The Trinity House of Deptford, 1540–1660* (1969).

For the Port of London, see Daniel Defoe's *Plan of English Commerce* (1728) and *Tour through Great Britain* (ed. Cole, 1928), McCulloch's *Dictionary of Commerce* (1832), James Elmes's *Survey of the Harbour and Port of London* (1838), J. Broodbank's *A History of the Port of London* (1921), and Ll. R. Jones's *The Geography of London River* (1932), G. M. Trevelyan's *English Social History* (1944), and J. Bird's *Geography of the Port of London* (1957).

CHAPTER 14   LLOYD'S

The history of Lloyd's during the era under survey is fairly well covered by the following works: *The History of Lloyd's* by F. Martin (1876), *A History of Lloyd's* by Wright and Fayle (1928), and *Lloyd's of London* by D. E. W. Gibb (1957). See also *Trade Winds*, ed. C. N. Parkinson (1947).

As regards the protection of trade in war-time, with which Lloyd's was very closely concerned, see A. T. Mahan's *The Influence of Sea Power upon the French Revolution and Empire* (1892), John Creswell's *Naval Warfare* (2nd ed., 1942), and Owen Rutter's *Red Ensign, A History of Convoy* (1947). A very interesting and illuminating contribution to this subject is an Admiralty MS, *Notes on the Convoy System of Naval Warfare* by D. W. Waters (1947).

CHAPTER 15   THE SOCIAL BACKGROUND

By far the most important authority on the social background of officers and men is *The Social History of the Royal Navy, 1793–1815* by M. A. Lewis (1960). Other works which may be consulted are the same writer's *England's Sea Officers* (1939), David Mathew's *The Naval Heritage* (1944), C. C. Lloyd's *The British Seaman* (1968), and P. K. Kemp's *The British Sailor* (1970).

For particular families, social circles, and geographical areas, reference may be made to a wide range of useful sources, both primary and secondary, among which the following may be named: *The Adventures of John Nicol, Mariner* by John Nicol (1822), *Public and Private Correspondence of Vice-Admiral Lord Collingwood*, ed. G. L. Newnham Collingwood (1829), *Memoirs and Letters of Captain Sir William Hoste* by Lady Harriet Hoste (1833), *Memoirs* by the Hon. Sir George Elliot (1863), *Personal*

Narrative of Events from 1799 to 1815 by W. S. Lovell (1879), *A Naval Career during the Old War* by J. Markham (1883), *A Sailor of King George* by F. Hoffmann (1901), *Nelson's Hardy* by A. M. Broadley and R. G. Bartelot (1909), *Jane Austen's Sailor Brothers* by J. H. and H. C. Hubback (1906), *The Wynne Diaries*, ed. A. Fremantle (1940), *Lieutenant Samuel Waters*, ed. C. N. Parkinson (1943), *The Story of Ilfracombe Harbour* by T. R. L. Green (1943), *Augustus Hervey's Journal*, ed. D. Erskine (1953), *Landsman Hay*, ed. M. D. Hay (1953), *Above and Under Hatches (Recollections of James Anthony Gardner)*, ed. C. C. Lloyd (1957), *Admiral Lord Hawke* by R. Mackay (1965), and *Life and Letters of Vice-Admiral Lord Collingwood* by O. Warner (1965).

CHAPTER 16   'SWEETHEARTS AND WIVES'

For the domestic side of the sailor's life, more especially for that of the officers, see Nicol, Newnham Collingwood, Richardson, Markham, Broadley and Bartelot, Hubback, Parkinson, Fremantle, Boteler, Erskine, and Gardner as above.

CHAPTER 17   JACK ASHORE

Most of the relevant information on this subject is to be found in contemporary memoirs such as *Landsman Hay*, ed. M. D. Hay (1953) and *Notes on the West Indies* by Dr. George Pinckard (1813), and also in later compilations embodying the observations of eye-witnesses, e.g. *The Royal Port . . . of Portsmouth* by Henry Slight (1843), *Free Mart Fair and Other Sketches* by W. G. Gates (1897), and *Naval Yarns*, ed. W. H. Long (1899).

CHAPTER 18   THE LETTERS OF SAILORS

The following works may be consulted for the correspondence of sailors:

Public and Private Correspondence of Vice-Admiral Lord Collingwood, ed. G. L. Newnham Collingwood (1829), *Memoirs and Letters of Captain Sir William Hoste* by Lady Harriet Hoste (1833), *Memoirs and Correspondence of Admiral Lord de Saumarez*, ed. Sir John Ross (1838), *Life and Correspondence of the Earl of St. Vincent* by E. P. Brenton (1838), *Memoir of Admiral Sir Edward Codrington*, ed. Lady Bourchier (1873), *The Life of Sir William Parker* by A. Phillimore (1876), *The Story of a Devonshire House* by Lord Coleridge (1905), *Jane Austen's Sailor Brothers* by J. H. and H. C. Hubback (1906), *Edward Pellew, Viscount Exmouth* by C. N. Parkinson (1937), *The Wynne Diaries* by A. Fremantle (1940), *The Private Correspondence of Admiral Lord Collingwood*, ed. E. A. Hughes (1957), *Nelson's Letters to his Wife*, ed. G. P. B. Naish (1958), *The Naval Miscellany*, IV, ed. P. K. Kemp (N.R.S., 1951), and *Admiral Lord Hawke* by R. Mackay (1965).

CHAPTER 19 STORY AND SONG

Daniel Defoe's masterpiece, *Robinson Crusoe*, was published in 1719; Tobias Smollett's *The Adventures of Roderick Random* in 1748 and *Peregrine Pickle* in 1751. Jane Austen's *Mansfield Park* was published in 1814 and *Persuasion* in 1818. Frederick Marryat's *Frank Mildmay* appeared in 1829 and was followed by *The King's Own* (1830), *Peter Simple* (1834), and *Midshipman Easy* (1836).

A considerable body of sea songs were collected by C. H. Firth and printed in his *Naval Songs and Ballads* (N.R.S., 1907). A large number of songs which are seldom or never heard today are quoted or cited in *Above and Under Hatches (Recollections of James Anthony Gardner)*, ed. C. C. Lloyd (1957).

CHAPTER 20 AFTERMATH

For the general situation in this country after the end of the Napoleonic War, see G. M. Trevelyan's *English Social History* (1944) and Sir Arthur Bryant's *The Age of Elegance* (1950). The following works illustrate particular aspects of the aftermath of the great struggle: *The Adventures of John Nicol, Mariner* by John Nicol (1822), *Nelsonian Reminiscences* by G. S. Parsons (1843), *Naval Yarns*, ed. W. H. Long (1899), and *The History of Portsmouth* by W. G. Gates (1900). For British naval policy in the early period of the peace, see *Great Britain and Sea Power* by C. J. Bartlett (1963). For naval construction, see *Sailing Ships, their History and Development* by G. S. Laird Clowes (1936) and *Rig in Northern Europe* by Sir Alan Moore (1956).

GLOSSARY

The definitions are for the most part derived from William Falconer's *Universal Dictionary of the Marine* (1769) and Admiral William Smyth's *A Sailor's Word-Book* (1878).

Aback. The situation of the sails when their surfaces are flatted against the masts by the force of the wind.

Abeam. Opposite the centre of a ship's side.

Aloft. Synonymous with up above the tops, at the mast-head, or anywhere about the higher yards, masts, and rigging of ships.

Alow. Synonymous with below.

Amidships. The middle of the ship, whether in regard to her length between stem and stern, or in breadth between the two sides.

A-trip. The anchor is *a-trip*, or a-weigh, when the purchase has just made it break ground, or raised it clear.

Bank. A rising ground in the sea, differing from the shoal, because not rocky but composed of sand, mud, or gravel.

Barge. A boat of a long, slight, and spacious construction, generally carvel-built, double-banked, for the use of admirals and captains of ships of war.

Barque. A three-masted vessel, with only fore-and-aft sails on her mizen-mast.

Beam-ends. A ship is said to be on her beam-ends when she has heeled over so much on one side that her beams approach to a vertical position.

Beams. Strong transverse pieces of timber stretching across the ship from one side to the other, to support the decks and retain the sides at their proper distance, with which they are firmly connected by means of strong knees, and sometimes of standards.

Bear, To. The direction of one object from the viewer.

Best bower. The bower anchors were the two most commonly used, being carried in the bows of the ship. They were of much the same size, the best bower being the one on the starboard side.

Bilander. A small merchant vessel with two masts, particularly distinguished from other vessels with two masts by the form of her mainsail, which is bent to the whole length of her yard, hanging fore and aft, and inclined to the horizon at an angle of about 45°.

Bow. The fore end of a ship or boat.

Bowline.　A rope used to keep the weather edge of the sail tight forward and steady when the ship is close-hauled to the wind.

Bowsprit.　A large spar, ranking with a lower-mast, projecting over the stem; beyond it extends the jib-boom, and beyond that again the flying jib-boom. To these spars are secured the stays of the foremast and of the spars above it; on these stays are set the fore and foretopmast staysails, the jib, and flying-jib, which have a most useful influence in counter-balancing the pressure of the aftersails, thereby tending to force the ship ahead instead of merely turning her round. Throughout most of the period under review, beneath these spars were set a sprit-sail, sprit-topsail, etc.

Box-haul, To.　An evolution by which a ship is veered sharp round on her heel, when the object is to avoid making a great sweep. The helm is put a-lee, the head-yards braced flat aback, the after-yards squared, the driver taken in, and the head-sheets hauled to windward; when she begins to gather stern-way the helm is shifted and sails trimmed. It is only resorted to in emergencies, as a seaman never likes to see his ship have stern-way. With much wind and sea this evolution would be dangerous.

Brig.　A two-masted square-rigged vessel.

Bring-to.　To check the course of a ship by trimming the sails so that they shall counteract each other, and keep her nearly stationary, when she is said to lie by, or lie-to, or heave-to.

Butt.　The joining of two timbers or planks endways. In large ships butt-ends are most carefully bolted, for if any one of them should spring, or give way, the leak would be very dangerous and difficult to stop.

Carry away.　To break.

Cat.　A ship formed on the Norwegian model, and usually employed in the coal and timber trade. These vessels were generally built remarkably strong, and might carry six hundred tons. A cat was distinguished by a narrow stern, projecting quarters, a deep waist, and no ornamental figure on the prow.

Chase.　The vessel pursued by some other, that pursuing being the chaser.

Close-hauled.　The general arrangement or trim of a ship's sails when she endeavours to progress in the nearest direction possible contrary to the wind; in this manner of sailing the keel of square-rigged vessels commonly makes an angle of six points with the line of the wind, but cutters, luggers, and other fore-and-aft rigged vessels will sail even nearer.

Club-haul.　A method of tacking a ship by letting go the lee-anchor as soon as the wind is out of the sails, which brings her head to wind, and as soon as she pays off, the cable is cut and the sails trimmed; this is never had recourse to but in perilous situations, and when it is expected that the ship would otherwise miss stays.

Cockpit.　A part of the orlop deck used in ships of the line as the midshipmen's berth; and, in action, as the place where the wounded are attended to; it was situated near the after hatch-way.

Commodore.   A senior officer in command of a detached squadron.

Compass.   An instrument employed by navigators to guide the ship's course at sea. It consists of a circular box, containing a fly or a paper card, which represents the horizon, and is suspended by two concentric rings called gimbals. The fly is divided into thirty-two equal parts, by lines drawn from the centre to the circumference, called points or rhumbs. This card is attached to a magnetic needle, which, carrying the card round with it, points north, excepting for the local annual variation and the deviation caused by the iron in the ship; the angle which the course makes with that meridian is shown by the lubber's point, a dark line inside the box.

Compass timbers.   Such as are curved, crooked, or arched, for shipbuilding.

Courses.   A name by which the sails hanging from the lower yards of a ship are usually distinguished, viz. the mainsail, foresail, and mizen. A ship is under her courses when she has no sail set but the three already named.

Current.   A certain progressive flowing of the sea in one direction, by which all bodies floating therein are compelled more or less to submit to the stream. The *setting* of the current is that point of the compass towards which the waters run; and the *drift* of the current is the rate it runs at in an hour.

Cutter.   A small, single-masted, sharp-built broad vessel, furnished with a straight running bowsprit, occasionally run in horizontally on the deck; except for which, and the largeness of the sails, they are rigged much like sloops. Either clincher or carvel-built, no jib-stay, the jib hoisting and hanging by the halyards alone. She carries a fore-and-aft mainsail, gaff-topsail, stay-foresail, and jib. The name is derived from their fast sailing.

Day's work.   In navigation, the reckoning or reduction of the ship's courses and distances made good during twenty-four hours, or from noon to noon, according to the rules of trigonometry, and thence ascertaining her latitude and longitude by *dead reckoning*.

Dead reckoning.   The estimation of the ship's position without any observation of the heavenly bodies; it is discovered from the distance she has run by the log, and the courses steered by the compass, then rectifying these data by the usual allowance for current, leeway, etc., according to the ship's known trim. This reckoning, however, should be corrected by astronomical observations of the sun, moon, and stars, whenever available, proving the importance of practical astronomy.

Dockyard mateys.   The artificers in a dockyard. In former times an established declaration of war between the mates and midshipmen *versus* the mateys was hotly kept up. Many deaths and injuries never disclosed were hushed up or patiently borne. It terminated about 1830.

Fair wind.   That which is favourable to a ship's course, in opposition to contrary or foul.

Fathom.   A measure of six feet, used in the length of cables, rigging, etc., and to divide the lead (or sounding) lines, for showing the depth of water.

Galliot.   A Dutch or Flemish vessel for cargoes, with very rounded ribs and flattish bottom, with a mizen-mast stepped far aft, carrying a square mainsail and main top-sail, a forestay to the mainmast (there being no foretopmast), with fore-staysail and jibs.

Graving-dock.   A dock used for inspecting, repairing, and cleaning a ship's bottom. It is so constructed that after a ship is floated in the water may run out with the falling tide, the closing of the gates preventing its return.

Ground-swell.   A sudden swell preceding a gale, which rises along the shore, often in fine weather, and when the sea beyond is calm.

Halyard.   The rope employed to hoist or lower the sail upon its yard.

Haul her wind.   Said of a vessel when she comes close upon the wind.

Haul off.   To sail closer to the wind, in order to get further from any object.

Head-wind.   A wind which will not permit a ship to sail her course.

Hoy.   A small vessel, usually rigged as a sloop, employed in carrying passengers and goods, particularly for short distances along the coast.

Iron-bound.   A coast where the shores are composed of rocks which mostly rise perpendicularly from the sea, and have no anchorage near to them.

Jib.   A large triangular sail, set on a stay, forward. It extends from the outer end of the jib-boom towards the fore topmast-head; in cutters and sloops it is on the bowsprit, and extends towards the lower mast-head. The jib is a sail of great command with any side wind, in turning her head to leeward.

Jib-boom.   A continuation of the bowsprit forward, being a spar run out from the extremity in a similar manner to a topmast on a lower mast, and serving to extend the foot of the jib and the stay of the fore topgallant-mast, the tack of the jib being lashed to it.

Journal.   Synonymous at sea with log-book; it is a daily register of the ship's course and distance, the winds and weather, and a general account of whatever is of importance.

Jury-mast.   A temporary or occasional mast erected in a ship in the place of one which has been carried away in a gale, battle, etc.

Jury-rudder.   A contrivance, of which there are several kinds, for supplying a vessel with the means of steering when an accident has befallen the rudder.

Keel.   The lowest and principal timber of a ship, running fore and aft its whole length, and supporting the frame like the backbone in quadrupeds.

Ketch.   A vessel of the galliot order, fitted with two masts—viz. the main and mizen masts.

Labouring.   The act of a ship's working, pitching, or rolling heavily, in a turbulent sea, by which the masts, and even the hull, are greatly endangered.

Lead.   An instrument for discovering the depth of water, attached to the lead-line, which is marked at certain distances to ascertain the fathoms.

Leeches.   The borders or edges of a sail.

Lee-tide.   A tide running in the same direction as the wind, and forcing a ship to leeward of the line upon which she appears to sail.

Leeward.   The direction to which the wind blows.

Leeway.   What a vessel loses by drifting to leeward in her course.

Lighter.   A larger, open, flat-bottomed boat, with heavy bearings, employed to carry goods to or from ships.

Longitude by chronometer.   The longitude was found by calculating the difference in degrees of arc between Greenwich time and the ship's time. Greenwich time was known from the chronometers on board. The ship's time was calculated from the altitude of the sun or a star, and the known latitude. To compute the longitude it was necessary to find the hour angle, or ship's time, by spherical trigonometry. The sides of the spherical triangle were represented by the polar distance (difference of declination from 90°), the zenith distance (from the true altitude), and the co-latitude (its difference from 90°). The ship's hour angle was the angle at the pole between the two sides of the triangle representing the polar distance and the zenith distance.

Luff.   The order to the helmsman, so as to bring the ship's head up more to windward.

Lugger.   A small vessel with quadrilateral or four-cornered cut sails, set fore-and-aft, and may have two or three masts.

Lull.   The brief interval of moderate weather between the gusts of wind in a gale.

Lunar.   The brief epithet for the method of finding the longitude by the moon and sun or moon and stars.

Magnetic needle.   A balanced needle, highly magnetized, which points to the magnetic pole, when not influenced by the local attraction of neighbouring iron.

Mainsail.   This, in a square-rigged vessel, is distinguished by the so-termed *square mainsail*; in a fore-and-aft rigged vessel it obtains the name of boom mainsail. Brigs carry both.

Master.   An officer appointed by the Commissioners of the Navy to attend to the navigating of a ship under the direction of the captain, and the working of a ship into her station in the order of battle.

Missing stays.   To fail in going about from one tack to another; when, after a ship gets her head to the wind, she comes to a stand, and begins to fall off on the same tack.

Orlop.   The lowest deck, consisting of a platform laid over the beams in the hold of a man-of-war.

Parallel sailing.   Sailing nearly on a given parallel of latitude.

Pink.   A ship with a very narrow stern, having a small square part above.

Pitching.   The plunging of a ship's head in a seaway.

Poop.　The aftermost and highest part of a large ship's hull. Even if, like a frigate, she has no poop, a vessel is said to be pooped when a heavy sea strikes the stern and washes on board.

Quadrant.　A reflecting instrument used to take the altitude above the horizon of the sun, moon, or stars at sea, and thereby to determine the latitude and longitude of the place.

Quarterdeck.　That part of the upper deck which is abaft the mainmast.

Rake.　To cannonade a ship, so that the shot shall range in the direction of her whole length between decks, called a raking fire.

Reef.　To reduce sail in proportion to the increase of wind.

Roadstead.　An offshore, well-known anchorage, where ships may await orders, as at St. Helens, Basque Roads, and others, where a well-found vessel may ride out a gale.

Rolling.　The oscillatory motion by which the waves rock a ship from side to side.

Royals.　The name of the light sails spread immediately next above the topgallantsails, to whose yard-arms the lower corners of it are attached; they are only used in fine weather.

Schooner.　A small fore-and-aft vessel of various classes, such as two topsail schooners, both fore and aft; main-topsail schooners, with two square topsails; fore-topsail schooners, with one square topsail. There were both two- and three-masted vessels called schooners.

Seamanship.　The art of managing a ship at sea.

Seamark.　A point or conspicuous object distinguished at sea; they are of various kinds, such as promontories, steeples, ruins, trees, &c.

Sheer.　The longitudinal curve of a ship's decks or sides.

Ship.　A three-masted vessel, square-rigged on each of her masts.

Shrouds.　The lower and upper standing rigging.

Sloop.　In a general way of speaking was a vessel similar to a cutter; the bowsprit, however, was not running, and the jib was set on a standing stay with hanks. Sloop in the Service was a term depending on the rank of the officer in command. Thus a frigate might be rated a *ship* when commanded by a captain and a *sloop* when only commanded by a commander.

Slops.　A name given to ready-made clothes and other furnishings for the seamen.

Snow.　A two-masted vessel which differs slightly from a brig. It has two masts similar to the main and fore masts of a ship, and close abaft the main-mast a trysail-mast. Snows differ only from brigs in that the boom-mainsail is hooped to the mainmast in the brig, and traverses on the trysail-mast in the snow.

Sounding.　The operation of ascertaining the depth of the sea, and the quality of the ground, by means of a lead and line, sunk from a ship to the bottom, where some of the ooze or sand adheres to the tallow in the hollow base of the lead.

Soundings.　Those parts of the ocean not far from the shore where the depth is about 80 or 100 fathoms.

Spanker.   A fore-and-aft sail, setting with a boom and gaff, frequently called the *driver*. It is the aftermost sail of a ship or barque.

Spritsail.   A sail formerly attached to a yard which hung above the bowsprit, and of some importance in naval actions of old, notably the battle of St. Vincent (1797).

Squall.   A sudden and violent gust of wind.

Stand, To.   The movement by which a ship advances towards a certain object, or departs from it.

Stay.   A large strong rope, extending from the upper end of each mast towards the stem of the ship, as the shrouds are extended on each side. The object of both is to prevent the masts from springing, when the ship is pitching deep. Thus stays are fore and aft; those which are led down to the vessel's side are *back-stays*.

Stays, In.   A ship was in stays when going about from one tack to the other.

Staysail.   A triangular sail hoisted upon a stay.

Stem.   The foremost piece uniting the bows of a ship; its lower end scarphs into the keel, and the bowsprit rests upon its upper end.

Stern.   The after-part of a ship or boat.

Stern-post.   The opposite to the *stem*; scarphed into the keel, and suspending the rudder.

Studding-sails.   Fine weather sails set outside the square-sails.

Swatchway.   A channel across a bank, or among shoals.

Tack.   To go about. It is done by turning the ship's head suddenly to the wind, whereby her head-sails are thrown aback, and cause her to fall off from the wind to the other tack. The opposite to *wearing*.

Topgallant-sails.   The third sails above the decks: they are set above the topsail-yards, in the same manner as the topsails above the lower yards.

Topsails.   The second sails above the decks.

Trysail.   A reduced sail used by small craft in lieu of their mainsail during a storm. Also, a fore-and-aft sail, set with a boom and gaff, in ships, synonymous with the spencers of brigs and schooners, and the spanker or driver of ships.

Turning to windward.   The operation of making progress by alternate tacks at sea against the wind, in a zig-zag line, or transverse courses; beating, however, is generally understood to be turning to windward in a storm or fresh wind.

Under way.   A ship beginning to move under her canvas after her anchor is started.

Variation.   A term applied to the deviation of the magnetic needle or compass, from the true north point towards either east or west.

Voyage.   A journey by sea. It usually includes the outward and homeward trips, which are called passages.

Wear (past part. *wore*).   In wearing, or veering, especially when strong gales render it dangerous, unseamanlike, or impossible to tack, the head of the vessel is put away from the wind, and turned round 20 points of the compass instead of 12, and without strain or danger, is brought to the wind on the opposite tack.

Many far-sighted seamen, like St. Vincent, issued orders to wear instead of tacking, when not inconvenient, deeming the accidents and wear and tear of tacking, detrimental to the sails, spars and rigging.

Weather.   To weather anything is to go to windward of it.

Weatherly.   Said of a well-trimmed ship when she holds a good wind, and presents such lateral resistance to the water, that she makes but little leeway while sailing close-hauled.

Weather-tide.   That which, running contrary to the direction of the wind, by setting against a ship's lee-side while under sail, forces her to windward.

Working a lunar.   Reducing the observations of the sun and moon, or moon and stars, in order to find the longitude.

Zenith.   The pole of the horizon, or that point in the heavens directly overhead.

INDEX